ASK AN AGENT

EVERYTHING ACTORS NEED TO KNOW ABOUT AGENTS

Margaret Emory

Back Stage Books
An imprint of Watson-Guptill Publications
New York

To climb steep hills requires slow pace at first.
—William Shakespeare

Senior Acquisitions Editor: Mark Glubke
Project Editor: Michèle LaRue
Cover Design: Steve Cooley
Interior Design: Michelle Thompson
Production Manager: Ellen Greene

First published in 2005 by Back Stage Books,
an imprint of Watson-Guptill Publications,
a division of VNU Business Media, Inc.
770 Broadway, New York, NY 10003
www.wgpub.com

Library of Congress Control Number: 2005931534

ISBN: 0-8230-8795-6

Manufactured in the United States of America

First printing 2005

1 2 3 4 5 6 7 8 9 / 11 10 09 08 07 06 05

CONTENTS

ACKNOWLEDGEMENTS

There are people to thank...

Mark Glubke for his enthusiastic support of my proposal for this book.

Michèle LaRue for thorough, dedicated, and smart editing.

Michelle Thompson for the classy look of the book.

Sherry Eaker for saying "yes" to the "Ask an Agent" column in *Back Stage*, and *Back Stage*'s Erik Haagensen for being a tough editor who keeps me honest.

Geddeth Smith for his erudite historical insights.

Sheila Levine—an enthusiastic and encouraging reader during the writing process.

Catherine Marks—whose good ideas never falter and never stop.

Dulcie, Barry, colleagues, clients, and students—past, present, and future—who gave me the material for this book.

And last, but not least, my parents—Nan and Martin Emory—who introduced me to the magic of theater by taking me to all those plays!

INTRODUCTION

This book came about through a series of columns that I write for the theater weekly *Back Stage*, in which I answer specific questions from actors. The information provided, offering insights into show business from an agent's perspective, is not readily available to actors and has proven very useful to them in developing their careers. When actors began asking me where they could find a collection of these columns, I began to think that some sort of manual about agents, actors, and the entertainment industry might be useful. This is that book.

I started out as an actress. I grew up in New York City with live theater as a staple of my cultural diet. First Broadway musical: *Hello, Dolly!* with Carol Channing. First Off-Broadway show: *Man of La Mancha* with Richard Kiley, in theater-in-the-round, no less! Larger-than-life performances. Magical moments. Threshold experiences. I was utterly transfixed.

After playing Mrs. Santa Claus in the kindergarten holiday show, I decided to be an actress when I grew up. For me, as for many other shy bookworms, theater and acting became an outlet for self expression. I could express my thoughts and feelings safely through the words and actions of an imaginary character on the stage. And I loved the sense of community I found in being part of a group of actors "at play," working together to create something special.

The summer between my freshman and sophomore years at Princeton University, I studied at the Stella Adler Studio with a lady named Pearl Pearson. She smoked very long cigarettes and said nothing to me the entire summer session, until I met her accidentally in the bathroom during the break of the final class. Having performed my monologue from Shaw's *St. Joan* earlier that night, I was eager to hear her assessment of my talent, but uncomfortable about asking for it given our present environment. To my surprise, she broke her customary silence to tell me that she thought I had promise.

Although Princeton had no performing arts major, I took every course offered in the Theatre Department, and I wrote my senior thesis on three contemporary playwrights: Christopher Durang, John Guare, and Arthur Kopit. I had become intrigued by the subject of irony in contemporary drama during my freshman year, when I played Bette in an unpublished black comedy called *The Marriage of Bette and Boo*. It had been written by a young MFA playwriting student from Yale named Christopher Durang, whom I met when he came to see the show.

At Princeton I performed in every possible venue on campus. Some of the best theater I ever witnessed or participated in took place in a small student-run theater: Theatre Intîme. It offered a variety of fare, ranging from Michael Weller's *Moonchildren* to Noël Coward's *Tonight at 8:30* to Stephen Sondheim's *Anyone Can Whistle*. These productions were extremely professional and drew an audience from the entire Princeton community. I don't know how I managed both my scholastic workload and thespian activities, but I think having them both in my life at that time helped keep me sane and balanced.

After college, I received my formal acting training at the Neighborhood Playhouse in New York City, which, for many years, had been the teaching home of the great actor and teacher Sanford Meisner. Though living with throat cancer and severely hampered by his artificial voice box, Mr. Meisner dropped into our classrooms occasionally. He always began these visits by asking who wanted to work. Most of the students, playing it safe, chose not to offer themselves up for sacrifice. But I was always ready and willing. I wanted to improve and trusted that the master's comments would help me. It was during one of these visits that I received the dubious distinction of being called by the great man himself, "an insult to my technique." I was in the midst of an "independent activity"—an exercise he devised to train an actor to behave instinctually rather than mentally, by performing a difficult but meaningful task—when he stopped the exercise to give his shocking pronouncement. I was devastated. *How* could he say such a hurtful thing? Didn't he see how hard I was working? Today I would question *why* anyone would say such a thing. What is the relevance of a comment like that? Egos can be such a problem. One would think that the Great Ones especially, with all their talent and wisdom, would help students become better actors in constructive ways. But that's not always the case. Great Ones are humans with flaws, just like the rest of us. It is important to learn the difference between constructive criticism and personal attack. The first you pay attention to; the second you disregard!

After graduating from the Neighborhood Playhouse, I went directly to the New Jersey Shakespeare Festival, where I worked for eight months as an Equity Membership Candidate (EMC). For decades, young actors have apprenticed themselves in the American theater by signing up for a season with a given company (usually a summer stock, outdoor, or regional theater) to work for free or for a very small stipend. In exchange these apprentices have learned about acting and other aspects of running a theater, and have had the opportunity to play walk-ons and small parts. Actors' Equity Association—the stage actors' union—systemized this traditional practice with the EMC program, under which young actors earn "points" toward union membership, by working backstage, playing small roles, and understudying larger ones at theaters around the country. Sometimes actors receive a small stipend for living expenses, but often no money passes hands.

How wonderful to go from the intense conservatory environment of the Neighborhood Playhouse to a fully functioning classical repertory company! I was reborn. It was revitalizing and inspiring to be thrust into the atmosphere of total theater. Founding Artistic Director Paul Barry cast his season with great actors, and during the rehearsal process he virtually left them alone to find the play. The productions were unencumbered by fancy sets and costumes, with attention instead paid to the intent of the playwrights as found in the text. During my first season as an EMC, my duties consisted of running lights for *Romeo and Juliet*, helping with props for *Cymbeline* (I handed Cloten's bloody head to the actor playing Guiderius), and participating in an a cappella singing group that sang madrigals to audience members as they walked up to the theater. In the third show, *Tartuffe*, I finally got on stage for the first time. I played Flipot, Madame Pernelle's maid, and did nothing but giggle stupidly in character as Madame shamelessly swatted me with her little pocketbook. Simultaneously, I took mental notes on the blocking of the actress playing Dorine, whom I was understudying. Being in the company of good actors, working on great plays, and hearing the words of Shakespeare every day was an irresistible introduction to the life of a professional actor. The New Jersey Shakespeare Festival educated me in the realities of the routine and regimen of an actor's life, and gave me a foundation of knowledge which has influenced my agent life.

The New Jersey Shakespeare Festival also gave me my first professional job as an actress. I got my Equity card when I was hired as a member of their Equity acting company. Every young actor is obsessed with getting two things: an Equity card and an agent. I had tried for the former earlier by going to an open call for *Oh! Calcutta!*, which was running on Broadway at the time. This was before I knew exactly what the show required. I'll save the story of my nude audition on the stage of the Edison Theatre for another time. Suffice it to say that I chose to return to the Shakespeare Festival and gain more Equity points rather than tour the United States in the buff under a non-union contract. Over the course of two seasons at the Shakespeare Festival, I had the opportunity to work with wonderful actors—many of whom I represent today—and play great roles like the Yellow Peril in *Da*, Nora in *The Plough and the Stars*, Jessica in *The Merchant of Venice*, and Lady Teazle in *The School for Scandal*.

Searching for jobs back in New York, I went to Equity Principal Auditions (EPAS) and Equity Principal Interviews (EPIS). These were open calls that the union required contracted producers and casting directors to hold, promoting casting opportunities for the members. Seeking an agent, I acted in many Off-Off-Broadway showcases. I did some commercials and some work on the soaps; and I waitressed and worked as a temp in countless offices. During the Reagan years I hooked up with a political satire group from Washington, D.C., and we performed our scripted material in clubs and cabarets in the tri-state area of New York, New Jersey, and Connecticut. After that I teamed up with a wonderful actor named Cal Winn, who had been an original member of the Oregon Shakespeare Festival. We ran and performed in a national Shakespearean company that brought assemblies and language workshops to grade schools, high schools, and colleges in nine eastern states. We began our program by performing a tapestry of scenes and monologues with minimal props, costumes, and sets. Then we infiltrated the classrooms to do language workshops with the students. Using two lines from the storm scene in *King Lear*, we guided them to create a raging "storm" from the sounds of the vowels and consonants in the words, thereby giving them a physical experience with poetic language. Like the fellow in that excellent film *Looking for Richard*, we believed, "You've got to *feel* the language" to understand the meaning. Time and again we proved our point that Shakespeare is meant to be spoken out loud or seen in performance for the complete experience. I learned a great deal about Shakespeare, and acting in general, from Cal and from the experience of bringing this material to life for young people.

I pursued an acting career for ten years, but—as many of you know from your own experience—much of the time was spent looking for work rather than being employed. A good friend of mine suggested that I look into other areas of the business, like casting and agenting, and I followed her advice. How I became an agent is a clear example of the showbiz maxim, "It's not what you know; it's who you know." First I sent résumés to casting directors, thinking that was an area of the business that I wanted to investigate. I made follow-up phone calls and had meetings—one with a casting director for whom I had auditioned many times. While the producing outfit she ran with her husband couldn't take on an eager assistant, she did phone me two weeks later with an interesting idea. A friend of hers who had run an agency for many years was losing her longtime theatrical agent, who was making a life change. She needed someone to take over for him immediately, and the casting director thought I might be an ideal candidate. She arranged a meeting between the two of us, which went very well.

While it was obvious that the owner of the agency couldn't hire me to fill the shoes of her longtime agent, I having no experience in this area at all, she did hire me as an assistant, and that was the agency where I learned the trade.

I've been a talent agent for fifteen years. I have represented actors for theater, television, and film projects; and have booked them on Broadway, Off-Broadway, in regional theater, national and international tours, on episodic television shows, soap operas, independent and feature films, and occasionally in commercials and voiceovers.

The first thing I noticed when I made the transition from actress to agent was how much useful information I had at my fingertips now that I was on the "other side." Each day I saw the breakdowns (detailed casting notices) for all of the projects being cast, complete with names of casting directors, directors, producers, writers, audition and production dates, and notes on which roles had already been cast. Remember, this was in the day before the information revolution propelled by computers, the Internet, and exclusive websites like Breakdown Express. I inherited a Rolodex of all sorts of industry players, many of whom I began to speak with on a regular basis. I learned, from the inside, about the process of the business: how projects get cast and produced and how an actor's career is built. An agent's perspective is very different from an actor's. I began to solve many mysteries. Like what really happened to all those photos and résumés that actors mail to agents. Or whether agents ever really attended showcases. Or how the actors who were actually working *got* those jobs. What process did they go through to book them? I had always wondered, for instance, why getting representation had been so difficult—and why, when I had it, getting auditions was still so difficult. Facing the realities of the business on a daily basis from the other side of the desk answered those questions, providing reasons and justifications that allowed me to accept the frustrations of the past and move on. In this respect, knowledge truly is power.

★

Now that you know a little bit about me—the person who, for the next two hundred pages or so, will be filling your head with her knowledge and insights about the business—let me tell you why I wrote this book, and what I want it to be for you!

★

This book is meant to demystify the inner workings of the industry for people who are not agents.

Once I began learning the inside information about being an agent and understanding how everything worked, I felt a real need to share this information with actors. I began thinking that the more answers actors get to their questions about the business, the better chance they have of moving forward in their careers. They should know what an agent does, how an agent works, what exactly the interplay is between casting director and agent, and how it affects the career of an actor. They should know how projects get put together, developed, and sold—in short, the realities of how business is done, from the perspective of a person doing it. For instance, everybody knows that a headshot should look like the actor. But why, really? And wouldn't it make sense for actors to know how, exactly, agents *use* headshots? And how that use influences what an agent looks for in a headshot? This information would certainly help actors to plan their next sessions with photographers. I say, why not gain the knowledge before the session, rather than afterwards? Then, armed with your great headshot, you can sit across the desk from an agent and develop a game plan for working together, rather than listen to her manifesto on what would have been the perfect photo.

So much of an actor's life occurs in a vacuum. You take actions which very often don't bring definitive results, leaving you unable to evaluate how to generate forward movement. To use another headshot example: Let's say you've sent yours to hundreds of agents and casting directors, and have gotten little or no response. You wonder, is it the headshot? The résumé? The cover letter? Now desperate, you agonize further: Did anyone look at it? Was it even opened? To whom should I send the next round of headshots?

Dealing with headshots is just one of many dilemmas befalling actors who *don't* have agents! How about all of you *with* agents, who wonder when and if you should call them for feedback on auditions, what to do when you haven't heard from them in weeks, or how to get submitted for projects in areas that are different from the usual?

This book answers these questions and many more, explaining why things are the way they are, so that we can all communicate better and help each other to fully reach our joint potential.

Nobody wants to live in frustration and disappointment. We all know that talent alone won't guarantee a successful career. Sometimes, in fact, talent doesn't even factor into the equation. Talent is indefinable, and the business is subjective: one agent's discovery is another agent's pass. I won't even try to define talent in this book—but I can certainly offer insights into how actors can create opportunities more quickly and less painfully, enabling their talent to come through in meaningful and fruitful expression. I truly believe there is no reason to spend time mired in wrong choices and bad decisions that could be averted with just one book's worth of correct information.

Research is an essential part of self-promotion; actors should be savvy about upcoming productions and their producers. The Internet has become a popular tool for finding out what's currently being cast, but many times pursuing this information only leads to frustration. It's important to understand the *business* of the theater and the context in which casting decisions are made. Broadway, for instance, will cast TV names to sell tickets, no matter how right you are for the role. That's the reality. Knowing and accepting this empowers an actor to focus on goals he can attain—goals that are more likely to bring him to the place of his highest dreams. This is a business of making and maintaining relationships over time, of taking small steps to ultimately cover large distances. There is no such thing as an overnight success. If you disagree, just see how long that success lasts. Being cast as the lead in a new Broadway musical as your first Equity job might seem to be an out-of-this-world opportunity. But if the show flops, the repercussions of this sudden reversal could throw you out of the show-business world completely. And coming back could take a long time. Having a realistic grasp of the industry and how business is done helps an actor make the correct choices and decisions that will save time, energy, and money in pursuing an acting career. It can promote good health, too!

This book is not just for actors looking for agents and for actors who have agents. It is also for the educators whose job nowadays is twofold: not only do they train students to be skilled actors, but more and more they find it necessary to prepare actors for lives as professionals. This is not England, which feeds its graduates from conservatories into a network of theater companies, giving young performers ample chance to find their balance. In the United States each year, a new crop of conservatory-trained actors hits the New York City pavements and Los Angeles freeways. They are well trained and talented, possessing lots of ambition and ready to take the industry by storm. What they don't know is how to get a job and how to work with an agent to accomplish that. While many actors do quite well without agent representation—especially outside of industry centers like New York and L.A.—sooner or later, an actor needs an agent in order to move up to the next level. This book is the manual on how to get one, work with one, and keep one—a unique exploration of the actor-agent partnership and the process of career-building.

A cautionary word: Agents don't have all the answers. Sometimes we are just as baffled by results as actors are. I remember one time I was working in an agency when a breakdown came in for a role in a feature film. A well-known actor whom the agency happened to represent at the time was listed as the prototype for this character. When we called the casting director to say we represented the "real deal," the response was, "Oh, no thanks. He's too perfect." Just try to explain that to your client!

A brief note about terms before we begin: In agent parlance, an actor represented by an agent is a "client." Casting notices are "breakdowns," published by a company called Breakdown Services, Ltd. that

agents and managers subscribe to. "Submissions" of clients are our responses to these breakdowns, which we give to the specific casting
directors ("CDs") handling the projects. We refer to these casting directors as our "accounts." Sometimes I also refer to actors as "talent,"
much as the production teams for television and film projects do on a
set. "Personal Managers" work in talent management—but while
agents generally are regulated by state business laws, and are fran-
chised by talent unions to solicit employment and negotiate monies for
clients, managers are not.

   This book is filled with anecdotes that illustrate the points being
made. Since I refer so often to my clients and the agency where I work,
I should tell you a little about the firm. For more than a decade I have
been an agent at a medium-sized agency in midtown Manhattan, which
has existed for almost thirty years. In the tough terrain of show business, where the struggle to survive reflects impossible odds, this is an
impressive lifespan. What's even more impressive is that the two sub-
agents—myself and a male colleague—have each worked at the agency
for more than ten years. The agency is located in an unusual environment: the ground floor of a townhouse, complete with greenhouse and
patio. All three agents (including the owner) work as a team representing a hundred or so actors in the areas of theater, television, and film.
Although our main focus is the "legitimate" side of the industry—
everything excluding commercials—we occasionally book a client in
a commercial or an industrial. We organize the workload by casting
director, each agent being the "point man" for breakdowns put out
by specific CDs. This has enabled each agent to build significant relationships with casting directors over time, which have benefited the careers
of our clients. Since it is an open office space (there are no partitions
at Dulcina Eisen Associates), and since the three of us have worked
together for so many years, we find that each speaks for the other in
a pinch. Our actor-friendly atmosphere and hands-on approach has
enabled me to learn every aspect of the agenting job from an up-close-
and-personal vantage point.

★

Standing outside the door of an agent's office in New York, an actor
reads in bold letters: DO NOT PHONE OR VISIT. Who *are* those people
on the other side of the door? What do they do all day with their time?
Will somebody *puh-leez* tell me, "What is an agent?"

Chapter 1

WHAT IS AN AGENT?

I first heard the word "agent" during my final year of acting school at the Neighborhood Playhouse, when my class was rehearsing its Senior Showcase for agents, managers, and casting directors—what the business commonly refers to as "industry professionals." I had no idea how an actor went about getting a job, much less how this audience factored into the process, so I certainly did not understand the opportunities that this showcase held for me in terms of my future as a working actress. Throughout its two-year program, the Playhouse, which looked askance at the commercial aspect of the industry, "shielded" its students from the harmful, competitive nature of the business by forbidding them to participate in shows outside of the classroom. Any participation in extra-curricular activities beyond the conservatory walls was grounds for expulsion. The school assumed responsibility for teaching its students how to be actors, not how to make a living—and it didn't recognize any connection between the two.

Although there had been no classroom education on the business of acting, I did pick up on the fact that inviting these personages to attend the showcase was very important. It also seemed clear to me that any future association with them depended on their favorable appraisal of my work. If they saw me and liked me, I assumed they would call me to meet me. I had no idea what they would do with me after that.

The class had grown very close during our two years of "boot camp," but it began to splinter as the big industry night approached. An undercurrent of tension swept through the rehearsals as our focus became consumed with grabbing time offstage to pore over contact sheets from headshot sessions and piece together our individual résumés. Our ignorance about the realities of show business led our curious minds to fantasize, and we began to single out the classmates who were destined to be big stars on TV, in films, or on Broadway. Our

Meisner training, with its good intentions of teaching actors to "work off each other" to produce a standard of honest acting with "real moments," went completely out the window as we stepped over the line into "showcase" territory. It was my first glimpse into the competitive playing field of the commercial world of show business.

Unfortunately, few industry professionals attended our showcase, and those who did weren't responsive, so nothing happened for most of the class. One student, however, got representation and booked a contract role on a soap opera. Several years later she was cast as a series regular on an irreverent, over-the-top sitcom. This surprised many of us because she hadn't worked on one comic scene at the Playhouse; she was enormously gifted as a serious actress. In retrospect, I wish I had known what I know today about the business, so that I could have made better use of the experience and opportunities of my Senior Showcase—I could have used this book!

First Encounter with an Agent

A few months later, I got to see an agent in action for the first time. I was working as an Equity Membership Candidate at the New Jersey Shakespeare Festival during the summer immediately following my graduation from the Neighborhood Playhouse. When the leading lady informed us that her agent was coming from New York City to see the show, the entire company sparked to the occasion. The dressing rooms filled with endless chatter in anticipation of the agent's arrival. All sorts of strategies were hatched to get photos and résumés into his hand, to arrange interviews with him back in the city, to make an impression and a connection. I figured this person must be pretty important, having incited more attention and frenetic activity than even the director had mustered during rehearsals. It was like Steven Spielberg was coming to town.

After the show, we huddled around the agent. He was a youngish man, very affable, beaming in the glow of his client's glory—and also, perhaps, in the glow of his own exalted position amid these polite and attentive actors. While he complimented the company's work in general, he made sure to pay great deference to his client, and found a few moments to go over details regarding an upcoming audition. He then dashed off to catch the train back to New York, bidding farewell with what I would come to hear often enough as a sign-off in agent-speak: "Marvelous job, darling. Let's talk on the phone tomorrow."

Seeing an agent in action gave me some clues towards deciphering this enigmatic role. I could see that an agent was a communicator and a diplomat. He was able to be personable and elusive at the same time. This particular agent had managed to make everyone feel good without promising anyone anything. His very presence had inspired a higher level of performance from the entire company. Gone was the usual post-performance griping on the state of the dressing rooms and lack of audience response. Everyone was definitely on their best behavior. I found it curious, however, that many of the actors, especially those who had planned to be aggressive in their outreach, gave timid performances when they approached the agent. Once-rabid actors turned subdued and polite in his presence.

The moment came and went—as did the agent. I don't think anyone heard from him again, except, of course, his client. What I took away from this encounter was an understanding of the relationship between an agent's actions and the continuity of an actor's employment. There was a connection between the agent's scheduling auditions and the actor's obtaining work. This agent came to see his client perform the job which he had helped her to get by securing her an audition. While the client was doing this job, the agent was busy submitting her for future work. That connection was very real and very important to the actress. She treated her agent with pride, like an honored guest, while also making sure that he was busy investigating future jobs for her.

Let's flash forward for a moment. A client recently flew me out to Denver to see her perform the lead in her first Equity show. While I was there I couldn't help but notice that I was playing the role of the agent whom I had seen in action so many years ago. My client was wonderful and the show itself was very good, so it was easy for me to relate to members of theater management and the acting company with warmth and enthusiasm. I was filled with enormous pride in my client's talent and assured her of my belief in her potential for a great career. As I complimented her wonderful performance and discussed upcoming projects and auditions, I smiled to myself, remembering the first agent I ever saw in action. I had definitely crossed over!

First Interview with an Agent

Not long after that summer at NJSF, I had my first interview with a woman who worked for a very large agency totally devoted to commercials. When I was ushered into the big room, I saw many agents sitting at desks, huddled over phones, talking a mile a minute. It was loud. It was busy. It was extremely hectic. My ten-minute interview with the agent consisted of a brief "getting to know you" chat, followed by her handing me some commercial copy to read. The interview was over before I knew it, and I couldn't remember what I said or what had been said to me. Let my experience be a lesson to all of you actors getting ready for your first interviews with agents: don't let the occasion get the better of you, as I did; try to stay "present" throughout the entire meeting.

About the same time I interviewed with the commercial agent, I met a legit agent in a courtesy interview that had been set up as a favor by a friend of the family. The relentless stream of phone calls that made conversation virtually impossible magically stopped for a minute, allowing me to do my monologue. The harried agent looked more exasperated than anything else, and I made the mistake of taking his lack of interest personally. Needless to say, the meeting didn't go well. Lesson number two: actors need to realize that the world they walk into when entering an agent's office has little to do with them. If an agent is having a bad day, seems stressed or preoccupied, that's his problem, not yours. When you understand this, you will be able to turn many negatives into positives.

While I was interested in establishing personal connections with agents during our meetings, I was also very curious to see what exactly they were doing for their clients when those actors called in. I felt like an undercover detective, participating in the interview while observing the agent at work.

DEMYSTIFYING THE DEIFIC BEING

So, what exactly is this deific being—the agent—at once so crucial to an actor's livelihood and so elusive? It is commonly believed that an agent is the answer to every problem an actor might have, although most of the time you'd be hard pressed to get a clear explanation of what an agent is or what he does. To be honest, I never really discovered all of that until I became one. Even the folks who have agents are often vague on the subject of what those agents do, exactly. They will tell you that their agents get them auditions. That certainly is true. But an agent does so much more…

My definition of an agent is "a business person who is responsible for getting an actor work." Everything an agent does for an actor is in direct response to this purpose. An agent's first and foremost priority is to provide opportunities for getting work. This means getting auditions for actors. An agent does this through a process of submitting and selling, which is discussed more fully in Chapters Five and Six of this book. Other duties, like negotiating contracts and offering advice, follow when these auditions are successful.

AN HISTORICAL PERSPECTIVE

Did you know that the first agents for actors were actually actors themselves? That's right. In the eighteenth century, play production in America consisted of repertory theaters employing companies of actors for entire seasons of plays. Actor-managers running the theaters sent actors to other theaters to broker deals of employment. The process went something like this: Actor A, having finished a season at Theater 1, is getting ready to go to Theater 2 for the next season. The actor-manager running Theater 1 wants to hire Actor B away from Theater 2, to be the older character man in his company's following season. Actor-manager 1 asks Actor A to approach Actor B with an offer of employment. If Actor A proves successful in brokering the deal, he'll receive some sort of financial remuneration for his efforts. That's how the process of "agenting" started.

My source for this historical perspective, an actor who moonlights as a biographer of great American stage actors, believes that by the end of the nineteenth century, when the repertory system was supplanted by long runs of single shows in centers like New York City, producers (many times the owners of the theaters), in order to save time and money, began negotiating with the actors directly. It didn't take long for actors to find representatives who would intercede for them, to work out the intricate details of an employment contract; and for producers to hire an in-house casting director to find the actors for hire. The jobs of agent and casting director were born.

Nowadays, prospective agents are required to file an application that includes sponsorship by the owner of the agency, and a work résumé, in order to be enfranchised as a sub-agent with each of the performers' unions. It is considered a conflict of interest for an agent to function as a producer or actor. For instance, I had to go on withdrawal from all three performers' unions when I became an agent. Although agents are not permitted to act as producers, many larger agencies get around this by "packaging" deals: providing a range of talent—such as writers, directors, producers, and actors—on a single project. In supplying such a large part of the creative team, the agency is essentially functioning like a producer.

The actor-agent connection is a symbiotic relationship. The actor depends on the agent to get him work, and since the agent gets paid on commission, she makes a living when the actor is working. Consequently, everything an agent does for an actor promotes possibilities for that actor's employment. The more jobs an actor books and the higher the salaries of these jobs, the better an agent does financially. The duties of an agent in accomplishing this work fall into three basic categories: submitting actors for projects and getting them auditions, negotiating terms of contracts, and offering actors advice and counsel on the development of their careers. An agent's success depends on the success of his client roster at any given time, as the two are inextricably bonded.

BACKGROUNDS OF AGENTS

Agents come in all shapes and sizes, with varied backgrounds and experience. In previous lives, many were actors, directors, stage managers, press representatives, casting directors, production assistants, talent coordinators, event planners, or publicity managers. Some come to the job equipped with degrees in accounting or law. Others have marketing and communication degrees. While studying law or accounting is not absolutely necessary, being able to read and structure contracts, and having a facility with crunching numbers can come in handy when negotiating deals. Agents possess skills in advertising, marketing, and sales, which they use to promote talent. Whether writing persuasive letters or chatting up actors on the phone to casting directors, agents know how to "sell" talent, and each agent has a personal style.

Some are loud and abrasive; others are soft and seductive. Many are everyday regular—whatever it takes to get the job done.

Having a thorough knowledge of the artistic and business sides of the industry helps agents act effectively in their three areas of responsibility—again: submissions, negotiations, and advice giving. Many agents know and appreciate firsthand the artistic side of the industry. Whether they are Shakespeare fiends or sitcom addicts, they know their territories backwards and forwards, and this enables them to make intelligent submissions. Many agents studied or pursued acting, directing, or playwriting at one time. Others know the history of theater, television, and film. All of this makes them knowledgeable and experienced players able to communicate and dispense advice to actors with ease and authority. You will find that, for the most part, agents work in areas according to their backgrounds and experience. It is no surprise, for instance, that I am a legit agent working with theater-trained actors for theater, TV, and film projects. This is what I studied and what I know from personal experience. There can be surprises too: behind many a commercial agent is a theater junkie whose client list consists of highly trained stage actors. Some actors value greatly an agent who knows the difference between Molière and Shaw; others are more concerned that their agent get them the best deal with the most money, and be available 24/7 to take care of problems that erupt on the set.

MULTI-TASKERS

As middlemen, agents must possess a solid understanding of human nature. They need to know how to manage different personality types in order to successfully interact and do business with highly creative and quirky individuals. Agents must remain cool under pressure in order to make the best of all occasions. Here's a story: Our client was on a national tour and had a week's hiatus. She had reminded the office that she would be in New York and available for auditions during this week. Although she had booked her next theater job, we were looking further into the future for work for her, and had secured some auditions. On the day of one of these auditions, we received a distress call from the actress. She wanted to cancel the audition because she hadn't had time to prepare the song. An agent in the office got on the phone and spent a long time talking her through her predicament, trying to salvage this important opportunity. A great deal was at stake here: not only the client's chance to audition for a very good job, but the agency's relationship with the casting director, which would be compromised if this audition were cancelled same day. At the same time, there was the consideration that a bad audition could have a detrimental effect on everybody. Many times actors need someone to prevent them from shooting themselves in the foot. An agent with an objective sensitivity can be just such a person. In conversing with our client, the agent realized that she was better prepared than she thought, so the agent strongly encouraged her to go to the audition. While the actress didn't book that job, she subsequently booked others through the same casting office.

It is not unlikely, on any given day at any given time, to see an agent at a desk, juggling three or more phone calls simultaneously. On the first line, a casting director is shrieking because he just found out that the agent pulled her client from the showcase booked yesterday, because the NBC pilot which the actress shot in the spring was just picked up and begins shooting next week. The casting director threatens to never see any of the agent's clients for any projects ever again; the agent must quell his wrath to protect their future working relationship. On the second line, a client is breaking up on a bad cell phone connection, making it very difficult to piece together her cryptic message, which sounds like, "I'm stuck up in Alaska missed my flight back not able to test for the contract role on *One Life to Live*." The agent must first soothe the hysterical and sobbing actress before determining when she will be able to get back to New York. The agent tries to get this information so that when she calls the casting director with the bad news, she might be able to pre-empt a negative response by suggesting a date for a re-schedule of the screen test. On the third line, a general manager is calling to make an offer to a client for a Broadway show. This, of course, is the money call that invariably comes when the other crises are in full bloom. All three calls happen at the same time. All are equally important. All require the agent to handle the intricate aspects and challenges calmly and thoroughly. She must work swiftly and diligently to soothe the apoplectic casting director. She must be attentive and think quickly to problem-solve with the frenetic client. And she must appear hassle free when taking down the terms of the Broadway offer from the general manager, so that she presents a position of strength from the start of the negotiation.

Commission industries, such as talent agencies, call for self-starters who are motivated and independent. Discovering talent is a large part of an agent's job. Agents build their business by finding talent that they market to the buyers—that is, the casting directors. To assess an actor's talent and career possibilities, an agent must be knowledgeable about the business and its demands. While agents' particular tastes may influence their final decisions, their knowledge and experience enables them to make educated assessments of an actor's casting possibilities and career longevity. If her assessment is favorable, an agent may then choose to meet with the actor to judge further whether they can work together. Their knowledge and experience also enable agents to give the good career advice on which their clients come to depend.

If agents appear elusive or aloof, it is simply because they can't represent every actor who approaches them, and they need to protect their right of selection. Some agents thrill to the courtship stage of representation; they love to chase after talent. Once they hook the actor, however, these agents tend to lose interest and leave the business of career building to their assistants. Some agents beam at opening nights or film premieres; they thrill to being part of the entertainment world. Others work from the objective position of "business representative," protecting clients from the nitty-gritty minutiae of business, enabling them to be the creative artists they were meant to be. Some agents are killer negotiators, some brilliant salesmen (or women); others have a pulse on discovering the stars to be. Most, it is safe to say, are extremely well organized and hard working.

WORK SCHEDULE

An agent's work schedule is always busy because there is always something to do—whether it is making another follow-up phone call to get auditions, reading scripts for clients, negotiating a deal, or meeting prospective clients. An agent must be available to deal with problems as they come up. (And they may come up at midnight if a client is working overseas.) Agents are the actors' advocates and will investigate any perceived injustice to see if it is real, then fight like crazy to get it fixed. One of our clients was rehearsing a Broadway show. When the company moved from the rehearsal studio to the theater, she learned that the entire female chorus was expected to share one dressing room. There wasn't sufficient mirror space for all the girls to put on their makeup. She called the agency to ask us what could be done. The agent who had negotiated the contract spoke to management, and together they came up with a solution to the problem.

Being an agent is not a nine-to-five job. It is much more. Some agents advertise that they are available to their clients 24/7. Others get to the office at 10:00 a.m. and are home at 1:00 a.m., having put in a full day's work followed, perhaps, by seeing a client in a show at 8:00 p.m. and then joining her for drinks or coffee afterwards to celebrate the performance and discuss subsequent career plans. Finding a mate who understands and appreciates this lifestyle is not always so easy.

TRAVEL

Agents travel frequently to see their clients when they are performing out of town, many times in neighboring areas but sometimes a plane ride away, and occasionally even overseas. This means a lot to the clients, who see this interest as support for their work. Seeing the work and keeping up with a client's development also helps the agent stay current when making his submissions. Plus, it's good for business: traveling to these theaters or film festivals enables agents to make friends with new producers or solidify already-established relationships. Many times agents will pick up new clients during these out-of-town junkets.

Lest you think an agent's life is opening-night parties and jet setting to film festivals in exotic locales, keep in mind that their hectic schedules can sometimes make them feel like their life is not their own; they are constantly servicing others. And, like actors, agents face a lot of rejection: not all of their "pushes" result in auditions; not every audition turns into a job offer. Constant selling can wear a person down. This is no job for the faint of heart. It requires constant interaction with people and ceaseless energy and ingenuity for problem solving. If you do not like problem solving and go to great lengths to avoid confrontation, then "agenting" is not for you!

THE TRAINING OF AGENTS

Since no schools offer degrees in talent agenting, hands-on experience is the best and only teacher. Many agents start out as interns or assistants, or in the mail rooms of agencies where they learn the trade. They read everything they can—creative material and trade publications like *Back Stage* and *Back Stage West*, *Variety*, *The Hollywood Reporter*, and *American Theatre* magazine. They go to plays, films, stage readings—everything they can—to become informed members of the industry they wish to enter. They may choose to get a business degree for additional credentials, but they know that there is no better way to learn the job than being on the job.

Even after being an agent for fifteen years, I still learn new things daily as I face different challenges. Each client, with his or her unique talent, brings a variety of needs. To meet these, the agent must skillfully improvise, as well as follow established patterns, formulas, and customary business practices. How these are proportioned for each client is the creative genius of an agent.

★

Hundreds of actors rise before the sun does to stand in line to audition for work. Others don't because they have agents. Hundreds of actors never dare to ask for more money when offered a job, for fear of losing the offer because they have asked. Actors with agents never face that fear directly. Hundreds of actors spend fortunes on coaches, consultants, and teachers to put together career-building plans that fall flat without the muscle of an agent to push them through. Clearly, an agent is a valuable entity in the life of a professional actor. Something so good must surely be hard to get.

Chapter 2

HOW DO ACTORS GET AGENTS?

Your Aunt Sally thinks you should be on Broadway. Your sister Sue can't understand why you're not on her favorite soap opera. Your high school drama teacher had you pegged for playing Romeo before you hit twenty-five. Everyone thinks you're very talented and can't understand why you're not further along in your career. You say, "But I need an agent." They ask, "How do you get an agent?"

They're not alone. I write a column called "Ask an Agent" for the theatrical newspaper *Back Stage*, and the question that actors most frequently email me is, "How do I get an agent?" In their correspondence they make impassioned pleas declaring how important acting is to them, and stating how badly they need to move to the next level in their careers—all the while implying that integrity, passion, and ambition entitle them to an agent. While these qualities may impress an agent, from her perspective, the decision to represent an actor will have more to do with the possibility of making business together than with fulfilling artistic ideals.

But aren't we getting ahead of ourselves just a bit? In order to land an agent, an actor must first attract her attention. This chapter is devoted to the ways and means with which he can do just that.

MAILINGS

An actor's customary method of introduction to an agent is mailing a headshot and résumé (which we'll discuss later in this chapter). Until an actor does so, he does not exist in the agent's sphere of activity. The purpose of mailing a headshot and résumé to an agent is twofold: to serve as a business card showing the agent what the actor looks like, while providing a summary of his work experience and training; and to attract an agent's attention, hopefully singling out this actor from the many others who are attempting to accomplish the same thing. An actor may have several different reasons for these mailings: requesting an interview, for example, or inviting an agent to a show in which he is currently performing, or asking to be kept in mind for casting opportunities as they arise.

One of the decisions an actor makes when doing a mailing is whether he is seeking "commercial" or "legitimate" representation. Commercial agents handle on-camera commercials, voiceovers, promos, and industrials. Legit agents cover everything else in the areas of theater, television, and film. All of these areas will be discussed in greater depth in Chapter 4: "How Do Actors Choose Representation?" What's important to note here is that the type of representation sought by an actor influences which headshot he selects to send out, what information he includes in his cover letter, and which agents he solicits. For example, many actors have two headshots—one for commercials and another for legit areas. How an agency is set up also influences mailings. Many agencies have separate departments handling different areas of the business. If you are seeking both commercial and legit representation from one agency, for instance, make sure to send a headshot to each department within that agency. The departments may work independently of one another and have totally separate and distinct client lists. Smaller agencies don't have different departments. They may have several agents who represent the clients as a single unit—as a team. Generally, actors need only send one headshot to a smaller agency, addressing it to one of the agents.

I always think it is a good idea for an actor to research the agents and agencies thoroughly when doing mailings. For instance, if you are just starting out in the business with some training but little experience, it makes sense to find out which agents handle talent at a level comparable to yours. Some agencies, usually the smaller-sized ones, are known for developing startup talent, while larger firms represent established performers. If you are interested in working in daytime drama, and feel you have a serious shot at booking those jobs, find out which agents cover that area. Remember that some commercial agencies have departments and/or agents who make submissions for roles on daytime dramas, although that area is mostly considered part of the legitimate side of the business. Actors who want to work in musical theater or regional theater should find out which agencies focus on those areas.

Over the years an agency develops a client roster that is based on the particular tastes of the agents working there. The industry knows this agency by the clients it represents. If highly skilled stage actors predominate, for instance, that's what the agency is known for. While the agency's profile may change as actors join or leave it, its reputation remains fairly consistent over time. That influences how the industry comes to regard both the firm and its clients.

Sometimes an actor can get information about agents through the casting directors with whom he has developed relationships. Because of their daily contact with agents, casting directors have this information at their fingertips. Knowing the agencies and their client lists as they do, the casting directors can accurately match up actors and agents. They will do this when they are fans of an actor.

"That's all very interesting," you say. "But how do I do the research if I don't have these significant relationships with casting directors? Where do I look for specific information on agents and agencies?"

Researching agents and agencies is tricky. The first place to start is *Ross Reports Television & Film*—an invaluable resource. Published bimonthly, this directory provides up-to-date profiles of New York, Los Angeles, San Diego, and San Francisco talent agencies, including their addresses and telephone numbers, their union franchises, the names of agents who work there, and their departments. It also gives similar listings for casting directors, network studios and offices, and television and film projects that are currently casting. Special issues add sections focusing on areas ranging from cable TV production to voiceover work. *Ross Reports* is available online at www.rossreports.com. The website lists agents and CDs throughout the United States.

Interview-style books on the market give accurate, though sometimes dated, information about specific agents—their backgrounds, philosophies, and preferences. The Internet yields tidbits too. You can google just about anyone these days to get some information on them. Organizations in major industry cities that offer seminars and workshops with agents and casting directors are valuable resources. And, of course, actors should never undervalue networking with teachers and fellow actors to pick up current information about the business and industry players.

When mailing to a talent agency, actors wonder whether they should send one headshot and résumé to each agent working at an agency or send just one headshot and résumé for the entire office. Some large agencies have lots of agents who work independently from their colleagues. As I mentioned earlier, usually smaller agencies have a team of agents who jointly represent all the clients. Each of these agents is accountable to specific casting directors and their casting needs. Mailing a photo and résumé to every agent listed in the *Ross Reports* is just plain unaffordable (and unnecessarily wasteful). For maximum cost-effectiveness, my suggestion is to narrow the field of your mailing according to your level of training and experience, particular skills, and personal game plan.

Most agency listings in *Ross Reports* conclude with a variation on the directive, "Do not phone or visit." Let's address the first part of this sentence: Agents need to keep their phone lines open for incoming calls from casting directors and clients. In the midst of a busy day, "research" calls from actors soliciting representation are considered interruptions and might get an abrupt reply. If you happen to be on the receiving end of such a response, don't take it personally. The agency where I work prides itself on not having voicemail. So any incoming call during office hours is answered by a real person. Sometimes only one of us is in the office at a time, handling all three phone lines. If I'm negotiating with a producer on one line and have a client on hold on another, imagine my response to a third call coming in when it turns out to be an actor wanting to ask which agent he should send a photo and résumé to. That's why I say direct phoning to agencies can be tricky; and that's why I advise actors, if they choose to make these calls, to get the answers to their questions quickly, saying "thank you" and "good-bye" directly thereafter.

When phoning a smaller agency, for instance, call to find out which agents handle the areas you're most suited for, or who specifically works with new startup talent. Perhaps an appropriate way to phrase the question might simply be, "I am an actor/singer/dancer seeking representation. To whom should I address my photo and résumé?" Depending on the attitude of the response you get, you might venture forth for more specific information about other areas, asking which agent handles TV and film, which legit theater—if you have not already found that information in *Ross Reports*. The more direct and specific your questions are, the easier it is for the person on the other end of the phone to answer them, and the more successfully you will obtain information. Call with a specific agenda instead of winging it on personality, which usually wastes everybody's time. Of course, if you happen to strike up a conversation with a willing intern, receptionist, assistant, or even agent, by all means make the most of it. Develop a relationship; sell what you have to offer. Just be sure to get the name of the person with whom you have enjoyed the chat, and log it for future follow-up. This is how relationships begin, and one never knows at the time where an encounter in this business will lead.

A side note: many actors call to make interview appointments. Sometimes they do this before they've even sent a photo and résumé to the office. Wrong action. Most agents need to see a photo and résumé first. If you choose to follow up on a mailing with a phone call suggesting an interview, use language as a hook to refresh the agent's memory of who you are. Many actors call to follow up on mailings. Their names do not ring bells, and when they mention nothing that the agent would remember them by, they're wasting everyone's time. Learn to speak in short sound bites with tantalizing language ("Steppenwolf actress with spiky brunette hair, recently re-located to New York from Chicago") that refers back to your cover letter or photo, distinguishing you from the many other actors who call the office.

The practice of "making the rounds"—dropping off your headshot and résumé to an agency in person—is discouraged in *Ross Reports* listings. When the industry was smaller, maybe fifty years ago, an actor could drop his photo and résumé off at a producer or agent's office with the hope and real possibility of turning this into an interview. These days, fast pace and lack of opportunity diminish the likelihood of such impromptu meetings. For smaller agencies without the shield of a front-office receptionist, these drop-ins are considered interruptions. However, it's still possible for an actor to leave his photo and résumé at an agency that has a receptionist, befriend that person, and a few years later end up with him or her as his agent or his entrée to a project.

Mailing to Commercial Agents

The general rule when sending to *commercial* agencies is to send to each agent listed in each department. One agent may speak for all the others in a department, or each agent may work separately. Since this information is hard to come by, it's a good idea to cover your bases and send to all the agents, especially when mailing your headshot and résumé to an agency for the first time. Make sure to send appropriate cover letters (discussed later in this chapter) to the specific agents, geared to the areas that they handle: on-camera, voiceover, promos, etc. Whenever possible, target your mailings to those specific agents or departments who work in your areas of interest and skill. It's an effective marketing strategy. I received an email for my column once from an actress who wanted to do voiceover work but didn't know where to start. Because she was a former Muppeteer with extensive puppet and voice experience, I suggested she send her photo and résumé to agents who worked in the voiceover area—especially in animation—and certainly to the casting directors of *Avenue Q*, at the time a hit Broadway show featuring actors who sing and are handy with puppets.

Because of the large volume and fluidity of commercial business, it's possible for actors to send photos and résumés ("do mailings") to commercial agents at any time and get response. These agents are always looking for new faces, working in volume as they do. They tend to call an actor in for an interview based on his look, type, special skill, or whether he happens to fit the requirements of a particular breakdown being worked on that day. (That's why it's very important to be specific and accurate when listing special skills on your résumé. One never knows when "sushi rolling" will be just the skill called for in a national ad campaign.)

For follow-up, actors should keep in touch with commercial agents by sending them photo postcards, especially when actors change their look or phone number, acquire new special skills, or make a jump in the business. Agents like receiving these postcards as follow-up correspondence. There's no need to open an envelope; it's a quick and easy way to see the face, name, and telephone number of the actor on one side, then flip it over to read any pertinent information on the other. The size of a postcard forces economy of expression, which is great. Inform agents of any significant bookings, callbacks, classes, and upcoming showcases. This is called relationship building. Actors should correspond with postcards only after having previously sent in a headshot and résumé with cover letter.

MAILING TO LEGIT AGENTS

It's a fact that mailings to *legit* agents, versus commercial agents, rarely lead to interviews in the office unless the résumé has top-notch credits that are current, or the mailing comes with a recommendation from an industry professional—casting director, director, producer, or sometimes even an agency client. "Top-notch" means Broadway, Off-Broadway, A-list regional theaters, contract or recurring roles on daytime TV, or guest-star or featured roles on episodic television shows or in feature films. The best time to mail to a legit agent is when you're appearing in something locally so the agent can see your work. If the agent finds your look, credits, and the show's flyer interesting, she might consider attending a performance. Of course, there are always exceptions to this rule. A mailing from a young and beautiful actress (or handsome actor) might get an immediate response from an agent who can assess the potential for submission and booking in daytime drama without needing to see a showcase.

HEADSHOTS

When I open a mailing from an actor, the first thing I look at is the headshot, or "eight-by-ten" (8" x 10"), as it is also called, referring to the actual size of the photographic paper. I think it has something to do with what I love about this business, which is the human element. I'm curious to see what the actor looks like. Quite honestly, if the headshot looks like a homemade job or is substandard in professional terms, it goes right into the circular file. I don't even read the cover letter or résumé. Receiving twenty-five to fifty photos and résumés in the mail each day can force an agent to make quick and slightly harsh judgments. There really is no time for charity cases.

When I first look at a headshot, I'm drawn to the eyes and try to read what the actor is saying through them. In the photo, actors are forced to speak through their eyes rather than words. Any number of attitudes can come through, ranging from welcoming to mysterious to worldly-wise to challenging. The more potent the attitude and the stronger the expression, the more likely a headshot will grab my attention. I also look at the other physical attributes, which give me a visual reading of the actor's age and type.

Knowing where they fit in the casting pool helps actors decide how to market their talents. Ingénues are different from character women; quirky is different from sexy. Although everyone is a combination of many essences and it's foolish to think one headshot will capture all the things you are, a headshot is more striking, and therefore more successful in catching an agent's eye, when it reveals one or two personality lines rather than three or four. If you have a huge range that goes from rural Americana to Park Avenue sophisticate, keep the looks separate and go for two or three headshots. This is easier for women to accomplish: makeup and hairstyle changes can provide new looks that suggest different personae. Men basically rely on facial hair to alter their look. I suggest that men take a roll of film with a five o'clock shadow, followed by a roll clean shaven.

Headshots are still the actor's single most important marketing tool. Be smart about how your photo portrays and sells you. Have a clear sense of who you are and what you're selling to the marketplace *before* you have your headshot session with a photographer. While the session may, indeed, be a journey of self-discovery, it shouldn't be approached as such. That could be an expensive trip resulting in lots of vague, in-between shots, instead of bringing forth a "you" that's clearly identifiable in the marketplace. One photographer I know advises her more inexperienced subjects to work with an on-camera acting coach before sitting for headshots. This is meant to help the actor clarify his type while giving him some experience in front of a camera.

It is understandable that an actor, frustrated by the lack of attention he is getting from his mailings, and from the business in general, might feel compelled to do something unusual, absurd—anything just to be different—in his next headshot session. In those moments of desperation, it's best to resist temptation. Photos are costly and money shouldn't be spent in ways that may give a "kick" to the moment, but prove to be expensive mistakes when trying to move a career forward.

Here are some quick critiques from an agent who has seen many headshots:

An 8" x 10" that is all face gives a distorted view, and an agent will have to struggle to *read* anything beyond the initial shock assault.

A headshot featuring an actor's body in the pose of a pretzel—crouching torso, arms akimbo, the head no bigger than a fingernail—doesn't provide agents, or casting directors for that matter, with much useful information.

Beware of oddly placed body parts—a floating arm without a hand, disembodied fingers holding up a chin. They steal focus from the subject: you, the person.

I often ask actors, "Why have a *head*shot that is three-fourths background and one-fourth face?" It should be the other way around.

Lastly, "open and vulnerable" does not mean vague and blank. Put some expression into those eyes.

Transformational actors who have the ability to play many things and be many people are challenged to come up with a headshot that markets this talent. Imagine a headshot of Robert De Niro that suggests the range of his creativity. Some actors use the composite (a combination of four poses laid out on one 8" x 10") to show their versatility. This might work in the commercial sector, specifically for print jobs and modeling assignments. However, it is not so successful in the legit world, where agents find that casting directors are more concerned with casting a particular role than finding the most versatile actor. I suggest that actors who consider themselves extremely versatile try for a neutral shot rather than force the issue one way or another, and let their résumé bespeak their acting range.

READING THE RÉSUMÉ

Depending on my initial assessment and interest from looking at an actor's headshot, I will or will not turn it over to read the résumé. When I do move on to the résumé, I become a private investigator, picking up clues as I go along. I read the résumé from top to bottom, first noticing the actor's name, union affiliations, height, weight, and hair and eye color. If vocal range is listed I think, "Ah, a singer, good," since so many opportunities are available for musical talent. I then look over the credits, picking up any details that strike a familiar chord with me. I notice theater companies, television shows, titles of plays and movies, roles, and directors. This is how I piece together the story of this actor's work experience and castability. Since I'm an experienced agent with a solid knowledge in all areas, I can quickly spot when an actor is padding the résumé. Most agents advise actors not to lie about their credits. We realize that everybody has to start somewhere, so there is no shame in being a beginner. If you are starting out and don't have any credits, list the roles you've worked on in class as "Representative Roles." This at least tells an agent and casting director what you are familiar with and how your teachers have cast you. (If you are an absolute beginner with no training whatsoever, you aren't ready yet to have an agent.) Once you start working, either on a professional or nonprofessional level, you can add those credits to your résumé and drop out the "Representative Roles." Credits on a résumé that are a decade or two old indicate that the actor is returning to the business from a hiatus. In most cases, résumé credits match up with a headshot; when they don't, the lapse of time can usually be explained. If I'm interested enough to meet the actor, I will learn his story during the interview.

On many of the résumés that I see, actors list a significant amount of work that they've done either at theaters out of town or in the Off-Off-Broadway venues in New York City, and in student or independent films that I don't recognize. At first glance the abundance of credits is impressive, but when I read more carefully I discover that I don't know how to interpret this unfamiliar information. Evaluating a résumé is easier when I know the plays, the roles, or the theaters, or some member of the creative team behind the films. At least then I can get a handle on how the actor has been cast and with whom he has worked.

When an actress's credits don't tell me much because they are either too few or for projects that are unfamiliar to me, I go to the training section of the résumé to see where she has studied. Every agent has his favorite training school and acting method that produce the actors whose work he likes. Some agents like Method actors. Others prefer Meisner-trained performers. Others go for Juilliard actors, or Viewpoints actors...the list goes on and on. Some agents have affiliations with the schools they graduated from many years ago and favor this year's crop of graduates over grads from other schools. By knowing where an actress has studied and what skills she has developed, an agent can begin to get a sense of her place within the industry and of casting possibilities for future submissions. For example, if Shakespeare training and experience are absent on the resume, the agent won't consider the actress Shakespeare ready.

Lastly, I glance over the "Special Skills" section to see whether anything unusual jumps out at me. Fluency in a second language may clarify an ambiguous ethnicity, for instance. I assume that the listing of specific languages, dialects, or instruments denotes a degree of proficiency. Be prepared: when auditions come up requiring a special skill, there usually isn't time to take refresher lessons. The casting director won't wait for your violin to be sent from home or for you to practice scales on a rental. List as special skills only those instruments that you play well or languages that you speak fluently. If you can't display a skill at a moment's notice but want to include it on your résumé, then accurately note your degree of proficiency. Your being able to drive an automatic-shift car or wear contact lenses means less to a legit agent than it might to a commercial agent. No special skill will prompt me to interview an actor, but any one skill could be a hook for engaging in conversation during an interview. Be creative, not outrageous, in your special skills section.

THE COVER LETTER

The cover letter accompanies the headshot and résumé. It is your written introduction to an industry professional—whether that be an agent, casting director, producer, director, or writer. Most industry professionals I know agree that it is absolutely necessary to include a cover letter with a photo-and-résumé submission. Actors need to understand that any submission they make is an attempt to build a relationship. Cover letters signify good manners and an attention to professional detail that befits a business person. Those names listed in *Ross Reports* represent human beings who like to be approached specifically as individuals. Letters beginning with "To Whom It May Concern" or "Dear Agent" invariably find their way into the circular file. Look at it this way: if an actor considers an agent to be one of the nameless masses, what's to stop that agent from having a reciprocal reaction towards the actor?

The cover letter is one element in marketing that can help an actor overcome the impersonal nature of mass mailings. In their marketing campaigns, actors can control how they express themselves. What they write, how they write it—even what they write it on—provide clues that an agent uses to profile a prospective client. A quickly scribbled note on a scrap of lined paper says something not very flattering about the person writing it and how he views the person he's addressing. Agents pick up on this. Looking for ways to separate the must-sees from the no-sees in the stacks of envelopes piling up on their desks, agents seize upon the cover letter as one of the first components to attack.

One agent, speaking on a panel to a group of actors, homed in on the cover letter. He stressed how important it is for an actor to do research before sending photos and résumés to agents. His pet peeve is receiving letters from actors addressing him as a commercial agent, although a variety of resources in the business clearly list him as a legit agent. Judging from how strongly he expressed himself on the subject, I definitely got the impression that he would not look past this error to review the headshot and résumé accompanying such a letter.

Actors hear conflicting things about the cover letter all the time. They wonder what they should "cover" in the letter. Should they try to be funny, interesting, personable? Should they describe how they see themselves and talk about the work they've done, or about the work they'd like to do? Should they keep it simple or make it detailed? They wonder what would be a big "turn-off" to an agent.

It's difficult to suggest a specific approach for the cover letter because agents, being individuals, respond differently to different approaches. One agent states that he wants to learn something about the "person." He responds to "clever," and looks for a winning opening line that brings him in immediately. He likes "candor," giving actors permission to talk about themselves as *people*. Another agent is interested solely in the "actor" and appreciates a clear and professional statement of purpose. Some agents like gimmicks; others think they are just so much foolishness. One actor doing a mass mailing to agents put confetti in the envelopes. He heard from one agent out of the hundred whom he solicited, who got a kick out of opening the envelope to find confetti flying all over her desk—so much so that she called in the actor for an interview. One wonders how many agents were annoyed at this ploy, yet it could be argued that, in the end, one interview with one agent justified antagonizing the others. What makes this business so unique is how truly difficult it is to separate the "actor" from the "person." When composing cover letters, revealing a little bit of both is probably the best way to go. Predicting the results of a marketing campaign is impossible. In short, the actor must decide on a format and content which he feels expresses himself in a truthful and an interesting way.

It's hard to specify what makes a good cover letter. Agents just know one when they read it. The letters I most remember are straightforward and to the point. They have an easy flow and a no-nonsense attitude. Pertinent details justify the intended purpose, which is stated clearly, with no apology. Any letter that *requests* a partnership rather than demanding one with a mistaken sense of entitlement always gets a better response from this agent. I would much rather read a sincere and honest letter coming from a person who is totally at ease with her place in the industry than a letter written with a puffed-up sense of self-importance.

For myself, I think in a cover letter it's important to *briefly* describe your training, experience, and career aspirations. Three short paragraphs (each two to three sentences in length) stating where you've been, where you are, and where you want to be provide a good structure. How you fill in the structure gives clues to your personality and business ethic. Having a show to promote is an excellent focus for the cover letter. A brief, enticing description of the production, stating the obvious—why an agent should invest her time in seeing it—gives purpose and focus to the initial mailing of a headshot and résumé, and paves the way for follow-up phone calls.

Beware of first lines that sound like Madison Avenue ad campaigns boasting of the millions you and the agent will make together. Avoid lines that express a false humility and the woebegone attitude of a lucky loser. These may work against your purpose. While agents appreciate actors who have a realistic understanding of where they are positioned in the industry, we'd much rather hear from someone who is upbeat and positive than from someone who accompanies each statement with an excuse or apology. Expressions of casual, personal intimacy or breezy nonchalance belie an insecurity better served with directness and real information. If you're young and just starting out, talk about your training and passion for acting. If you're experienced and well trained, describe future goals. If you've just moved to New York from Chicago, returned from a national tour, or are in a master class with one of the great teachers—start there and proceed.

Refrain from flights of fancy or page-long artistic manifestos. They have limited success in attracting an agent's attention because no agent has time to read them. Save the big story for the interview. When writing your cover letter, your interior monologue should always be, "What do I have that's unique that would make an agent want to meet me?" Figure out what separates you from the masses, then find your special way to express it. The economy of a cover letter will force you to come up with a sharply defined and purposeful approach—a "hook."

Perhaps your hook is a special gift, like being a triple-threat, well-trained Shakespearean actor, or a fearless comedienne. Noting your "type" by celebrity name is just so much cookbook programming. It's fine to express admiration for a celebrity and suggest your work's likeness to hers, but to condense your "sell" of your special talent into something akin to a Hollywood screenplay pitch ("I'm a Renée

Zellweger/Cameron Diaz type") actually throws the focus on the celebrities rather than on you. Because our culture is so "celebrity conscious," once we hear or see a "name," images of that person flood our consciousness and we travel off on a personal fantasy with the star, which hardly leaves room for an unknown like you. "I'm a ____ _____ type" is a marketing shorthand that everyone uses to cut corners, but it ultimately diminishes the possibility of an agent's making a new discovery: you.

When actors mention in their cover letters that they are seeking *new* representation, the first thing I do is look at their credits to determine their place in the business. If the credits are impressive, my curiosity is piqued. Perhaps in his letter the actor will go on to give his reason for seeking new representation. Maybe his agent is retiring, closing offices, or moving to another city. Once I opened an envelope and saw the photo of an actress whose brilliant performance in an independent feature film I had seen just a week before. She wrote that she was seeking new representation because her former agency had closed offices. Thrilled, I immediately picked up the phone to set up a meeting.

Actors wonder if presentation makes a difference. Put yourself in an agent's shoes. We get twenty-five to fifty photos and résumés in the mail each day. They usually pile up on our desks until we can stand it no longer. In a flurry of activity, we open the envelopes, take out the photos and résumés with accompanying cover letters and flyer invitations, and sift through them. Consider what will attract our eye more: A cover letter on colored paper? Or on a sheet ripped from a spiral notebook? Will a letter that's typed in a clear and interesting font be easier to read than one written by hand in poor penmanship? Does a busy agent really have the time to read a two-page, single-spaced personal biography? Common sense and business savvy will lead you to make correct decisions in these matters.

How much influence these letters have in actually making an industry professional pick up the phone to set up an interview is hard to determine. What is absolutely certain, however, is how necessary they are. Make sure to date them (agents like to keep current when responding to solicitations), to address specific people by name, to sign them— and to include your phone number!

REFERRALS

First of all, make sure that the referrals you mention in your cover letters are truthful and accurate. Mentioning a referral here is not to be confused with listing directors' names on your résumé. Those exist as objective fact, and may or may not spark the reader's interest. A referral invites the agent to verify that the person you've mentioned recommends you and your work. Agents pay close attention to referrals from casting directors, for instance, and will always track down a recommendation mentioned in a cover letter. One reason for this is the assurance that the casting director who is a "fan" will call an actor in for auditions. Getting auditions for an actor is always half the battle for an agent, so a casting director's predisposition to see the actor is a strong selling point. One of my pet peeves is actors' dropping names of casting directors whom I don't even know. ("So-and-so suggested I contact you.") A reference from a stranger, whatever his title, tells me nothing about the actor and his work—except, perhaps, that the actor does sloppy research or has a vivid imagination. I become suspicious and will most likely send his résumé to the circular file without review. Check your sources: Make sure there is a definite connection between the CD and the agent you're approaching. And make sure that the casting director was sincere in his recommendation; get his okay before using his name in your cover letter.

Agents take client recommendations very seriously too, although we know that actors "share" their agents for all sorts of reasons. The most sincere and effective reason springs from genuine respect and interest in another actor's career. If a client of mine has worked with an actress or has an extensive knowledge of her work and recommends her to me, I will strongly consider the referral and probably meet the actress. If the introduction is merely a gesture of good will on my client's part, I will receive it as such and take action according to my interest and whether or not there is an opening in the client roster for the actress. In the end, no matter how strong the recommendation, I would still want to see the actress's work before deciding whether or not to represent her.

One final note: if someone gives you permission to use him as a contact, by all means do so. If your outreach doesn't get a response from the agent, you may then ask your "benefactor" to follow up for you, perhaps making a personal call to the agent to urge a meeting.

ACTOR REELS AND COMPACT DISCS

Since most legit agents do not have time to view unsolicited demo reels or DVDs, or to listen to compact discs, I would advise actors against including these marketing tools in their initial mailings to agents. The exception would be when soliciting representation from voiceover agents, who *expect* to find a voiceover demo tape in an initial mailing. In the voiceover field, the demo tape is equivalent to a headshot and résumé elsewhere. Reels, DVDs, compact discs, and demo tapes are good to have for follow-up purposes, too. Sometimes an unsolicited photo and résumé pique my interest in an actor who is not performing in New York. I look to see whether he lists any TV and film work. If there is a substantial amount, I will call him to request a demo reel.

Actors should make sure to include only professional television or film work on their demo reels. Including inferior-quality student films, videotaped scenes from acting class, or a community theater's production of *Hello, Dolly!* will only work against you. Provide a variety of clips, start and end with your strongest work, and try to keep the reel no longer than five minutes. Make sure the quality of the tape or DVD is the same from start to finish—it's very disconcerting for the viewer to go from a very clean clip to one in its third generation. An obvious tip, but one worth noting: choose clips in which the focus of the camera is on you and not on the other actors. An actor once sent me a tape with a selection from a low-budget film in which his back was to the camera the entire time. He might as well have been off camera for all the good this clip did him.

The best demo tape I ever saw had five short clips from a sampling of television and film work. The clips were very different in subject matter and tone, and each ended with a cliffhanger. The tape left me wanting more—precisely the response a demo reel should elicit—and I was excited to meet this actor. Another tape featured a compilation of scenes from an actress's stint as a recurring player on a soap opera. Each selection centered around a cup of coffee. Although the tape lacked variety of subject matter, the running gag was humorous. Many years (and many tapes) later, I still remember it. I would, however, discourage actors from compiling a reel using one character. This was a special case.

For musical talent, a compact disc of songs is an extremely valuable marketing tool. Many times after hearing an actor sing at an audition, I want to get a better sense of his range. Listening to a compact disc with a sampling of different material gives me just that. Legit, pop rock, country—an agent needs to hear the quality and range of an actor's musical talent. Of course nothing can compare to watching a live performance in a show, but in this section we're talking about marketing tools to attract attention and entice interest. I once heard an actress sing at an "audition" night. (These evenings, produced by firms located in the various industry centers, offer actors and singers an opportunity to pay a nominal fee to audition for an agent. See "Pay to Play Auditions," page 28.) I liked the actress's voice very much, but questioned its strength and range. The next day I called her to ask whether she had a compact disc demo of her singing, because I wanted to hear more. She did and brought it to my office. It was a wonderful sampling of many different styles, simple but extremely well produced, focusing on her voice and without a lot of complicated instrumentals. Singers stand forewarned: don't overproduce your demo CDs. Agents want to hear the voice and the song stylist, not the band. When this actress came in to sing for the other agents in the agency, at my invitation, I was beaming: she sang the songs I suggested (I knew her repertoire better by this time, having listened to her CD) and really sounded great—with a gloriously full and vibrant soprano. I would never have followed through to bring this actress into the office had I not heard her demo CD.

Showcases

Most legit agents like to see an actor's work before signing, freelancing, or even meeting him. Agents may respond to photos received in the mail, or set up interviews at a client or casting director's recommendation, but invariably the conversation leads to, "I'm interested in working with you, but I need to see your work." For agents needing to see talent perform live, showcases—productions specifically produced to display the work of actors to industry professionals like agents and casting directors—fit the bill. Preferably the performances should be at an accessible location, in a safe area, at a reasonable hour, and at no cost to the agent. Avoid inviting agents to see you be "great" in a mediocre showcase. Remember that agents put in a solid day of work before going out at night to see theater. Although seeing a showcase is free entertainment, it is "work" for an agent. Don't count on their coming to see your ten minutes of comedy at Carolines, at 2 a.m.

It is not easy for actors to land a quality showcase in a convenient location at a time of year when industry professionals aren't bogged down with priorities like pilot season (when the test television shows are cast), or the student league presentations (in which graduating students from acting conservatories and college theater departments descend on the industry centers looking for agents), or the holidays (yes, agents have families). Even a dream showcase—an exciting new play with a fabulous cast and director—will not attract an agent if it's in a non-air-conditioned black box in an out-of-the-way location during a record-breaking heat wave.

When to Invite the Industry

Actors are ecstatic when they get cast in a showcase: finally they have something to which they can invite an agent. Unfortunately, however, many actors never know whether the showcase they're in is any good while they're in it. They can sense how they're doing, but can't objectively judge the production as a whole. Their ultimate question is whether or not they should invite agents and casting directors to see the piece. What should they do if they're great but the evening is long? Or if they're not sure about the other actors' performances? Should they invite industry people anyway? Actors are eager to have their work be seen by these industry folk, but certainly don't want to make enemies of potential allies before even meeting them.

Bold actors invite agents and casting directors no matter what, and consider any promotion of the showcase valid and valuable, whether or not they succeed in getting industry to the show. Agents are impressed with self-starters who are motivated to generate work for themselves. They hope the quality of the showcase will match the moxie of the actor.

Cautious actors hold off on mailing flyers, sometimes missing the opportunity to get industry folk to see them in a quality production. These actors vacillate during rehearsals, wondering whether or not to invite people, then realize on the final weekend of performance (after a best friend praises the showcase) that it is too late to promote the show to agents and casting people.

Many times actors ask me where I think they should draw the line in promoting their showcases. Here's what I think: actors should spare agents and casting directors from mediocre evenings of theater. Agents expect showcases to be professional so they can assess an actor's talent within a context similar to what they would submit him for. Agents don't want to devote two hours of their extended workday to making educated guesses about what an actor can do. ("I think the actor would have been better if the material had been better"—things like that.) Showcases are meant to prove hunches about an actor's talent, not to create more questions.

Respecting an agent's work hours and tolerance level buys good will. If you push an agent to see you be "great" in a less-than-professional, uneven, or just plain bad piece, the agent's negative response to the production will overshadow any recognition of your "brilliance." Some actors who appear only in the first half of a showcase will even suggest that agents "first-act" it. This is a generally accepted practice, although I still feel guilty when considering whether to leave at intermission.

To sum up, showcase etiquette advises actors to be all-inclusive when advertising the product, but selective when pushing for attendance. Send those invitations to everyone, but only make follow-up phone calls when you are sure that you and the piece are worth viewing.

SELF-PRODUCED SHOWCASES

Many actors turn to producing their own showcases to market their talents. In doing so, they should first decide which industry people they want to attract. If you're seeking commercial representation, for example, why not produce a fifty-minute light-hearted scene night featuring actors with commercial looks, types, and attitudes? If you're an incredible singer, gather a group of musically talented friends and perform a cabaret show. Legit agents are always looking for top-notch musical talent, so these evenings, if well produced and well advertised, are bound to attract industry professionals. Classical actors beware: A showcase of *Macbeth* is hard to sell. Agents avoid showcases of classical work like the plague because at this level their quality is generally inferior, and at any level they are long. (Ever seen a Shakespearean play run under three hours?) I've often thought that an evening of classical scenes interlaced with songs might attract an industry audience. This format might soften an agent's customary prejudice against classical fare by providing an opportunity to canvas classically trained actors and musical talent simultaneously.

Agents generally like to see more than two actors perform in an evening. It helps them justify their investment of time. So one-man (or -woman) shows, although a great showcase for an actor, fail to draw industry folk. I received an email for my column from a producer once who was frustrated by the lack of response to a big campaign she had made to get industry people to see her husband in his one-man show at an Off-Broadway theater. She had received two responses to the 150 invitations she'd sent out. She wondered why it was so hard to get people who are supposed to be looking for new talent interested in viewing a critically acclaimed show. I told her that a one-percent response rate is normal for mailings, and that the two responses she received were actually a success. I also remembered receiving the package. The presentation was very professional and the materials were, indeed, enticing. However, they came across my desk at a time when I was out every night covering clients in shows and had no free night to devote to seeing an unknown actor in a solo performance. An agent's first priority is to see her clients in shows. Unrepresented actors can use this fact to their advantage: getting in a show with actors who have representation brings you closer to the possibility of having an agent see your work.

Regarding the efficacy of solo shows, there is always an exception to the general rule. I remember when I was just starting out as an agent, I saw a well-produced showcase of an intriguing play which featured a very good, young cast. I thought one actor in particular was brilliant. I very much wanted the agency to represent him, but I needed to find an opportunity for the other agents in the office to see him perform. Shortly after the showcase, he was booked to do his one-man show, which he had been developing over the years, at a club in downtown Manhattan. I very persistently encouraged the owner of the agency to accompany me to see him in this production. Luckily, he was great and my boss was sold! We started representing the actor immediately.

Keep in mind that many senior agents don't even attend showcases. But junior agents, assistants, and interns do. Actors should invite and push these industry players to attend their showcases. A junior agent using you to raise his stock in his boss's esteem can only benefit you and your career. Plus, yesterday's intern can become tomorrow's studio head.

Actors should target casting directors, along with agents, to see their showcases. It is the casting directors' job to constantly acquaint themselves with the ever-renewing pool of actors. Establishing a relationship with a casting director not only leads to employment opportunities but to possible introductions to agents.

THE INVITATION

When inviting industry professionals to a show, send a current headshot and résumé with a flyer or postcard advertising the production. In your cover letter be very clear about arranging tickets and transportation, if necessary. Make sure it *is* an "invitation." An agent never expects to pay for tickets, cover charges, or drink minimums when prospecting new talent. That's true across the country: from Broadway and Off-Broadway in New York, to CAT in Chicago and BAT in San Francisco, to films, comedy clubs, and cabaret shows. It is assumed that the word "invite" means complimentary tickets, but be sure to clarify this in your cover letters. The best way to get agents to see your work if you're performing out of town is to take care of everything. That means transportation, housing, and tickets. How could an agent refuse such a generous offer? It might sound like a large cash outlay, but remember that the expense is tax deductible. More importantly, it will set the correct tone between you and the agent from the very beginning of the relationship, showing how you value the agent's time and comfort when soliciting her attention. Of course, a large marketing investment like this makes sense only when what you're doing is a must-see. This is assessable only on a case-by-case basis.

In your cover letter and phone follow-up, find a hook beyond the opportunity of seeing your work with which you can sell the production. Justify to the agent why she should devote her one free evening that week to seeing your showcase above all others. If the production is really good and you can substantiate that claim with a review from the leading newspaper, or with a well-known producer's interest in moving it, get on the phone and start selling. Offer limo rides, dinner—whatever enticements you can imagine—to get those agents and casting directors in the seats!

"PAY TO PLAY" AUDITIONS

For most legit agents in New York, live performance is the only true litmus test to determine whether they want to represent an actor. Being able to say, "I saw so-and-so play such-and-such, and she was brilliant," legitimizes our "pushes" to casting directors. Along with attending showcases, many agents participate in "audition" or "pay-to-play" evenings, which they view as good beginnings that can lead to representation for the actor down the road. Organizations exist that specialize in mounting these evenings, sometimes featuring agents, sometimes casting directors. In these settings actors essentially pay to show their work to industry professionals, and agents or CDs "sell" their expertise to actors.

Some actors question the legitimacy of pay-to-play auditions. In defense of these evenings, I can only speak for myself and how I approach them. If an actor is paying to meet me, I will make that meeting worth his while. That does not mean the actor will automatically acquire an agent. I reserve the right to choose whom I represent. However, I think these evenings are valuable simply because they offer actors an opportunity to meet and perform for industry players. Before these forums existed, agents were just names in *Ross Reports*. Now, in these evenings, we are human beings in the flesh, accessible one-on-one for seven to ten minutes. Think about it: The purpose of a mass mailing to agents is to get an interview with an agent. When an actor signs up for one of these evenings, he accomplishes that goal without the huge expense of a mailing. The actor pays for a definite meeting that would have only been a hoped-for possibility with the mailing. Do the math: Let's say you send a mass mailing to a hundred agents. That would *maybe* elicit one response that *might* lead to an interview. Say that mailing your headshot and résumé plus a cover letter costs sixty cents. Multiply that by one hundred and you get $60—and that's not even factoring in the price of the envelopes, stationery, photos, and résumés. The going rate for audition evenings is $35 a pop, which makes them cost effective. For about half the price of a mass mailing, an actor is guaranteed the chance to show one industry person his work: either a monologue or a song—sometimes both—which wouldn't necessarily be true in an interview in an agent's office, where an actor is lucky to utter a complete sentence amid workday interruptions and the constant ringing of phones.

Actors always want to know about agents, what they look for, and how they do business. The question-and-answer period that usually begins these evenings provides a valuable forum for discussion. The success of this session depends largely on the actors' participation. However, many times I find that I walk into a room full of nervous actors waiting for their chance to audition and "get" an agent. Sadly, they remain frozen, don't ask questions, and neglect to take full advantage of this time with an agent. I begin by stating very bluntly that most likely none of them will "get an agent" that night. I am there to canvas new talent; to answer questions about the agency, myself, and the business in general; and to give honest feedback on each actor's work as I see it from my perspective as an agent—an industry player who represents talent of a certain level that can book work in certain areas. I invite talent to keep in touch with me by sending me invitations to showcases whenever they perform in the city.

These pay-to-play evenings are for making impressions. What impresses me is a positive attitude, sincerity, and a passion for the work; and work that is specific, truthful, and creative. Talent will win every time. Keep in mind, however, that one agent's estimation of talent is another's reason to pass on an actor. It's all subjective.

Actors should have a collection of monologues ready for these pay-to-play evenings, ranging from comic to serious, classical to contemporary—agents might ask for a contrasting piece. Singers should have a book of material ranging from legit to pop/rock, opera to country, Rogers and Hammerstein to Jason Robert Brown. Always be prepared to deliver on a request for an additional monologue or song. Never try out a new monologue or an uncoached song at one of these evenings. In fact, if you have a monologue that you've actually performed in a show and are very comfortable with, I would suggest using that, so your audition experience is less stressful. Know, however, when a monologue has gone stale. Either figure out how to revitalize it or trade it in for a new one. Dress appropriately and look your best. First impressions are key moments in relationship building.

Some actors complain that these evenings can at times turn into "workshops" (work sessions as opposed to auditions). They do, quite frankly, for me, when the performer's level of skill and experience does not meet my requirements as an agent. I suppose I could just say, "Thank you," and move on to the next actor. However, most seem to appreciate the honest and constructive feedback I offer. I'm allotted a certain amount of time with each actor. He first performs the monologue and/or song. In the remaining minutes after viewing the work, I give him the choice of telling me something about himself or getting my feedback. If he asks for the latter, I start by asking him what he intended to "show" me, the agent, in terms of his talent and marketability. I then tell him whether or not he was successful in his purpose. I think this is more constructive than a polite, "Thank you."

MUSICAL AUDITIONS

One back-door entrance into an agency exists—for musical talent. Since musicals are an overwhelmingly popular form of money-making entertainment these days, the need for musical talent in a legit agency's stable is greater than ever. Many regional theaters begin their seasons with musical revues; Broadway and Off-Broadway are filled with musical vehicles; movies and television are re-embracing the musical for product. Why, even the cost of a ticket to New York's City Center Encores! series, which has popularized concert-staged readings of musicals, is approaching Broadway prices. Every day more and more breakdowns of musical projects come across my desk. From Equity workshops of new musicals, to TV movies of classic Rogers and Hammerstein to, at this writing, the making of the movie of the musical of the movie *The Producers*—seeking good musical talent is financially imperative for an agent.

With this in mind, many legit agencies offer musical comedy performers the opportunity to audition. Where there is little or no time for an actor to perform monologues in an agent's office, agents will make the time to hear two contrasting songs showing vocal range and acting ability. This is done in various ways. Some agencies have a piano in the office and set up evenings during which they provide an accompanist for the auditioning actors. Other agencies book space in a studio and schedule talent to audition in five-minute slots. For that matter, an actor can suggest setting up time with an accompanist in a studio so that an agent or group of agents can hear him sing. This is an especially good follow-up when an agent responds positively to the CD demo of songs that you submitted to her.

A musical audition for an agent is different from auditioning for a specific project. Agents want to see in the song a full range of vocal quality, ability, and technique, along with the equally important level of good acting. I usually suggest that an actor bring in two full songs (to fill a five-minute audition) that are contrasting and show vocal as well as acting range. When agents say "contrasting," we mean it. One time an actress brought in two songs that were both dark and driving. While she had a thrilling voice and was very committed to her choices, she showed us her passion but not her range. We would have had a hard time deciding how to submit her for any kind of character that was different from the one she showed us. We wondered, for instance, whether she had a sense of humor and could play comedy. Auditions are most successful when they include material that contrasts by 180 degrees. Try to honestly show as great a range as possible— in the style, sound, or acting levels of each song. If the pieces are a traditional musical theater up-tempo and ballad, make sure that your up is hilarious and your ballad very sweet and poignant. Create a similar contrast with pop/rock and legit selections. Or country and operatic. Agents need to see the full range of your abilities in these auditions so we can make a complete evaluation of talent, technique, and casting possibilities. We are seeking information that will help us in the future if we take on the actor and submit him for projects.

When auditioning for agents, bring in your tried-and-true audition material. Don't experiment with new songs; that will cost you big time. Recently we saw a fellow who excelled in his first song but was very unfocused in his second. When I asked him how long he had been using this song for auditions, he admitted that his coach had just given it to him. It was a shame that he chose to bring this under-rehearsed piece to an audition for agents. Despite his fine performance of his first selection, his less-than-professional rendition of the second cost him the chance to work with a group of interested agents, because they worried about his auditioning skills.

When agents hold musical auditions, they expect to see acting values within the singing. After all, a song is like a monologue set to music; the heightened event of the situation forces the character to "burst into song." Like an audition monologue, an audition song should have a journey with a beginning, middle, climax, and resolution. By the time an actor gets through the door of an agent's office to sing for her, the agent expects his voice to be developed and trained. This is the minimum standard in the business. Agents want to know what you have beyond that; specifically, we are looking at vocal quality, technique, strength, musicality, acting choices, and personality. This is why we need to hear full songs, not just sixteen bars showing your money notes.

A few tips about auditioning for agents: Dress for the occasion, as you would if you were auditioning for a Broadway show. Bring a sense of confidence and fun into the room. Make sure your music is attached properly so that the accompanist has no problem reading it. Make sure your instructions to him are clear and concise. Make sure he knows the tempo you want, and don't expect him to make key changes on the spot. Be gracious and appreciative; he is an important ally. Be professional. Don't make excuses, and try not to show nerves. After all, if you're nervous when auditioning for your potential agents, how are we to think you'll be when you audition for Sam Mendes?

THE AGENT INTERVIEW

Before an actor has his first interview with an agent, he wonders, "What should I wear? What should I say? How should I come across? What questions will the agent ask me? What are some appropriate questions for me to ask? What is expected of me?"

Actors spend so much time and energy trying to obtain interviews with agents that it's a shame many fall short of making the most out of the opportunity when they finally get it. What I mean to do here is offer some insights about what to expect in an interview and how to prepare for and handle the meeting to your best advantage every time.

Regardless of whether you are being called in from a mailing or after an agent has seen you in performance, research the agent and agency before the meeting. If your interview has come from a mailing, you have presumably already done the research and are ready to go. If not, learn the size of the agency, how many agents work there, how long it's been around, what it's known for, and, more specifically, the background of the particular agent you're meeting. Resources available for this research include the Internet, interview books, trade papers, and your fellow actors. This information gives you a knowledge base and position even before you walk into the office.

Wear something simple and clean, with accents that suggest your personality. Suits are not required for men, but unless you want all your submissions to be for punk rockers, leave the facial piercing jewelry at home. Wear what you'd wear to an audition or headshot session.

Be prepared to wait. Agents are very busy people, constantly on the phone, dealing with "situations," and racing deadlines. The chance that you'll be seen "on time" is slim. Accept this; don't take any delay personally. If you have another appointment to go to, mention this to the receptionist, then call your other appointment to say you're running late, and go back to listening to your Walkman or studying lines for tomorrow's audition. Getting all hot under the collar won't do you any good, and it won't get the interview started any faster. Such behavior will only get you labeled as "difficult" before you even say "hello" to the agent. Stay positive through any obstacle, especially during the interview when the phones are ringing off the hook and there doesn't seem to be any chance for real dialogue between you and the agent. If the agent seems particularly stressed, or if you have an important audition to go to which you are in danger of missing, it's perfectly acceptable to suggest meeting another day.

An agent usually starts the interview by asking for a photo and résumé. Make sure you have a few of these on hand in case you meet the other agents in the office. "But I sent it to you in the mail," or, "It was in the press packet for the showcase you saw me in," are no excuses for showing up empty-handed. An agent feels lost without this record of who you are and what you've done. The headshot and résumé anchor the interview, offering visual reference points for discussion and providing an agent with something tangible to use for taking notes.

Be prepared for immediate feedback on your photo. If the comments are negative, make note of them and ask for ways to improve. Ask for suggestions of favorite photographers or for the agent's preferences: natural versus studio lighting, three-quarter versus standard headshots, digital versus regular film, color versus black-and-white. Try not to react defensively to the criticism. Use the negative comments as a springboard for a discussion of headshots from which you come out learning more than you knew before.

Interviews with agents are both personal and professional. The agent might start off with, "So, tell me about yourself." This throws many actors into a state of befuddlement. They wonder if they should talk about their acting? Their personal life? Childhood? Hobbies? What is the agent fishing for? For such occasions have ready a prepared script—a personal monologue giving a brief history of where you grew up, your family, what got you interested in acting and what you want to do—that should seem utterly spontaneous when you "deliver" it during the interview.

An agent might ask you about your personal history: Where are you from? What do your folks do? How many siblings do you have? Is anyone in your family in the business? You are your own barometer as to how personal the information will be that you choose to share. There's no need to dwell on traumas; however, if a traumatic event has played or is playing a major part in your development, you might wish to share it, depending on your comfort level.

Try not to "recite" your résumé. To make conversation the agent will allude to teachers or directors, to projects and experiences that are familiar to her. It's your job to elaborate on these points and highlight the areas about which you are passionate. For example, if Shakespeare is your "thing" and you just finished a Shakespeare course in London, by all means say so. The agent might be able get you auditions for Shakespearean festivals.

Actors are encouraged to "act natural" and be themselves during the interview, while the agent observes and silently critiques how they present themselves. (There's a challenge!) The agent reads your "look" and personality to determine casting possibilities. She assesses your interview skills to see whether you appear comfortable and appealing, whether you come out of yourself and offer something. She wonders how you would do sitting across from a panel of network executives. She is also trying to determine whether you are responsible and will make your auditions and pay your commissions.

Actors should treat the interview like a conversation. Take notes if you must, but don't make it a science project. This is a chance for two people to explore working together. Ask questions and use the answers as a springboard for more discussion. Here are some questions an actor might ask: Do all the agents represent the same client pool, working as a team, or does each agent have a list of his own? Are the agents assigned specific casting directors or particular territories? If the agency has a commercial and legit department, do they work together? Would both departments sign you, or could you sign with one only and do your other business elsewhere? Is the agency bicoastal, or does it have affiliates? How does that work, exactly? What does each coast promise the other for its exclusive clients?

If the meeting is going well and the agent seems interested in working with you, you might ask what your competition is within the agency. You may also ask what kinds of projects the agent would submit you for. However, it's up to you to offer a full account of all your talents and special abilities, of your preferences, and of where you see yourself in the industry vis à vis your strengths and weaknesses. The interview serves as a chance for the agent and actor to get on the same page from the start. If you come in selling yourself as a quirky comedienne and two weeks into the working relationship complain that you're not being seen for *Medea* on Broadway, red flags will go up in the agency. In your discussions with the agent, be general to maximize opportunities for submissions, and be specific to clarify territories that are off limits.

At some point during the interview you will begin to wonder what comes next. Will they offer to "sign" you? To "freelance" with you? Or to get back to you? "Signing" and "freelancing" are two levels of representation available to an actor. The first pertains to management contracts that are sanctioned by the performing unions and signed by the agent and actor; the latter denotes a more casual relationship not bound by written contract. (See Chapter 4 for further details.) Go ahead and ask these questions. It's an excellent way to illuminate your upbeat and savvy professionalism. The agent will respond in one of several ways. She might indicate interest and suggest freelancing. She might say she needs time to process the information from the interview, to which you would respond by asking how she would like you to keep in touch. She might suggest that you meet the other agents/ departments, leading you to ask if you should schedule those meetings now. She might say that she needs to see your work and suggest you get into a showcase. Regardless of the response from the agent, be positive, thank her for her time, and then leave graciously, without apology or excuse. Always leave on an "up" note. The last impression is just as important as the first.

The smartest advice given to actors in terms of their interviews with agents is to encourage them to share the responsibility of running the interview. After all, it's a partnership you're developing, right? Even though the meeting takes place in agent territory, the actor must reach out to make something happen. Make conversation. Ask questions. Talk about yourself, your passions, what you want in your career. Be active, not reactive. Interested and interesting. If it's a game of twenty questions, make sure you ask at least ten of them.

★

You're stapling together your winning headshot and stunning résumé. The cover letter you've composed is short, snappy, and totally you. You've targeted the agents who are going to receive this mailing. Hopefully they will see something that makes them choose you... What will it be?

Chapter 3

HOW DO AGENTS
CHOOSE ACTORS?

As I write this chapter I am sitting on a train traveling to Philadelphia, where I will see a young actress perform in the world premiere of a new musical. Let me fill you in on the history of our relationship. I met this young performer at one of those "pay-to-play" audition evenings in New York. She was young, attractive, had a winning personality and a glorious voice. As I listened to her sing and watched her act, I was not only assessing her musical gifts and level of training, but also the range of her casting possibilities. As I usually do when prospecting new talent, I compared her to the clients I already represented, as a way of gauging her place in the industry at large and at the agency in particular. Was this actress ready to be sent out on professional calls? Could she beat out the competition and book jobs? Would she be competing against many of the young women we already represented? Was this an actress in whom to invest the significant amount of agency time and energy required to build a career? These are some of the questions an agent asks herself when deciding whether to represent an actor.

I was very excited, as I always am when I discover an exceptionally talented performer, and I invited this actress to sing for the other agents in the office, which she was glad to do. After the audition, the consensus among the agents was that while this actress was very talented, she was a little green and needed seasoning. To be honest, her audition in the office lacked the spark she had shown when I saw her the first time. I think she may have been nervous, putting unnecessary pressure on herself to do well on account of my seeing her first and then bringing her in to the other agents. Although I was disappointed that she had not done the best for herself, I was still very supportive—because it was my belief, as it continues to be, that talent doesn't go away, and that nerves are merely a challenge an actor can learn to handle with training and experience.

I told this actress the truth: that we thought she was very talented, but that she needed more experience before we could start sending her out on auditions. We felt that additional professional work would give her that much more confidence in her auditions and her work in general. We also knew that additional professional credits signifying work experience on her résumé couldn't hurt our agenting when it came time to launch her into a larger market. They would make her a much easier "sell." Casting directors question an actor's experience when he lacks professional credits; agents must compensate for this by conveying the excitement of discovering a phenomenal talent. I urged this actress to keep in touch with me, to let me know from time to time what she was doing, and to certainly invite me to anything she was performing in locally. I also said that we would be happy to hear her sing again in six months. She took the feedback very well. I think she may have realized that she had let her nerves get the better of her at the audition in the office, and she was thankful for the honest feedback and the promise of continued interest from an agent. Her positive response encouraged an ongoing relationship, keeping the doors open for future business.

Flash forward to a year later: I received a mailing from this actress inviting me to see her perform in a new musical at one of Philadelphia's premier theaters. In her letter, which accompanied an updated photo and résumé, she mentioned that she was playing a lead role and was very excited about the show. She graciously offered to pay for my transportation to Philly, along with securing me a complimentary ticket for the show. It was obvious that she very much wanted me to see her work. When I realized that she had won the role over some of my best clients, I was naturally impressed and curious. I decided to make the journey. As I sit here on the train, writing this chapter about how agents choose the actors they represent, I am thinking that if this young actress is at the level where I imagine her to be, I will definitely begin working with her. Her good will, talent, and recent professional experience will have already factored into my decision.

As a legit agent I am looking for actors whom I can submit in the areas of the business that I handle. Legit representation covers all areas of theater, television, and film, excluding commercials. That includes Broadway, Off-Broadway, and regional theater; high-profile but low-paying New York showcases, workshops, and readings; episodic TV series, daytime drama, movies of the week, and pilots; and studio and independent films, plus the occasional grad student film. Sometimes a casting director will call me with a breakdown for a commercial, but that is usually when she is seeking strong actors with theater backgrounds, as opposed to "commercial types." In those circumstances, I will submit clients who are not signed for commercial representation with other agencies. Because the competition for legit jobs is so fierce and the demand for A-list actors so high, an agency's selection of new clients requires a careful, in-depth approach and is never taken lightly. How can an agent legitimately "push" (sell) an actor to a casting director against a television personality with box office pull if the actor doesn't have fine training and exhaustive experience that the agent can point to in order to justify her push?

ASSESSING AND CHOOSING TALENT

I choose talent from many sources: I consider referrals from clients, casting directors, directors, and producers. I go to shows, showcases, and audition nights. Headshots and résumés received in the mail may attract my attention, but I need to see someone in action before I can even think about representing him. I have to know what I'm selling, and the only way I feel truly confident about my judgment is by seeing an actor perform in a show. An actor "acting" provides the living proof of the experience and training that appear on the résumé. What convinces this agent will hopefully convince a casting director. Within the business, my reputation depends on the fact that I submit for projects actors whose work I've seen; there is experiential proof behind my pushes.

An actress was referred to us by a client who had shot a commercial with her and thought she had "something special." Attractive and personable, she had training and modest out-of-town credits. We explained to her our agency policy of working with actors only after seeing them perform, and advised her to get into a showcase, which she did. When we attended a performance, we were delighted to discover that the actress was, indeed, very good. Every element of the evening, from the well-written material and convenient location to the talented cast and good direction, worked to the actress's advantage. We immediately started submitting her for projects.

Not all agents stipulate that they must see actors perform in shows before deciding to represent them. Some agents have very busy schedules and complex personal lives. They don't have time to prospect new talent in showcases at night, so in their offices during the day, they make the time to see actors do monologues, sing songs, or show demo reels. Other agents respond to photos and résumés they've received in the mail, calling in actors for interviews and making the decision to work with them based on a hunch.

Sometimes all it takes is a strong referral and a good interview for agents to start working with actors. One time a client of our office recommended one of his best friends, who was seeking new representation. This actor had very good credits and had recently worked with another of our clients who also recommended him highly. He had been with the same agent for many years, and when she retired, had struggled unsuccessfully to feel comfortable with the other agents at the firm. Since we came highly recommended to him through two sources, he approached us. After meeting with him we chose to take a leap of faith. There were enough "sure things" in the mixture to make representing him a calculated risk: good credits, casting director recognition, his realistic expectations about his career. Within weeks after we started working together, this actor booked a very good job.

Talent is the primary aphrodisiac in the romance between agent and actor. Whenever I see an actor perform brilliantly, I immediately want to represent him. Then I start to think objectively and weigh the possibilities of making business together. I have to assess whether I can truly provide enough opportunities for steady employment for this actor, and I need to determine whether I think he is a "booker"— i.e., will he indeed book jobs from these auditions? Since I seek to establish long-term relationships with actors, I also have to assess whether I saw a one-time fluke or a typical performance. In essence, I am evaluating whether there is a career to be had that translates into the long-term success of many bookings over time. Usually an agent, because of her knowledge and experience of the business, can make these assessments and formulate opinions quite easily.

UNUSUAL CASES FOR REPRESENTATION

Sometimes agents decide to break from the pattern and represent unusual talent. Following are two interesting cases that have come my way. I relate these to give hope to those of you who feel you might not fit into the conventional mold.

The first year I was an assistant agent, I canvassed all of the league presentations that the graduating acting students from national and oversea conservatories and acting programs gave in the spring. Since I was an "agent in training" with limited knowledge of the business with respect to casting and booking—how an actor gets work and makes money—I previewed the talent and selected my preferences according to what I knew: acting. I saw some great actors, but had no sense of whether they would book jobs and have careers. For instance, I remember seeing a Pakistani actor who was absolutely wonderful. In his two scenes he was handsome, sexy, dynamic, and well trained, plus he had a comic sensibility that was irresistible. I thought he was just fabulous, but I had no idea how an agent would find work for this actor. I was so green that I couldn't get past what I thought to be the challenges of his ethnicity. So I got cold feet and didn't call him in. A couple of years later I moved to another agency, where I was delighted to discover that he was a client. I found out that he had been working consistently. Obviously, an agent with vision had trusted his belief that this unusual actor, classically trained and very talented, could find work in many different areas. Nowadays, this actor is having a very successful career on the West Coast, playing several recurring roles on noteworthy episodic television dramas.

One time a client invited me to a showcase of a new play that he had written and directed. He wanted me to check out one particular actor whom he thought was extremely talented and deserved an agent. I was absolutely taken by the actor, who happened to be a dwarf. By this time I had become more secure as an agent, and I decided to jump right in to represent this gifted and unusual actor. Opportunities for him seemed to just sprout up out of nowhere during the time we worked together. Projects materialized where I couldn't have even imagined them. I'm sure this had something to do with his being well trained, highly creative, sexy, and funny. People loved working with him, and to this day he has never stopped working. He has a huge network of friends who are always generating projects. One of these actually became a big success, providing the vehicle that propelled him into celebrity.

WHAT AGENTS LOOK FOR

Now that we know what situations lead agents to choose the actors they represent, let's focus more closely on how they make their choices—more specifically, on what they look for in an actor. Such a discussion will naturally turn to the question of when actors should seek representation and how they should market themselves correctly. Let me preface this discussion by reiterating that this is a crazy business with no absolute formulas for success. There are, however, certain steps to take which should all be familiar to us by now: for instance, we all know that to get an agent an actor needs a headshot and résumé, training, and experience.

Agents *choose* to be agents. And agents have the freedom to choose what actors they wish to represent. The selection process often comes down to a matter of subjective taste. Unfortunately for actors, making all of the right moves—getting new headshots, doing showcases, etc.—doesn't guarantee that they will get an agent. It's not like taking a test in which memorizing the facts usually brings about a good score. This business is as much a game of chance as it is anything else. Talent and hard work don't always win. Learning and accepting this lesson was hard for me as an actress, and I continue to wrestle with it as agent. It is usually the source of many an actor's—and agent's—frustration.

An actor once asked me if I thought he would have more success by narrowing the focus of his capabilities when marketing himself to agents. He claimed to be a classically trained character actor who could do anything. According to type, a character actor doesn't fit the conventional mold of ingénue or leading woman (for women), or juvenile or leading man (for men). Character actors possess slightly unusual traits; sometimes these are physical, sometimes they are other qualities—gifted comedian, for example. Since where to cast a character actor is not so obvious, it might take some time until his career gets rolling. Once it does, however, he can use his everyman persona and great skills of transformation to continue working for a long time. This particular actor's dilemma, however, as expressed in his email, was one that I imagine many actors must face when soliciting the attention of an agent. Versatile actors wonder whether spending all those years (and dollars!) in perfecting their craft and gaining experience to become well rounded and complete performers is what it takes to sell themselves successfully to an agent. They wonder whether "well-rounded actor" signifies longevity of career to an agent. And when their mass mailings to agents don't get any nibbles, they wonder whether their abundance of riches may have been confusing.

In addressing these questions I would like to first distinguish between "art" and "show business": Art is the activity of human creativity. Business is the activity of making money. The combination of the two—show business—is a complex and contradictory hybrid. Business people have little patience with the artistic temperament, and artists rebel against the commercialization of their art.

As an actor, you may be blessed with natural talent and develop that talent through many kinds of training, but the moment you wish to turn professional—i.e., make money at your craft—you have entered the marketplace. And what you trade in that marketplace is yourself. Because actors so outnumber jobs, competition is fierce. That Shakespearean monologue you've been working on in your studio apartment in Queens becomes a commodity of commerce in a highly competitive arena: it's not as much about being a brilliant Shakespearean actor anymore, as it is about beating out the competition to *get the job!*

Each audition is like a job interview for a particular position, in which you pit yourself against other applicants whom you must vanquish in order to get hired. How does one do that? By being the "best" applicant for the job. Now, we all know that "best" in showbiz terms doesn't always mean most talented, most trained, or even most qualified. In show business, "best" is often based on a set of subjective criteria which is influenced by personal taste, circumstance, and sometimes timing. Or it refers to specific physical attributes that are beyond an actor's control—two inches taller, twelve pounds heavier, one shade darker, being a few examples. That the criteria for selection should be so literal or based on the whims and fancies of others drives both actors and agents crazy. Take this particularly maddening example: No matter how sensible an agent is in justifying why his client should get hired for the job, if the producer wants his own daughter in the picture instead—guess what? She's in the picture.

Pretend you're the classically trained actor mentioned on page 41. You've done comedy; you've done tragedy. You do Shakespeare; you can even sing and dance. You've studied at all the major studios in New York City, yet no agent has responded to the numerous photos and résumés you've sent out. What's wrong? What's to be done? One thing not to do is throw up your hands in disgust and dismay. That won't solve the problem. What I might suggest is that you focus, instead, on what you can control. Perhaps the abundance and range of talent, skills, and experience listed on your résumé is actually obscuring the "hook" that will get you noticed by the agent and casting community.

Sometimes agents need to be shown how they and actors can make business together. Here are three steps that might help you in focusing your marketing campaigns:

Step One—Assess your talents, realistically, against the backdrop of the competition in the city where you've chosen to build your career. Sure, you were the greatest tap dancer back in Sioux Falls, Iowa, but you just might need to get up to New York speed at one of the dance schools in the city before auditioning for *42nd Street* on Broadway.

Step Two—Decide what's most marketable in your arsenal of skills, i.e., what's going to beat out the competition. Figure out where you are most likely to book jobs. Then, go to…

Step Three—Sell that to an agent. Create marketing campaigns based on your strengths.

Performers often ask me if I look for a certain "type" of actor. There's no doubt an agent goes "shopping" with an eye on particular industry demands and on what the agency might need at a certain time. I remember once hearing an actor ask a panel of agents if it were true that most of the roles up for casting on television breakdowns were really for actors between the ages of eighteen and twenty-five. The agents unanimously answered in the affirmative and made it clear that they were looking to acquire talent that would fill the demands of that market. There are agents who look for actors to fit the casting trends observed in breakdowns, and there are agents who look for actors whose careers they wish to build through the breakdowns. A subtle difference, but one worth noting.

As a legit agent working in the fields of theater, television, and film, I look for actors who are well trained, with range, experience, and a variety of skills, and who can work in all media. Why? More chances to book jobs, more opportunities to make money. I like an actor who makes unpredictable choices. That's exciting. Many times I think that's what keeps casting directors honest, waking them up during casting sessions, forcing them to take notice to discover a new talent. My favorite actors are those who, whether they're playing comedy or tragedy, Shakespeare or Simon, invest their work with the same painstaking specificity to create characters rich in depth and detail. They make it look so easy, investing each moment with the same Zen of intensity and focus. This usually comes from years of performing.

I respond well to actors who have an honest sense of where they fit in the marketplace. They know their general type and age range, and possess a confidence and ambition that are based on a firm grasp of reality, not on some sort of puffed-up invention of desire. While I think it is important for an actor to have an accurate sense of type regarding how the industry will cast him, I am not suggesting that I am a champion of "types." In fact, when an actor sits across from me during an interview and asks me what type I think he is, I refuse to pigeonhole him. I usually throw the question right back at him to see whether he has a realistic sense of himself. You'd be surprised at the extent to which desire and ambition can cloud the vision. I don't like the limiting connotations of type any more than you do. However, the industry uses "typing" as a tool for clarification and selection in the casting process, and I choose to work with it as a means to an end.

I once attended a showcase of scenes performed by the graduating class from a prestigious acting school and was, quite frankly, appalled by the prevalence of type casting. In an effort to entice us industry folk (believed to be prowling for our next meal tickets through these "hot" stars of tomorrow), the material included scenes from then-current movies and television shows. The showcase, catering to the most commercial aspects of the industry, left nothing to the imaginations of the agents and casting directors attending. The banquet of talent offered was a misconceived recipe wasting flavorful ingredients, rather than a fine stew celebrating the talents of dedicated artists who had devoted three years to rigorous conservatory training in Shakespeare, Molière, Shaw, and Ibsen. It seemed odd that all that training should come down to a two-minute sampling of the latest Quentin Tarantino flick. While type casting exists, and there's no way of escaping it, using it as a basis for showcasing talent gives actors little opportunity to display their creativity and uniqueness—qualities equally important to agents and casting directors.

When an actor approaches me for representation, the first thing I usually try to figure out is how we are going to make money together. This translates into how I'm going to get him or her working. The answer to that question will usually have something to do with the strengths of the particular actor. Once I've plugged him into the industry and he's distinguished himself as a winning talent by booking jobs and building fan clubs of casting directors, I will be justified, in the eyes of the industry, in expanding horizons and pushing the envelope. The famous soap star who gets a chance to star in a Broadway musical exemplifies this progression. Some agent was responsible for getting this actor started, and perhaps that same agent is responsible for building that career to the point where the actor now has entrée into other arenas.

I have also been fortunate to work at agencies where a large number of resources are devoted to the development of well-trained actors who are just starting out. At the beginning of a career, the name of the game is to get work. That's what it means to be a professional. Then, when an actor has reached a position of prominence, he can call the shots. Bette Midler started out singing in the baths of downtown New York City. She didn't just wake up one day with her own sitcom and her first name sprawled across the MTA busses in Manhattan. Audiences first saw Kevin Kline singing and dancing in a small role on Broadway. We now see him as a major actor in films. These are character actors with diverse talents. They both had to start somewhere, and you can see that their particular strengths early on landed them the jobs that kicked off their careers. An everyman character actor who can use his skills to change into many different types of characters will work forever, once he starts working. The challenge for actor and agent alike is to capitalize on strength and start the ball rolling; then they can enjoy the fruits of a healthy long-term career and relationship.

THE AGE FACTOR

Many actors wonder whether age is an important factor when agents consider taking on a new client. Age becomes a factor when considered in direct proportion to training and experience. It's a fact that actors face age-related challenges in every decade of their careers. In your twenties, you're young, vital, and talented, but lack experience. In your thirties, the talent pool you're competing against is the largest it will ever be during your career. In your forties, if you're a man, you're still in demand as an actor, but the competition gets even tougher and lifestyle issues start to limit your freedom of choice. For women at forty, the opportunities definitely start to dwindle. The fifties separate the men from the boys. Those who have "made it" are still making it; those who haven't have found other ways of earning a living and generally view acting as a sideline or hobby. Those actors who are still working over sixty and are proven commodities with impressive credits and plenty of energy, face a shrinking market and a professional lifestyle that gets harder and harder to embrace as the years go by. In short, when you're young and willing, you have no experience but lots of opportunities; when you're older and more knowledgeable, you have lots of experience but few opportunities. That's showbiz.

When I look at a photo and résumé I've received in the mail of a forty-year-old actor or actress with modest credits, I can tell that this is coming from a person who has decided to embark on a second career. No matter how great the look (soap opera beautiful or handsome, blue-collar everyman), performers at this age are hard sells if they come to an agent without significant credits from well-known regional theaters or TV/film work. Everyone in the industry expects teenagers or twenty-somethings to have slim credits. After all, they're just beginning. (Child actors are another story.) It's very difficult to plug someone who is "mystery thirties" into the business. He will be competing against a large number of actors, many of whom have been working in the business for ten years and have already compiled a list of impressive credits. As I've said before, casting directors don't generally take chances on actors whose inexperience they deduce from a résumé of modest credits—no matter how many classes and seminars are also listed on the résumé. Professional experience really makes a difference.

Let me put it to you this way: Why would an agent invest her time and energy into jumpstarting a newcomer's midlife career when this agent is already struggling to get auditions for the fine actors she's been representing for ten to twenty years? Where's the financial sense and loyalty in that?

Whether returning to the industry after being away for a period of time or embarking on acting as a second career in midlife, the best thing an actor can do to help himself "get connected" is to first and foremost adjust his expectations to a realistic level. The woman who is taking acting class for the first time at age thirty-two and wondering if getting an agent will be a problem is actually getting ahead of herself. She really shouldn't even be thinking about getting an agent yet. She's not ready. Instead, she should concentrate on building her résumé to the point where it will eventually attract the attention of an agent because it represents a viable commercial entity. True, careers can happen at any time, and this business has a place for late bloomers. What's more to the point is the fact that for the most part there are no shortcuts. Actors develop careers over many years. Overnight successes, at whatever age they occur, are flukes, and usually don't last too long. Recently, for example, I read that an actress who won a Tony Award as a preteen for her first prominent role discovered that by age twenty-five she was perceived by the industry as a has-been. Fyvush Finkel, on the other hand, kicked around the business for years before he became a TV star on *Picket Fences* at the age of sixty. His story is more the norm, plus the flourish of a Hollywood finish.

If you are an actor wanting to enter this profession in the middle of your life, hear this agent's words of advice: enjoy the process; live for the journey. It's best to allow yourself the satisfaction of reaching short-term goals. Focus on making new contacts and rebuilding your résumé with any kind of experience you can get. Know that the competition is tough and there are many obstacles to surmount. Own this reality happily and persevere. You will get an agent when you're ready to have one. As an agent, I can't express to you how delightful it is to meet actors who have a realistic understanding of how the business works, and of how and where they fit into it at any given time in their careers. As one agent once told me, "It's not enough to be very good these days; you have to be great just to be competitive. And greatness comes with experience."

WOMEN AND MOTHERHOOD

I want to spend some time focusing on the problems that actresses face in the business. The plain fact is simply that more roles are written for men than for women. The opportunities offered now are certainly better than in Shakespeare's day, when boys played the female parts and women weren't even allowed to be actors. But we still have a disparity: only occasionally does a Broadway success like *Dancing at Lughnasa*—in which most of the characters are women—fan out through regional theaters in a single season. And only a few celebrity women, like Goldie Hawn, take the bull by the horns and produce their own vehicles offering abundant roles for women. Women can easily feel like second-class citizens in this industry. Older men work more than older women, and the few women's parts written are skewed towards younger actresses. It's a cruel irony that after the chicks have flown the nest and an actress is finally free to return to a career that she put on hold for twenty years in order to raise a family, she finds herself returning to a landscape that's entirely changed and not particularly welcoming. How does one break back into the industry? Who's going to take a chance on representing, much less hiring, *Mrs. Rip Van Wrinkle?*

The business doesn't give a break to mothers-to-be either. One client praised our agency for signing her when she was noticeably pregnant with her first child. This differed from other agents she had met, who questioned whether she would ever really work again, or for that matter even want to work again. I remember we chose to sign her based on the work we had seen her do in an Off-Broadway play, her demo tape of clips from several movies and television shows, her impressive credits, and her upbeat personality. We believed her when she said that she fully intended to continue her career after giving birth. Based on the pleasant experience she had with us, she advises women to tell their agents when they're pregnant and not keep secrets. Actresses should present their pregnancy as a good thing, not a problem, which might sidetrack them for a while but won't prevent their quick return to work. Our client had an actress friend who never told her agents she was pregnant. This actress made excuses for months as to why she couldn't go out on calls. When she finally had to disclose the truth because she couldn't hide it any longer, her agents were very upset with the deception. She had created exactly the situation she had hoped to avoid.

On an interesting side note, our client was eight months pregnant with her second child when she was requested for a role on a Los Angeles-based television show that was coming to New York City to shoot some exteriors. The role was a woman in the borough of Queens who was the neighbor of the episode's victim. The scene took place in autumn and the script called for the woman to rake leaves in her backyard while being questioned by the star of the show. We were thrilled that our client had been requested, but with some trepidation informed the casting director of the pregnancy. Our client felt she could do the physical activity without harming herself and her baby. The casting director asked the producers in Los Angeles if this was alright, and they replied that they would hire her despite her "condition." The fact that the producers allowed for this meant that they really wanted our client for the role—which, of course, speaks well of her.

REPRESENTING SIMILAR TYPES

Many actors wonder what happens when an agent finds a client whom he likes, but already represents several clients of a similar type or look. Speaking for myself, and I assume for other legit agents, I respect my exclusive relationship with my signed clients. I can't take on new talent indiscriminately. However, if I feel I can truly offer enough potential activity to a prospective client while keeping my current clients satisfied, I will establish this new business relationship. To start, I might propose freelancing to test the waters. Another possibility is a three-month exclusive relationship that leads either to an evaluation at the end of the term or to the actual signing of agency papers when the first job is booked—whichever comes first. (Please note that these degrees of representation will be discussed further in Chapter 4.) I can understand an actor's trepidation about signing with an agency without knowing how many similar clients it represents. Therefore, I think it's perfectly permissible to ask where you would stand in your new "home," and I think a smart agent will answer the question honestly. I know I would.

Whenever the situation arises of taking on an actor who is competitive with a current client, the agent will more than likely ask that client's permission, or at least feel him out on the subject. We represented an actress who was doing very well. An opportunity to represent a friend of hers who happened to be her contemporary came our way. When we asked our client how she would feel if we started working with her friend, she replied that it would be fine. I imagine that because she saw the two of them as being on separate career tracks, she felt comfortable enough to grant us permission. Another time we had the opportunity to bring in a very talented singer-dancer who was similar to a client we already represented. Luckily both girls booked very good long-term work and therefore were not competing against each other for any length of time. One of them booked a national tour and the other a Broadway show.

Truthfully, at the end of the day, an agent never really knows which client is going to "make it." That's one of the reasons why an agent can and should represent more than one actor in each age range, look, or type.

WHY CAN'T I GET AN AGENT?

Most actors struggle to understand how agents choose the talent they represent, especially when they are not among the chosen. For my column in *Back Stage*, an actress once sent me an email that read like a primer on "how to get a legit agent." A member of four performers' unions, she had worked jobs under all contracts except Broadway's, and had booked jobs through Equity Principal Auditions (EPAS—auditions required by Actors' Equity Association) and referrals. She described to me in great detail everything she had done in the past twelve years to obtain legit representation. Here's her list: She had sent out mailings, worked in student films, performed in developmental theater companies, and done staged readings. She said she had training, was very professional, got great feedback, followed up, and built relationships. She had spent thousands of dollars on requested new headshots, and had her own website. She had tried to get to know legit casting directors by taking workshops with them so she could impress agents with a list of casting director contacts, which she felt was key for new clients to have. In the end, she wondered why she had had no luck getting an agent, and asked me for advice. I truly sympathized with this industrious actress's predicament. She made such a persuasive case for being an ideal client—i.e., she looked good on paper. However, no agent had sparked to her. Why?

Another actress wrote that she was very discouraged. While she had a high rate of callbacks, she felt she was not getting access to the auditions she needed to move her career forward. A casting director had given her the "helpful" advice that she needed an agent to get seen for those projects. This actress had tried all of the classic strategies to land an agent. She had even had several meetings with one agent who was interested in her but, to her great disappointment, had insisted that she change her look entirely and be somebody else. This actress felt that if she could limit the scope of her search and learn the things she really needed to know about agents in order to get a sense of which one would be "right" for her, she would be on the right track. She asked me if there were times I had misread a prospective client, and she asked what I would recommend for a well-trained actor who was running out of patience with the business but didn't want to carry those resentments into auditions.

While I had no specific solutions for either of these actresses' dilemmas, I did offer some thoughts that came from my personal experience, both as an actress who had sought representation and as an agent who is besieged daily by actors seeking representation. I'd like to share them now with you.

As an actress, I too did all the right things—headshots, mailings, showcases, referrals. I even formed my own theater companies. The most important thing I learned when I crossed over to the side of agenting was how foolish it was to think that an agent would call me up for an interview having only received and reviewed my photo and résumé. From the other side of desk, I now see how important it is to show an agent your work.

First of all, I have to applaud the actress who is aware of her own growing resentment, yet has a keen sense of not wanting to bring this in with her to meetings and auditions. She knows how important it is to stay positive and make a good impression. That's good. However, I feel compelled to address several statements of faulty logic in her letter: It is important for actors to know, especially when talking themselves up to agents, that agents don't necessarily believe a high rate of call-backs justifies submissions for higher-level jobs. Callbacks signify good auditions and being in the running for a part. Booking jobs means beating out the competition. We are interested in meeting and working with the actors who beat out our clients and actually book the jobs. To interest agents in themselves, actors must prove that they are *at least* at the level of the actors already represented by those agents. The time to move upward on the project ladder is when you are consistently *booking* jobs at a certain level. Then you can use your booking record to convince an agent of your readiness to enter a more competitive arena.

Second, the "right" agent for an actor is the one who wants to represent the actor. It's that simple. Actors and agencies match up. For example, some agencies tend to represent musical talent that is equally comfortable in straight plays and musicals. These actors go from Sondheim to Shakespeare in one season. Other agencies look for big voices that they place in the ensembles of Broadway shows or national tours, ever hopeful that these actors will move up the ranks to play principal roles. Either path is fine. It just depends on the individual talent. Researching agents and the "business" through the Internet, books, newspapers, and seminars can point actors in productive directions. Research reveals to singers which agencies specialize in musical talent. Further, it helps performers distinguish the agents who look for actors who sing from the agents who look for singers who act—note the subtle but important difference. This is an example of how research can identify which agents are more likely to choose you. Those agents who are most interested in what you do best are those you should target when you go looking for representation.

Agents look for actors whom they think will work, and actors look for agents whom they think will get them work. While research can help an actor target his search, the real challenge remains of getting an agent interested in representing you specifically. Agents respond to talent, marketability, and professionalism. Upbeat attitudes and realistic expectations don't hurt, either. The agent who is most excited by your talent and feels confident about building your career is the right one for you.

Third, as I write this we are in a recession, which means fewer jobs for fewer actors. An actor I know who works consistently just had the worst year of his career. In tough economic times, everyone feels the pinch as casting gets more and more "inside," and "short lists" get shorter and shorter. Actors are taking jobs that are down a notch from those they're used to doing. Opportunities that existed for aspiring actors in more prosperous times have evaporated. One actress perceptively acknowledged, "When Ileanna Douglas takes a one-scene role on an episode of *Law & Order*, it's clear why getting on that show is so difficult." Every week we submit at least thirty actors for the episode currently being cast, and there's no predicting which client will get an audition. Having a realistic perspective can help an actor maintain a healthy head and heart.

It certainly seems normal for an actress to wonder whether agents sometimes "misread" prospective clients, especially if no agent has responded to her. In addressing the question in the second actress's email, I have to reiterate the fact that we are in a subjective business. And subjectivity works both ways: Agents choose which actors we want to represent, but we don't always get them. Sometimes our hunches work out; sometimes they don't. Many actors now performing on Broadway were passed on by our agency years ago. We don't see this as "misreading" their talent. We're happy for their successes, and we feel that these have no bearing on our taste in talent.

I suppose one could say that an agent might misread an actor's ability to audition—the maturity of his audition technique. When we make our decision to work with an actor based on a performance we've seen in a show, the thing we don't know about him is how he auditions. But that's not really "misreading" an actor. That's just lack of knowledge. And we'll learn soon enough after the first few auditions.

I can't explain why the actresses that emailed me questions leading to this discussion haven't found legit representation; I've never seen their work. For that matter, I can't explain why some casting directors won't see some of my clients for their projects; they've never seen their work. Agents know not to take the lack of response from a casting director personally. So many factors are beyond our control. We function in a business climate of lists: lists of specific actors requested by directors, producers, and writers. When our clients are not on these lists, it's hard to get them seen. Agents have only one choice: to continue submitting and pushing their clients. Actors must be as resilient. They must learn how to withstand the shock of rejection. They must learn to value constructive feedback from reliable sources, but not to let the opinion of others rule their lives. It can take years to get an agent. Actors will continue to seek representation as long as they can tolerate rejection.

Dreams and expectations balance the harsh realities of life in show business. Actors possess them both, but run into trouble when they base their expectations on fantasy rather than reality. For instance, just because an agent says she wants to see your work doesn't mean she will attend the very first showcase you invite her to. And if and when she does attend, her attendance doesn't guarantee that she will want to represent you.

To these two actresses who emailed and others like them: Continue doing what you're doing. Take classes, do workshops, network, keep your skills up and ready for when opportunity strikes. When seeking legit representation, try not to demand results. As one agent I know postulates: if actors spent the same amount of time taking class and working that they spend pursuing agents, they would sooner be ready for an agent to discover them. Try to balance expectations with reality, and know that the principle of free choice works for actors as well as for agents.

An exhilarating aspect of this business is that things can change overnight. Let's say an actress has sought representation from an agency for some time, but the agency claims to have too many women in her age range. Suddenly, the agency finds itself looking for actresses in their thirties because several of its clients are becoming mommies. The door that was once closed is now open. This actress would never know it had opened, however, if she had let her networking activity lapse. Being out there consistently increases the odds for fostering lucky situations. As a gambler would say, "You have to be in it to win it."

★

Let's say you won! An agent is interested in representing you. The interview is set up for Thursday afternoon. It's Tuesday now. There's no time to waste. You should know what types of representation are available out there; and how to decide whether this is the right agent for you.

Chapter 4

HOW DO ACTORS
CHOOSE REPRESENTATION?

S o far in this book we have concentrated on the job description of an agent, the various ways and means that actors can use to acquire agents, and how agents choose the actors they represent. It is time now to focus on the *relationship* between an agent and an actor, in order to understand more fully how they work together to advance the actor's career. In this chapter we will explore the various levels of representation available to an actor, the structures of talent agencies that provide that representation, and the many combinations of representation that an actor can put together for himself through agent-actor relationships.

THREE LEVELS OF REPRESENTATION

The metaphor most often used to describe the three levels of representation that agents offer actors is one of romantic progression: "freelancing" is likened to dating, "going exclusive" to getting engaged, and "signing" to marriage. An actor's age, experience, and specific skills determine the level of representation an agent may choose to offer him. Of course, actors have a say in the matter, too: Some are rambling souls; they enjoy the freedom afforded by freelancing, which enables them to play the field with more than one agent at a time. Others prefer a long engagement; they work exclusively with an agent for many years, never signing a management contract that validates or protects their relationship. Others want to settle down; they desire an agency home and a signed piece of paper to secure an exclusive relationship with an agent.

Dating, engagement, marriage—is the representation for a year or for life? How long and how far do these relationships progress? The answer lies in the unique match between two given individuals: an actor and an agent. Some actors and agents enjoy a freelance relationship for many years without ever progressing to something more exclusive. Others begin their relationship with freelancing and progress to a more exclusive level as their association starts to bear fruit. (An agent, for instance, may invite a freelancer to sign with the agency at the time he books his first job through the agency.)

FREELANCING VS. SIGNING

When I am interviewing actors about possible representation, one of the questions they ask most frequently is, does the agent freelance with actors or work solely with signed clients? Most legit agents have a policy of representing signed talent only. Some, however, freelance with talent with an "eye to sign"—meaning they will begin representing an actor on a freelance basis with the intention of developing the relationship into one of exclusivity. Others work mainly with signed talent, but will freelance in specific areas like musical theater. Agents have particular reasons for determining which level of representation they offer an actor. Knowing how agents make these choices can help actors correctly decide about their own representation.

FREELANCING

For many agents and actors, the freelance arrangement is a testing ground. Did you ever meet someone you really liked, who liked you, too...but you just weren't sure enough about him or her to make a commitment? So you figured you'd get to know each other better and see what happens? That's what agents' freelancing with actors is like— only on a business level, of course. It allows agents and actors to have casual working relationships that can grow into more serious ones.

Freelancing provides a structure in which to explore and develop associations. Those actors fortunate enough to start working with an agent on a freelance basis—or with several at the same time—should know that the representation they receive from an agent is different from the representation offered to a signed client. An agent's first priority is to her signed clients. Whether she is submitting or pushing, they always come first; that's what being signed means. Further, although agents usually consider type when submitting actors, they generally are more creative when submitting signed clients. Thinking creatively— going beyond the obvious casting choices—requires additional time and effort. Until an actor is signed by an agent, he will most likely be submitted only for the obvious choices. In short, while gaining the freedom and variety of working with several agents at the same time, freelancers sacrifice the dedication, commitment, and creative risk-taking of one legally bound agent.

Many older character actors, as well as those actors returning to the business after either raising a family or caring for a sick loved one, appreciate the submission coverage offered by freelancing with several agents. They are happy for any submissions made on their behalf, and believe that the more agents keeping them in mind for projects, the better. Whether staying in circulation as casting opportunities narrow, or jump-starting a career that was put on hold, these freelancers aim to be "up for" as many projects as possible.

Some legit agents freelance in the area of musical theater because they feel they can do so without taking opportunities away from their signed clients. Given what's playing on stages on and Off-Broadway, in regional theaters and overseas, clearly the call for musical talent is great. The abundance of opportunity in this arena justifies an agency's decision to freelance with musical comedy performers. Including musical projects and freelance musical talent puts agents in a position to submit more actors for more roles on more projects. In an economic climate of recession, some agencies relax their "signed talent only" policy, hoping to book more clients from a wider range of submissions, thereby bringing more money to the firm. As a result, more actors get the chance to establish working relationships with agents, which can lead to signing opportunities as relationships develop.

CLEARING THE FREELANCE CLIENT

To eliminate double submissions to casting directors, agents "clear" their freelance clients each time they submit them for a project. Here's how the process works: When I get to the office in the morning, I go through the breakdowns and decide which clients to submit for the various roles listed there. As I've mentioned previously, "breakdowns" are the casting notices that agents and managers receive via the Internet, from Breakdown Services, Ltd. If I see a role that is right for a freelance client, I call to clear that actor for the submission. I am essentially calling to ask permission to submit him for the project. When I call, I usually get voicemail and leave a message saying something like, "John, this is Margaret from Eisen Associates. I'd like to submit you for the role of Chris in the production of *All My Sons* at the Denver Center Theatre Company. Please call me back to let me know if I have you on this project."

Now, John is freelancing with several agents, right? So he might get calls from his other agents that morning to clear him for the same project. What does he do? The general rule of thumb is for the actor to give clearance to the agent who calls first. It's important for him to keep an accurate record of his clearances. He certainly wouldn't want to be the cause of any mini-wars between the two most important categories of people in his professional life: agents and casting directors.

That being the case, it is easy to see how clearing actors for projects can turn into a time-consuming phone-calling race. Agents whose work days extend into the night tend to lose out against the early-bird agents who always get to the actors first. If an agent finds that she is consistently losing an actor on projects because he is being cleared by other agents first, she will lose interest in working with the actor. Realistically, an agent who can never submit an actor for projects can't really make anything happen for that actor. There's no possible basis for working together and developing a relationship. It's very frustrating. I think many agents object to freelancing because, quite frankly, they don't want to devote their time to the phone calls required by the clearing process. They'd rather service their signed clients instead, knowing that their efforts are protected by a legal contract. No agent wants to share with other agents the financial benefits that result from introducing actors to casting directors. This is why many agents refuse to freelance, instead working only with signed talent.

EVALUATING YOUR FREELANCE RELATIONSHIPS

After several months of freelancing with a number of agencies, an actress may choose to evaluate these relationships by reviewing and comparing her submissions from each agent. Which agents call to clear her for comedy projects? Which for dramatic? Which for musicals, theater, TV, or film? If she's musical, which agents submit her for ensemble positions on national tours—what some might consider low-maintenance, commission-collecting jobs? Conversely, which submit her for career-building projects—like those high-profile, low-paying workshops in New York, where the hottest director on the Great White Way is developing his take on a classic Rogers and Hammerstein piece? (To be honest, however, it is very unlikely that an agent would submit a freelancer for such highly competitive, non-commissionable jobs. He would, more than likely, reserve these opportunities for his signed clients.)

An actress may also evaluate the ratio of auditions to submissions. If ten clearance calls have yielded but one audition, she could begin to have doubts about an agency's effectiveness. Actors should be aware, however, that it sometimes can take fifty submissions to get one audition, especially if the agent is trying to move an actor forward by submitting him for jobs on a higher, more competitive, level. As for turning submissions into auditions, when an agent is given the opportunity to push a client, he will most likely choose a signed client over a freelancer. An exception would be when a breakdown calls for something specific and a freelance client fits the bill; then the agent will seize the opportunity to get that client the audition.

Freelancing with multiple agents enables an actor to view how each agency functions on a daily basis. Which agents return calls? Which agents seem to lose interest when there are no callbacks? Is the client-agent interface warm and pleasant, or impersonal and abrupt? For their part, agents have a chance during this time to evaluate an actor's professionalism, business etiquette, industry recognition, and competitive edge. Are the casting directors picking up on the submissions and calling this actress in for auditions? Is she showing up for her auditions? Is she getting callbacks? Does she seem to be a high- or a low-maintenance client?

A warning to the freelancer looking to get signed: an unfortunate event could befall you during this dating period, but you can easily avoid it. If you are freelancing with several agencies but prefer one above the others, by all means tell that agency so. Our agency was freelancing with a very talented actress who was doing quite well. She was being seen by numerous casting directors and we were getting great feedback. We felt for sure that it was just a matter of time until she booked a job. We called to clear her for a project one day and were struck dumb when she told us that she had signed with another agent. When we asked her what had happened, she said that she really liked us best, but since we hadn't asked her to sign, she had gone with the agency that had. We explained to her that she could have told us of the other agency's offer and at least given us a chance to invite her to sign, which we most likely would have done. But it was too late. This lack of communication was costly for all of us. We at the agency never capitalized on the efforts we had made during the dating (freelancing) period, and she ended a relationship that she had very much enjoyed and had wanted to make exclusive. When you reach this level as a freelancer, don't wait until after you've signed with another agent to let the preferred agent know that she missed her chance. Inform the preferred agent of the other agent's proposal and see if she matches it. If she does, great—you have finessed the deal that you wanted. If she doesn't, no problem—you still can accept the first offer.

WHY AGENTS SIGN ACTORS

As I've already noted, many legit agents refuse to freelance with actors. They take very seriously the responsibility for their clients' livelihoods that comes with the exclusive management agreement. They feel that freelancing intrudes on that representation. They also don't wish to share their actors with other agents. They want to protect their good agenting efforts through a contractual agreement of exclusivity. Let me explain this further:

Each year, graduating acting students from conservatories all over the world flood industry centers like New York City, Los Angeles, and Chicago to showcase their talents. Most agents interested in one of these actors would choose to sign him rather than freelance with him, because they know that launching a career is hard work. It can sometimes take six months to a year before these talented and well-trained, but inexperienced, actors actually book jobs. Agents want to protect their investment in these young actors. They don't want other agents to benefit from efforts made early on towards establishing a young actor's career. Take this example: An agent talks her heart out trying to get the head of casting at CBS to meet her latest discovery, a freelancer, for a specific project. When the casting director finally gives in to the agent's haranguing and meets the actress, his response is, "I love that girl. She's fantastic. I'm going to bring her in for the very next thing she's right for." How do you think the agent will feel if the next project this actress auditions for at that network is through the clearance of another agent? Let's take it two steps further: say the actress books the project and it becomes a major hit series. Some other agent will reap great financial rewards resulting from the original agent's initial phone call made to push the actress to the casting director. This is why agents protect their efforts to build careers by signing their young clients. It is the only way they can legally ensure collecting commissions on jobs booked through their agenting efforts.

It's helpful for actors to know that when a legit agent says he only works with signed clients, it usually means that his clients are either very experienced or highly trained. Younger actors signed by these agents often come out of undergraduate acting conservatories or graduate acting programs where the training gives performers the skills necessary to be a professional—i.e., to book jobs in the industry. An actor who is neither very experienced nor highly trained needs either to look elsewhere for representation or to get experience by working at jobs that would make him a more credible candidate to a legit agent. It's that simple—harsh, perhaps, but simple. Maybe he will approach the agency later on, after he's built up his résumé with more training and credits. Actors should make a practice of responding to a "rejection" positively, by keeping a connection with an agency viable for possible future dealings.

Most actors want an agent home. Even so, marriage can be a big step. Actors respond in many different ways when agents ask them to sign. Some shriek with glee, some look stunned and befuddled, others hem and haw—which an agent reads as "weighing options." An agent is flattered and gratified to hear the response, "I thought you'd never ask," but also understands, "Thank you—this means a lot, but I need some time to think about it." Don't keep an agent waiting too long, however. Unlike fine wine, the offer does not improve with age.

THE EXCLUSIVE ENGAGEMENT

You may wonder how an agent handles an actor who is skittish about signing. One way to deal with the shilly-shallying is to suggest working together under an exclusive agreement for three months, at which time both parties will evaluate and decide how to proceed. This "exclusive agreement" is the same as signing, but without the formality of union contracts. Usually a simple letter of agreement between agent and actor has been drawn up by the agent to stipulate the terms. Both parties conduct themselves within the relationship as if they were doing business under an exclusive management contract. The agent doesn't need to clear the actor for projects because the actor has agreed not to work with other agents. The actor agrees to pay a commission to the agent on all work booked during this time. Another proposal an agent may offer is to sign exclusive management contracts (agency papers) for a year's term and draw up an additional rider signed by both parties. This rider states that the actor is free to "break papers" (terminate the contract) after a certain period of time, usually stipulated as six months (half of the contracted term).

As a marriage contract does for marriage, the exclusive management contracts between an agent and an actor state the rules and regulations of talent management. They delineate an agent's responsibilities in terms of submissions and general business practices, and an actor's responsibilities in terms of commissions. Each of the three major actors' unions publishes its own version of the agency contract for the protection of union members. For the most part these documents are very similar. Actors' Equity Association provides one agency contract that covers representation in all areas of the legitimate theater. SAG, the union with jurisdiction over film work, and AFTRA, the union governing videotape and radio, have two separate contracts each: one for commercials and the other for theatrical (everything else). The initial term for SAG's contracts is one year. AEA and AFTRA allow for an initial term not exceeding eighteen months. In all three unions, the term for renewal of the contract can be up to three years. Each contract includes a "termination" clause that gives the agent a ninety-day (or ninety-one-day) time limit to find work for the actor before the actor can elect to terminate the contract. It's interesting to note that because these agency contracts are written by the actors' unions, they generally tend to protect the rights of the actor over those of the agent. For instance, the contracts delineate very specifically the business practices that agents should follow. However, they do not define in any such detail the professional conduct of actors in this relationship—other than stating a performer's obligations to pay commissions to the agent on all work booked under contract. (An exception might be the controversial "General Services Agreement" that some L.A. agents began offering to SAG actors in 2002. It differs significantly from the standard union contracts in many areas.) The actor and agent sign the contracts in triplicate; the actor keeps one copy, the agent another, and the third is filed with the relevant union.

SIGNING
When it comes to signing with an agency, an actor has several choices. One of the most common is whether to sign across the board within a single agency, or to sign in different departments at different agencies. Another consideration is whether or not to look for an agency that is bicoastal. Each potential choice offers advantages and disadvantages in terms of an actor's relationships with agents and the degree of representation offered. Let's see how an actor might investigate these possibilities beforehand in order to choose knowledgably for himself.

AGENCY STRUCTURES
The structure of an agency—the way its office or offices are organized—determines how it promotes its clients. In order to make a well-informed

decision about signing with an agent, an actor should know the agency's setup. For instance, do all of the agents function as a team in representing the clients, or does each agent have a separate client list? Perhaps the agents handle projects by medium—theater, television, or film. Or by casting director. Is this strictly a commercial agency, or does it have departments for every area of the business? Does this agency handle only actors, or actors, directors, choreographers, and producers?

More specifically, if the agents in an agency work as a team, find out which agent handles what areas. For example, learn which agents cover musical theater submissions, submissions for regional theater, Broadway, Off-Broadway, tv/film, daytime drama, etc. Discover which agents speak to which casting directors. With commercial agencies, find out who handles on-camera commercials, voiceovers, promos, and daytime drama. A little bit of research can tell you a lot about how an agency does business. Knowing this information will save time and everybody's patience; when you call your agency with specific questions, you'll be able to direct them quickly to the responsible agent.

It also helps to have a sense of whether the agent who brings you into the agency is a "lifer," or whether he has a history of agency hopping. I know an actress who signed with an agency right after graduate school. Shortly afterwards the agent who brought her into the agency moved to Los Angeles, leaving her high and dry in New York, with an office of agents who didn't really know her or her work.

Actors should try, as best they can, to find out if any internal shifts are occurring at the agency at the time of signing. Is the agent who is bringing you into the agency on the brink of retirement? Remember the actor who was represented for years by an agent who owned her own agency? She decided to merge with another agency, and very soon after retired from the business. The actor struggled for a while to continue his association with the firm through the other agents, but the connection was never the same after his longtime agent retired. He eventually had to find an entirely new office to represent him. Imagine if this had happened to an actor shortly after signing with an agent.

If one agent brings you into an agency, it's a good idea to establish relationships with the other agents in the office, so you can maximize the efforts of the entire agency in representing you. By doing this you also protect yourself against the possible departure of your primary contact. Personalized correspondence, telephone conversations, coffee or lunch meetings—these are some of the methods an actor can use to develop relationships with the other agents in the office. Of course, any opportunity to show an agent your work is always preferred. Perhaps you might offer to do monologues or songs in the office. If that's not an option, suggest bringing in for the other agents cassettes or CDs of your singing, and demo reels of any tv or film work.

Many agencies owe their day-by-day existence to the revenues coming in from their lucrative commercial departments. Their office policy is to sign talent to both their commercial and legit departments, in an effort to encourage a healthy cash flow. For the actor, choosing whether or not to sign across the board with an agency depends on how well he gets along with the agents in both departments. If, for example, he feels very happy with the agents in the legit department but has better relationships with agents in a commercial department elsewhere, this would influence his decision.

SIGNING ACROSS THE BOARD

Signing across the board at an agency can give an actress a sense of clarity and security. She knows that one organization is responsible for handling all of her business. If you sign across the board at an agency, be aware that the department in which you are most successful will often control your career opportunities. For instance, let's say you book three national commercials in three months. The agents in the commercial department will be hard pressed to keep you from going out of town to do regional theater jobs, although that experience might be just what you need to get your TV and film career rolling. Sure, Steven Spielberg might spot you in a commercial and decide to cast you in one of his films. But the way it works, most of the time—for New York actors especially—is that an actor first builds the legit side of his résumé. The casting directors, impressed and assured by the number of credits on his résumé, bring him in for the New York theater projects that offer the exposure necessary to move up the legit ladder into the TV and film area. In New York, still considered by many a "theater town," when it comes to selling talent to the casting directors of prime-time dramas, agents stand a much better chance of getting a client seen by talking about his latest job at the Guthrie Theater than by citing his current spot for Cingular Wireless. Agents determine how to sell their clients according to what the casting director is buying. Television dramas call for references to serious stage drama. Promoting that Cingular commercial might be more effective in securing sitcom auditions, because sitcoms are referenced to the lighter fare of musical theater and commercials.

LARGE AGENCIES AND CLOUT

Being "chosen" by one of the big or mega-agencies in town—the ones with many departments, divisions and agents, representing hundreds of actors—is an ego boost. The representation at such firms can offer opportunities that are not necessarily available at a mid-sized agency, where three agents, for example, handle a hundred actors; or at a "boutique" agency, where one agent reps twenty-five to fifty actors. Perhaps an agent at one of these huge firms will "piggyback" you on the coattails of one of his celebrity clients, opening a door that would not even have been visible at a smaller agency. I worked at an agency that represented a few "name" actors. Whenever a casting director

called for one of them, the agent would take the opportunity to persuade him to meet a few "hot" up-and-comers.

Agents with "clout"—those who work in big agencies representing celebrities, especially—can sometimes make a difference in an
actor's career. This is not always the case, however. Sometimes an
agent will talk big, but deliver small. Say he lacks a sense of urgency
because his yearly overhead is already paid for by the commissions he
earns from his celebrity clients. He may never pick up the phone on
your behalf, simply because he doesn't have to. An agent with clout is
only as good as how much of that clout he is willing to use to advance
your career. Sometimes that agent's interest in the actor depends on how
many auditions turn into jobs. If the actor doesn't book, he can quickly
fall through the cracks and be forgotten. Such was the case with an
actress who chose to go with one of the big agencies when she finished
graduate school. She had received many offers from various agencies,
but chose the big one for its power and prestige. After a few auditions
that didn't lead to bookings, she was quickly "forgotten," and she
spent a year trying to figure out why she never heard from her agents.
Now signed with a smaller, and more patient, dedicated agency, she
rarely spends a day between engagements—even during engagements—
when she isn't auditioning for the next project. And she has booked
an impressive twenty regional theater jobs in seven years!

If truth be known, most large agencies aren't interested in building
the careers of start-up talent. They become interested in that talent
once the career gets rolling—which is usually after a smaller agency
has put in the "building" time. Low-paying Small Professional Theatre
contracts and Letters of Agreement that offer young actors the chance
to become players in the marketplace mean little to these agencies.
They would rather keep a client close to home and available for that
"big" audition than send him out in the field to get experience by acting in plays.

Hungry Agents

Just as there are pros and cons to having an agent with clout, there are
pros and cons to having a hungry "baby" agent—an agent making her
climb in the industry. Whether employed at a large or small firm, this
agent will submit you across the boards, be aggressive on the phone,
and fight like a terrier to get you in. She might use you to boost her
own career by taking credit for your successes when "talking you up"
to casting directors—but, hey, if it gets you an audition for a TV
pilot, who cares! This agent might send out a hundred of your photos
and résumés in a month and come up with only four auditions. But if
these are four auditions more than you would have been able to get
on your own, and if they are for projects that were seemingly out of
your reach before, then I say, working with that agent is a consider-
able step forward.

Let me further illustrate this point by sharing with you an email I received for my column. An actor—we'll call him "John"—wrote that he was asked to sign with a small, well-established literary agent who was starting to represent actors. Although the agent did not have a presence in New York, John had developed a good relationship with her, respected her, and thought she would work really hard for him. In his email he asked me whether he should give signing with her a shot or keep looking for other representation. I encouraged him to give it a try. He had already booked a fairly big job through this agent, and even though she didn't have a presence in New York yet, I agreed with him in thinking that perhaps she would build her New York office around her star client—him—in the near future. These days, agents are global. those in New York have good relationships with casting direc tors in Los Angeles who, in turn, work for producers overseas. Many Los Angeles casting directors, in fact, are transplanted New Yorkers whom the New York agents knew way back when. I told John that I thought this agent's enthusiasm and perseverance outweighed any lack of presence or experience she might have in the New York playing field. Agent and actor could journey forward together.

SIGNING WITH MULTIPLE AGENCIES

Many actors choose to sign with separate agencies for their commercial and legit representation. Not every large agency signs talent across the board. In some firms, the different departments function separately, each with its own client list. I know for a fact that a commercial department at one of the large agencies in New York regularly sends its clients to legit departments at other agencies when those clients are seeking legit representation. An actor may choose to sign with two firms: a big commercial agency specializing in commercials that gets him the greatest coverage in that area; and a smaller agency that offers more personal attention for its legit representation. This choice reflects how different the business can be in each specialty. The commercial arena, though highly competitive, is vast and full of opportunities. I've heard it said that to book one national commercial takes a hundred auditions. That's an awesome statistic until you realize how much activity exists in this area. It makes sense for an actor to be represented by an agency specializing in commercials. He stands the chance of being submitted five times daily by each of many agents. The legit world, on the other hand, is highly selective and therefore extremely competitive. Any kind of career-building effort requires the exclusive personal attention of a few dedicated agents, which more often than not is found in a smaller agency. Signing with two different agencies for representation in these separate arenas not only can provide better coverage, but can eliminate any conflicts of interest among the agents. The commercial agents of one agency have no connection to the legit agents of the other. Each works to acquire the most activity for the client. Not a bad deal for the actor!

BICOASTAL REPRESENTATION

Many actors wonder about the importance of signing with an agency that offers bicoastal representation. The truth of the matter is that choosing the right agent has a lot to do with where you are in your career now, and where you want to be in five, ten, or fifteen years. For actors starting out in the business, the goal is to get work quickly and start building a résumé. Young actors with great looks and personality who want to do television and film should go straight to Los Angeles and find an agent there, where most of that activity centers and the youth market reigns supreme. On the other hand, students entering the job market after training at one of the theater conservatories should seek a New York office that can place them in the territory they've trained for: the theater. The access that a New York legit agent has to the casting of theatrical productions, and of television and film projects (such as daytime dramas, feature films, sitcoms, and episodics) shooting in New York, offers a wide range of opportunities for the young actor who is transitioning from student to professional.

From a New York agent's point of view, the logical career progression for an actor starts with establishing his presence in the marketplace (making allies of casting directors), then building upon that presence (stacking up regional theater, Off-Broadway, and Broadway credits) until the time is right for a move to the "other" coast. New York actors are found popping up as series regulars on Los Angeles-based television shows, for example, after having been seen in several Broadway shows or as contract players on daytime dramas. On the other hand, West Coast film and/or television actors find their way onto Broadway stages when their name value can stimulate box office revenue. In response to this curious pattern of career progression, a young East Coast actress recently decided to move out to Los Angeles to get TV and film credits so she could eventually come back to New York and fulfill her lifelong dream of working on Broadway.

Most actors assume that an agency promising the widest range of submissions would be the best choice for representation. A bicoastal agency ostensibly offers actors coverage on both coasts. What actor wouldn't want representation by an agency with offices in New York and Los Angeles? It sounds so all-inclusive. There are several cautionary realities, however, to keep in mind when signing with a bicoastal firm.

Signing with a bicoastal agency is similar to signing across the board at a large agency in which the department that brings you in guarantees you submissions, while the other departments don't. When signing with a bicoastal firm, remember that the coast that signs you is the one more committed to working for you. That office may be obligated to set up a meeting for you with the office on the other coast should you go out there, but you have no guarantee that the attention you get there will equal your primary agents'. How could it? First of all, the new office would need to get to know you and your work, if you aren't already known in the business. Secondly, a lot would depend on where you fit within the new office's current client roster. If you present conflicts to their existing talent pool, the new agents aren't going to jeopardize their relationship with these clients by taking you on. Should your reception at the other coast's office turn out to be chilly or noncommittal, you may terminate your relationship with that office only and seek representation from an entirely different firm on that coast, by following the procedures stated in your union contract.

Here's an interesting story: Recently a student from one of the acting conservatories came to New York with her graduating class for their senior showcase. After a series of positive interviews with a legit agency that had an office solely in New York, she was asked to sign. At the same time she had an excellent meeting with the New York office of a bicoastal agency that expressed interest in working with her. In weighing the pros and cons of signing with either agency, this student had the luxury of knowing that she'd be able to assess the interest of the bicoastal agency's office in L.A. when she and her class did their senior showcase there later that month. The solely New York agency couldn't force this actress to make a decision before she had the opportunity to fully evaluate the interest of the other agency's L.A. office. The New York firm let her go "explore," and its agents were very happy when she decided to sign with them after all. Perhaps the second firm's Los Angeles office responded less enthusiastically than its New York office, so this actress decided to go with the agency that had expressed enthusiasm and interest in her all along. This unusual set of circumstances arises from the unique timing of the senior showcases. Most actors don't usually have the chance to evaluate interest on both coasts before deciding to sign with a bicoastal agency. Having signed with one office, they must hope that when the time comes the agents at the other office will service them with equal diligence and zeal.

AFFILIATES

An actor signed by an agency with an office on only one coast is free to hook up with an entirely different agency on the other coast. When an actor tells his New York office that he wants to try his luck in Los Angeles, the office may offer to make introductions to agencies there with which it has "business relationships." These agencies are called "affiliates." Although agents can negotiate contracts for employment taking place anywhere in the world, the handling of day-to-day business is difficult without a physical presence in that geographical location. New York agents can't make lunch meetings at film studios in Hollywood, and L.A. agents don't have the contacts in New York necessary for placing clients on Broadway. Therefore, an agent on one coast looks for a trustworthy business partner on the other coast with whom she can agreeably share clients when the need arises.

Affiliate relationships between agencies usually spring from two agents' past familiarity. Perhaps they worked together at a third agency early on, or studied and performed together back when they were actors. The affiliation is based on similar taste in talent and business practices, and on an agreed-upon split of commissions. Once the primary office has introduced an actor to its affiliate—either by cover letter with photo and résumé, or by phone—the primary office cannot *force* its affiliate to represent that actor. The affiliate is free to decide whether or not it can take on the actor as a client. Actors should plan to live in the affiliate's city for at least three to six months so that the affiliate agent's investment of time has a chance to pay off financially. The decision to include another agency's talent in a roster has much to do with the realistic opportunities that an agent senses she can promise the actor—given his type, training, and experience, and the likelihood of his competing with exclusive clients. One Los Angeles agent only took on New York actors who could guarantee "top of show" (highest salary amount offered) money. She saw no financial sense in splitting commission with the east coast agent on money that came in below that ceiling. This same agent, however, did decide to take on a well-trained but inexperienced young African American actor because there was an opening for his type in her talent pool. He quickly booked a supporting role in a popular summer film and became a lucrative client as his film career progressed. So you see: there are no set formulas, just general rules to be followed—and, at times, broken.

PILOT SEASON

Some New York-based stage actors, finding themselves on the West Coast in national tours or plays, sometimes hook up with agents there and book spots on episodic television. L.A. loves New York stage actors— there's still that mystique. (However, it seems the traffic does not move both ways: New York theater does not embrace the L.A. actor with similar passion—unless, of course, that actor is a TV or film star, past or current, who can stimulate box office.) Other New York actors have meetings with L.A. agents, but don't stick around long enough to cultivate any real activity. Actors from all over—New York, Chicago, Boston, the Twin Cities, Atlanta, etc.—consider going to Los Angeles for pilot season. It's like the Gold Rush and, like all those '49ers, they think they will strike it big. Any knowledgeable legit agent will tell these actors that unless they have a solid reel of TV/film work or are currently in something that offers significant exposure to industry professionals like agents and casting directors, the *worst* time to go to Los Angeles is during pilot season. The L.A. agents are less likely to make any effort to include newcomers at this time, because they are obligated to their signed clients. A better time to go to Los Angeles, I've been told, is during the summer months. Episodic television is in full swing then, offering more opportunity for solid and castable New York talent.

✳

Your interview with the agency was a big success. They offered to sign you and you said, "yes." What happens now, you wonder.... It's a good thing you brought those twenty headshots and résumés along. The agents will need them to start submitting you for projects.

Chapter 5

HOW DO AGENTS SUBMIT ACTORS?

BREAKDOWNS

One of the first things I do when I get into the office in the morning is turn on the computer and download the breakdowns from an Internet website called Breakdown Express. "Breakdowns" are casting notices published by a company called Breakdown Services, Ltd., which was established in 1971 to serve as a casting system linking casting directors and talent representatives throughout North America. Specifically, a breakdown gives a written synopsis of a project with character descriptions of the particular roles being cast. It also includes pertinent information about the project, like the names of the producers, writers, director, casting director, location, and time frames for rehearsals, performances, and/or shoot dates. Provided by casting directors, these breakdowns cover a range of projects including television episodics, pilots and movies, feature films, student films, interactive videos for the Internet, and theater of all kinds. A separate division called Commercial Express sends out breakdowns for commercials and industrials to agents via email.

Whereas in the past actors found out about casting calls and upcoming productions through listings in theatrical trade publications like *Back Stage*, the *Theatrical Index*, *American Theatre* magazine, and union listings, they never had access to the actual breakdowns that agents and managers received through Breakdown Services. These were published as copyrighted information with a directive prohibiting any kind of duplication and dispersal. With the advent of the Internet, actors can now find out about castings of projects from individual websites. (I know an actor in Atlanta who logs onto two websites providing information on projects specifically casting in his area.) But many of these websites provide information that is secondhand, filtered, confused, or mistaken. What seems to be more legitimate are the breakdowns that actors can access through Actors Access—an arm of Breakdown

Services specifically geared to publishing breakdowns for actors. These are mostly for non-union projects with casting directors who don't mind receiving submissions directly from actors.

Illegal break-ins into Breakdown Express through borrowed codes from "friends" in the business (interns, assistants working in agencies) generally lead to frustration. Because casting directors continue to look mainly at agent submissions for their projects, agents still stand a much better chance of securing auditions from their submissions. Some casting directors even go so far as to state very clearly on their breakdowns that they will not open any submissions sent to them by actors. Look at it this way: There are approximately a hundred agencies in the New York City area alone. Let's say each submits two actors for a role on a project breakdown. That would already be two hundred photos and résumés coming to the casting director. For that one role only! Add to that the number of actors requested to be seen by the director, the writer, and the producer of the project, and it's easy to see the impossibility of actors' submissions being accepted into the casting pool of possibilities—especially when the time allotted for casting the role is only four hours on one day! (It happens.)

Because they want to make a good impression on the people hiring them, casting directors carefully choose the talent they bring in for auditions. The sheer imbalance of the number of roles for actors and the number of actors for roles forces casting directors to be selective. They must draw the line somewhere in making their selections, and the most natural line seems to be at agent representation. Presumably, an actress submitted by an agent has already been favorably evaluated by a professional in the industry: the agent. Therefore a casting director feels more secure about showing that actress to the creative team than he would an actress promoting herself. With competition so fierce just to obtain *auditions*, actors can see how crucial it is to have an agent submit them for projects. Any actor accustomed to lining up at seven a.m. in front of the Actors' Equity building in New York City to sign up for EPAs certainly knows the value of an agent submission in saving time and energy.

These days, the breakdowns are launched onto the Internet website from the Los Angeles office of Breakdown Services during the morning hours. Because of the three-hour time difference between Los Angeles and New York City, these breakdowns start popping up on computer screens in Manhattan during our afternoon. Another development made possible by the Internet also affects how agents receive breakdowns: the service constantly updates itself, posting new information continually (Monday through Friday, from 10:00 a.m. to 6:30 p.m. west coast time) as it arrives from the casting directors. This is to accommodate the CDs, who may now submit breakdowns to the service at any time for an immediate posting rather than adhere to a specific posting deadline. Agents, who pay for this service—casting directors use it without charge—find themselves changing diehard routines in order to work with this new system. In the past, agents received the breakdowns in an envelope that was delivered to the office before office hours. Agents used the morning hours to make their submissions and the afternoon to make follow-up phone calls, call out audition appointments to their clients, negotiate deals, and do other agent business like interviewing prospective clients. Now, although we still devote our mornings to doing the breakdowns, we must be flexible multi-taskers—forced, for example, to drop everything in response to a *Law & Order* breakdown that comes in at 5:30 p.m., rather than return the backlog of phone calls from clients.

Selecting Actors for Submissions

There I sit at my desk, with my morning cup of coffee and the breakdowns, ready to look over the agency's client list—an alphabetized, gender-based listing of the names of signed clients and freelance clients, totaling around a hundred—to decide which actors to submit for the various roles listed. How do I choose which breakdown to tackle first? I usually make that decision according to the audition date of the project. I want to make sure that my submission gets to the casting director's office in time for her to go through it thoroughly to select my clients and include them in her casting session. The timing of this varies according to the project medium. Television projects such as episodic dramas are cast very quickly. In fact, by the time the breakdown is posted online, a casting session responding to the director's, producer's, or writer's requests has already been set up. In order to get any action on a TV breakdown, it's crucial for an agent to respond immediately. We may quickly fax a cover letter to the casting director with our list of suggested actors for the roles, then follow up with a packet of photos and résumés messengered overnight. Theater projects usually allow for a week between the breakdown's appearance and the audition date. The time may be shorter if the casting is for an immediate replacement in a show that is rehearsing or up and running. Casting for films can stretch over many weeks—sometimes months—depending on the shooting schedule and length of the project. The Los Angeles casting director might make a swift trip in and out of New York in order to audition the talent pool there. This occurs especially if some of the film takes place in New York and will be shot on location, offering acting opportunities to New York actors. This is similarly true for any film shooting on location. The Los Angeles casting director puts out a breakdown and receives submissions from those agents representing the talent at the target location—Boston, Las Vegas, Miami, etc. Then he chooses the actors he wishes to meet and perhaps put on tape for the director during his two-day visit to the city. Many an agent, having missed the mail-in submission deadline, will fax suggestions to the casting director or drop them off at his hotel in hope of slipping some clients into the session.

Back to the morning breakdowns: I pull out the first breakdown from the pile on my desk that I have prioritized according to audition dates and project importance—which is usually determined by commission. Money-earning projects always take precedence over freebies, unless it's a workshop for something like a new Adam Guettel musical. How many actors does an agent submit per role? How do I choose which actors to submit? Does the type of project—theater, television, or film—make a difference? What about an actor's training, experience, or credits? At this point I turn into a casting director, using my knowledge of casting to select the best talent available for the job at hand.

While I believe that every actor is essentially a "character" actor, with unique gifts and abilities that he uses to transform into different characters, I've been around long enough to know how this business works: In the real world, as opposed to acting class in conservatory, roles are cast according to age range, type, and look, with talent appropriate to need. For example, when *Third Watch*, a New York-based "firefighter drama," was looking for a seventy-year-old Japanese man, the casting people found an actor who looked seventy years old and was Japanese, not Chinese or Korean.

Agents choose talent according to the appropriateness of look, training, and experience. They submit actors whom they think are most likely to get the audition. Sometimes a breakdown contains extremely specific qualifications—5'2" tall and blonde—sometimes it is general, as in "all ethnicities considered." Agents will select clients according to the information provided in the breakdown. For instance, when the project is high profile, the agent knows to submit actors who are "known" in the business. This is true especially if the breakdown specifically asks for "names only" (meaning actors who are easily recognized by the public). An agent knows not to submit unknowns for such a project, because their chances of being seen are so slim. Other times it is clear that the project is one for actors who are just starting out. These are usually theater jobs at small companies out of town that offer low salaries.

Generally speaking, in making a submission, an agent aims to be selective but inclusive at the same time. For example, while the casting director in me wants to zero in on the most accurate choice of actor for a role, the agent in me refrains from submitting too narrow a selection of actors—so that getting an audition is possible for a range of clients. Of course, I can't overload my submission with talent for two reasons: Number one, I don't want to admit to casting directors that so many clients are jobless; and two, I don't want to make the casting director's job more difficult than it already is, by giving him too many actors to choose from. Sometimes the more specific a breakdown, the easier it is to choose talent to submit. It can be a relief getting a breakdown that's specific according to age range, look, or type.

REPRESENTING SIMILAR TYPES

Actors sometimes wonder whether a given agent represents similar types. I think they want to know how much competition they would have when this agent's clients are submitted to casting directors. Truth be told, an agency's longevity depends on the depth, as well as the range of its client list. ("Range" alludes to variety of types—"from young adults to octogenarians." "Depth" refers to the number of clients within a type—representing two or three African American ingénues rather than one gives an agency depth.) Knowing this, AEA, AFTRA, and SAG permit agents to represent more than one actor of any type, which is a good thing; if we couldn't, we'd be out of business fast. Actors' Equity, in fact, goes so far as to state in its Exclusive Management Contract that an agent may represent actors of similar qualifications who can play the same parts. It even stipulates that prospective clients of the agency may ask to look at a client list—usually considered top-secret information—before signing with the agency. It is presumed that the actor would be researching the list to see if he recognized any actors who are similar in type.

An agent goes through a fairly complex thought process in deciding whether to take someone on who is similar to an exclusive client. Let's assume that I like an actor because I've seen his work, have assessed his career possibilities, and anticipate a comfortable working relationship. Next I would have to decide whether I could realistically promise this actor sufficient activity (submissions and auditions) without jeopardizing the opportunities for my current clients. In deciding whether to represent an actor who might potentially conflict with some of my existing clients, I also consider my current clients' positions within the industry. Actors work their way up the ladder of opportunity. They make their industry climbs by choosing certain opportunities, and every job turned down presents a potential opportunity (or opening) for someone else. Let's take an example drawn from regional theater. A little background information first: Certain regional theaters across the country are members of an association called the League of Resident Theaters (LORT). This organization is the bargaining agent that represents member theaters when negotiating with the unions to establish items like salaries, health-care costs, and working conditions. Salaries for Equity actors are determined by box-office capacity and are named in categories according to the alphabet. The smallest theaters (i.e., those with smallest box-office capacity) are labeled LORT D theaters, with the scale going up to LORT A, the largest within the League. When an agent refers to a client as having worked her way up the LORT ladder, he means that she started out at the smaller venues and moved up (usually through connections and experience) to the highest-level theaters. Using this client as our example, let's say she now books a "run of the play" contract on Broadway or in a national tour. Suddenly she is no longer available for any regional theater jobs for an entire year. Her agent—whose livelihood depends solely on commissions earned from actor bookings—must be able to submit other actors when the casting directors call with their breakdowns for the fall regional theater slots. In cases like this, it's in an agent's interest to represent actors of similar type.

Agents determine which clients to submit for certain projects according to the clients' positions within the industry. For instance, some clients decide it's time to concentrate on New York-based projects, declining opportunities to work out of town; other clients absolutely refuse to understudy in New York. With their agents, actors make these decisions based on how they want to position themselves in the business.

If agents don't continually replenish their client lists, they can easily find themselves empty-handed. That's why agents are always on the lookout for new talent: they never know which clients are going to move up a rung on the ladder, or when. Nor do they know which clients may have to get off the ladder for a while. Sometimes, for instance, actors take a leave of absence to care for a sick loved one, or to go back to school. Sometimes they just plain leave the business altogether. Situations like these, in actors' personal lives, affect how their agents submit them for projects. Given the possibility of such developments, it's very important for an agent to protect himself. We need to continually meet new talent and entertain the possibility of representing them, despite any potential conflict with the existing talent pool, so that we can stay strong and stay in business regardless of the situations that come our way.

Expectant Mothers

Another circumstance that agents deal with is actresses becoming expectant mothers. Even though they say they'll be ready to work practically the day after they give birth, we agents know that's not going to happen. We can count on their needing at least six months to enjoy motherhood and figure out just how to return to an actor's lifestyle with baby in tow. The industry generally assumes that expectant actresses will lessen their activity during pregnancy and return to the business two to six months after giving birth. Some casting directors (for commercials especially) have a "pregnant actress" file for those occasional jobs calling for an expectant woman. Legit agents submit their pregnant clients for jobs that can accommodate their appearance and physical condition. For the most part, this translates into short-term television and film. When I asked one of our clients, a mother of one, to share her thoughts on this subject for a column I was writing, she mentioned how grateful she was to her agents for submitting her for television, film, and voiceovers well into her third trimester, even for non-pregnant parts. She particularly enjoyed walking into an audition for a police detective on a television show, eight months pregnant. (An example of an agent's creative submission: the police detective was on desk duty, so it made total sense that the character could be pregnant.)

Most of our clients spring the news of their pregnancies on us with a mixture of joy and apology. Excited by upcoming motherhood, they realize this life change will affect our business together (and they worry about how it will alter the career that they see as a full-time job). Generally agents embrace the news positively and leave it up to the client to determine how far into the pregnancy she can handle the activities of an actor's life, and what those activities can be.

Auditions and workload depend on the individual woman. All agents ask is that they be told the parameters within which to work. A client of the agency received an offer to do a play at a theater out of town with her husband—also an actor—during her second trimester. Many elements made this offer enticing: the role, the play, the director, and the theater, plus the opportunity to live and perform with the father of her child. The offer also came without her having to audition! This being her first pregnancy, she didn't know what to expect, but since she felt fine, aside from slight morning sickness, she decided to accept the offer. The role was very physical and the job became increasingly challenging as her pregnancy progressed. Despite the development of some potentially dangerous physical problems related to her pregnancy that made this job a nerve-wracking experience, my client felt grateful to be a working actress at this time. Still, she advises women to think twice before accepting theater jobs during pregnancy— a physical state that another client's Ob-Gyn described as being full of hairpin turns impossible to predict.

Agents realize that only the actress and her body can tell them to what extent she can continue her "actress" life while pregnant, and how soon she can return to the workforce once her baby is born. Actresses would do well to remember that showbiz is a constant; it's not going away. Although taking time off from a career does pose certain challenges—growing out of young roles or losing recognition due to inactivity—none are automatically insurmountable. The actor's lifestyle is actually one of the most flexible. While a young mother might not be able to afford working on an Off-Broadway salary after paying childcare expenses, many out-of-town theaters offer two-bedroom apartments for mother, infant, and nanny (often the grandmother), plus a variety of childcare options. How well you adapt to your new life as mother depends on how successful you are at putting together a good support system of babysitters you can call in a pinch! With understanding, and patient partners and *agents*, an actress can continue crafting a career while enjoying motherhood.

Agents trust that actresses will adapt to their new lives of arranging babysitters, toting babies in backpacks, and coping with the omnipresent state of sleep deprivation, in order to make auditions and do jobs. We know that last-minute auditions won't work for a young mother's schedule, and that a lead time of at least twenty-four hours is needed to set the support system in motion towards making the audition. I never cease to be impressed with these moms who are able to organize and accomplish so much in order to make auditions and take jobs—especially when I compare them to the young single actors who freak out each time they get an audition and have to find someone to take their shift at the restaurant!

CREATIVE SUBMISSIONS AND CROSSOVER TALENT

How creative are agents when it comes to submitting actors? Most are very literal minded and subscribe to the tenet, "seeing is believing." For instance, if I start working with an actor who has heavy musical credits, you can bet that I will submit him for musicals at first. Why? Because that's where the auditions will be for him. However, having said that, I still believe that actors are actors first and foremost, whether they sing or not. The role of Billy Bigelow requires just as much heavy-duty acting as Chris in *All My Sons*. The only difference is that one of these fellows must have a killer baritone in his back pocket.

From the perspective of a legit agent in New York, finding actors who sing and dance triples the number of auditions and job opportunities available. Being a triple threat is the fastest route to getting work and exposure in New York—which, in turn, is the fastest route to getting work on TV and in films. So much musical product is found on and Off-Broadway, in regional theater, and on tour. A musical theater actor can make a good living in *Phantom*, but there comes a time when he wants to explore other areas, as well he should. Actors who have agents want to know whether they support this goal of crossing over to other areas. Here's where I stand on the matter: I believe that musical theater requires good actors and actresses who can sing well—very well. For the most part, these actors are just as strong as actors who get hired on episodic television shows, feature films, or straight drama. However, as an agent I would need to see someone perform a dramatic role in a straight drama before submitting him for a role in, say, the Broadway production of *The Crucible*. Such a submission, unsupported by evidence, would be illogical, and would reflect badly on my reputation as an agent. No casting director will "take a chance" on bringing in for *The Glass Menagerie* a performer with heavy musical credits unless his résumé boasts a good showing of straight drama credits. To justify his agent in submitting him for a crossover role, an actor must build his résumé. Someone who's been in Broadway musicals for the past five seasons, for instance, might need to take a couple of roles in the regions to gather experience in straight plays; or do a freebie in town that shows off his dramatic ability. Such forays would make him marketable in the area of straight drama: additional credits substantiate his dramatic talent and prove his case to agents and casting directors alike. I represent a fellow who has been very successful in musicals. I booked him in the premiere of a drama at a theater in

Philadelphia, and this opened doors not only in the world of theater but also in television and film. It challenged and expanded his abilities as an actor, and gave him a significant credit on his résumé that moved his career forward.

From Cabaret to Primetime TV

An actor once wrote to the column asking whether agents would be able to see a cabaret act and imagine the artist in other mediums, i.e., consider submitting him for non-musical projects like television and film. I think it would be valuable to spend a little time now on how agents and casting directors interpret a performance seen in a cabaret act. Cabaret is a specific art form. What it is to musical theater parallels what standup comedy is to comedy. When I see a cabaret performer, I hear her voice and vocal style, take in her "look," and get a sense of her personality—just as when I see a standup comic perform, I hear how he tells a joke, see what he looks like, and get a sense of his personal style of comedy. Whatever my impressions, I wouldn't necessarily feel justified in submitting the comedian for a part on, say, *Law & Order* unless the breakdown called for his particular skills (like the role of a standup comic in a comedy club). Cabaret performers are a similar case. Even after seeing one in her act, I would feel unsure about submitting her for the lead in a new William Finn musical at Lincoln Center Theater. "Selling" a song in a cabaret setting is different from singing a song in a musical. In cabaret, we don't necessarily get the throughline, character development, and relationship that are part of the dramatic structure of a play. What I do learn about are the performer's vocal technique, style, and special abilities (like dance, puppetry, or magic tricks), as well as her personality—in her patter to the audience between songs. The unanswered questions are whether she could (1) play a character from start to finish and (2) relate to other actors in a scene. Having said this, I did once take in a cabaret act to check out an actress who had been highly recommended to me by a casting director. In her show, the actress played a fictional cabaret performer who had seen better days and was making her comeback. The actress used the songs that the character sang in "her act" to flesh out the character's story. That clever framework enabled me to assess the actress's voice, vocal style, acting ability, and comic gifts. I could see she was talented and accomplished in many areas, and that I would have no problem submitting her for both musical and non-musical projects. (Of course, the casting director's recommendation was a bonus.)

Ethnic Submissions and Nontraditional Casting

When speaking of making creative submissions, it's important to discuss the topic of nontraditional casting and its affect on submissions. Ethnic actors are always asking agents how they approach the subject of nontraditional casting. The answer is this: When a breakdown specifically asks for "multi-ethnic" talent we will take that opportunity to suggest every ethnic actor we represent, in a way forcing the issue and holding the casting director to his word. As for nontraditional casting—an African American actor playing Hamlet, the Danish prince—and even colorblind casting—African American offspring of Caucasian parents—agents make these submissions in cases where they feel a casting director is likely to respond. It is not an agent's responsibility to guarantee nontraditional casting to clients. We submit and push, but the casting director is the person who ultimately decides which actor gets the audition.

Ethnic actors also want to know whether an agent represents more than one actor of a certain ethnicity. Here, too, the agent could check out possible competition with existing clients before making that decision. While agents do not work with quotas, they do take a cautious approach to representing several actors within a specific ethnic group. When an agent feels certain that she can provide each actor of a certain ethnicity an equal number of job opportunities, she will sign more than one. Recently our agency signed two African American actors out of a first-rate acting conservatory. Despite their similarity in age and training, we felt there was enough difference in "type" and special abilities for the office to represent them equally well. Sure enough, one actor quickly booked a job that took him out of town for six months. So it proved fortunate that the agency had the second actor in this category to suggest when a call came in from another casting director. A year later, one of the actors actually left the business, further confirming the fact that agents need to build depth into their talent pool along with range. Actors must accept that they'll be competing against friends of similar type, and they have every right to know the "complexion" of their agency's talent roster.

Ask any actor of color what his professional life has been like and he will answer, "challenging." Finding work within an industry that boasts an eighty-five percent unemployment rate is hard enough. Add the lack of opportunity available to ethnic actors, and you can understand the frustration.

The good news is that things are getting better. Doors once shut are opening thanks to the efforts of artists whose perseverance and success have paved the way for greater diversity in casting. These actors fought to create and seize upon career-making opportunities that launched them into the mainstream. B.D. Wong, a regular on television's *Oz*, first gained recognition by appearing in *M. Butterfly* on Broadway. Similarly Jesse Martin, who partnered with Jerry Orbach and Dennis Farina on *Law & Order*, was an original cast member of *Rent*. Whoopi Goldberg's career was propelled by her 1984 solo show *Whoopi Goldberg*, which Mike Nichols brought to Broadway. From there she became a successful actress, director, and producer. As a legit agent in

New York, I've seen theater (especially in New York) be the launching pad for many ethnic actors' careers in television and film. I define these areas as mainstream due to their wider degree of exposure; actors may be known within the theater community for their appearances on Broadway, but once they show up on a primetime or daytime drama, or in a feature film, they gain national and international recognition.

Playwrights also help the cause by creating work for ethnic actors. Nilo Cruz, August Wilson, and David Henry Hwang are pioneering playwrights who write roles specifically for ethnic actors. Television shows reflecting the urban landscape require ethnic diversity in casting. Casting directors purposefully search for an ethnic mix, balancing the degree of opportunity for Caucasian and ethnic actors.

Depending on the flexibility of an ethnic actor's specific physical attributes and characteristics, like skin color and accented speech, agents will submit him in one of two ways: either embracing, promoting, and politicizing his ethnicity by positioning him into his racially specific arena; or submitting him nontraditionally in an effort to break casting barriers. Racially specific submissions garner auditions; African American actors get seen for August Wilson plays. Keep in mind, however, that the more specific the ethnic pool, the greater the competition within it.

A submission based on ethnic identity can set an actor up for increased disappointment when the project he is "right for" is cast with actors who do not fit the accurate racial profile. One of our Hispanic clients, a Cuban by birth, was distraught to discover that the film he auditioned for, *The Perez Family*, which dealt specifically with a Cuban family's story, hired mainly Anglo actors. Moreover, as near as he could tell, the few Hispanics who *were* cast were not Cuban. The irony that my client recognized at being excluded from this film, apart from his obvious disappointment of not getting the role, points to how a policy of diversity in casting can sometimes work against its objective of inclusion when different nationals within a specific ethnic group—Cubans, Puerto Ricans, Mexicans, in this case—compete against each other.

One agent advises her ethnic actors to establish themselves as a "Someone" through obvious casting routes before trying to break down barriers. By leveraging their fame and box office appeal, ethnic actors can create the vehicles which will broaden their scope of professional work. For instance, James Earl Jones, a well-known African American actor whose roots are in the theater, returns to Broadway in a nontraditionally cast revival of *On Golden Pond*. The success of this project is guaranteed to have an effect on creating more opportunities for nontraditional casting.

The second approach to submitting ethnic actors—nontraditional casting—succeeds when ethnic actors of consummate talent and skill are hired. After seeing a wonderful African American showcase of Tennessee Williams' *The Night of the Iguana*, set in the Caribbean, I decided to start working with three of its actors—based on their performance, not on their ethnicity. After viewing an all-Asian version of *Our Town*, I began working with the young actress playing Emily, who was not only glorious but accent-less. She enjoyed a wide range of submissions during our time together. I tried to stretch the envelope on as many submissions as I could when suggesting these particular actors, because I had firsthand experience of seeing them in non-traditional roles and felt they could compete effectively.

Agents know to look for nontraditional casting opportunities for their clients in classical theater productions and on television shows. Recently a classical theater company in New York City searched specifically for an ethnic actress to portray the ingénue in a play. In its productions of Shakespeare plays, the Public Theater of New York continues to uphold the policy of nontraditional casting established by its founder, Joseph Papp. Every breakdown for a television pilot invites multi-ethnic submissions for at least one series regular. Episodic television shows and sitcoms regularly employ ethnically diverse casts.

When submitting actors of mixed race, agents must find ways to cut through the casting community's quibbling about which particular ethnicity an actor "represents." We do this by submitting talent that is so superb as to make the "confusion" irrelevant. After his musical had been given a staged reading, a writer told me of his struggle to persuade the director to audition a marvelous ethnic actress he knew for the lead. I asked the writer how this choice supported the world of the piece, which was nineteenth-century New England. He explained that casting the *ensemble* multi-racially had created a homogenized society that included his choice of leading actress. Attention was placed on the acting and singing requirements of the piece, rather than on issues of race that had no bearing on the subject matter.

Although it sometimes seems that actors of every race have little control over their careers, they *can* control their training and skill level. Getting work is about beating the competition. These days, it is not enough to be "good." As one agent has remarked, an actor has to be "great," with impressive credits, especially when it comes to soothing the fears of cautious producers, directors, and writers, whose priority is selling tickets or getting high ratings. Decision-makers invariably play it safe and cast traditionally. If they do stray from the norm to cast nontraditionally, most likely there's a commercial motive behind the choice.

My advice to ethnic actors is this: study to be the best actor, singer, or dancer you can be. Follow every possible lead to get work. And look for that agent who believes so strongly in your talent as to submit you boldly and creatively.

Agent Submissions
Before I describe how agents actually make submissions, and the tools they use for this purpose, it is important to note that actors can and

do get jobs through their own personal contacts. In fact, agents encourage actors to network with directors, writers, other actors, and theaters, knowing that work begets work. There is, however, a whole range of projects that an actor would never be "up for" without an agent's submission—projects, for instance, that don't get cast through the breakdown service, that don't even surface on the Internet, that come together purely in a phone conversation between an agent and a casting director. And I'm talking Broadway shows, television shows, films, and commercials. I remember when the casting director for *Law & Order: Trial by Jury* called for help with a few lingering roles in an episode. She gave us the breakdowns and accepted our ideas by phone. Four actors got auditions from one phone call. Many day-player and under-five roles on soap operas are called out to agents in this manner by casting directors.

An agent's written submission, which is addressed to the casting director of a project, consists of a cover letter listing the roles and the names of the actors suggested for each, plus photos and résumés of those actors. These letters can suggest several actors for one role, respond to a project casting thirty roles, or submit one specific actor for a single role. The letters get to the casting director either by mail or messenger, depending on location and time frame.

The times they are a-changin', and technological advances have initiated a movement to make the entire submission process electronic, with agents submitting their clients to casting directors via the Internet. At the time this book was published, this system—already in use for commercials on both coasts, and for film and TV projects in Los Angeles—was infiltrating all areas in New York. While most legit agents in New York retrieve their casting breakdowns through the Internet, they continue to submit their clients the old-fashioned way, with hard-copy photos and résumés. When agents do make an electronic submission, the casting director asks that actors bring hard copies of their headshots and résumés to auditions. Actors also continue to use these in mailings soliciting the attention of agents and casting directors.

SUBMISSION TOOLS: THE HEADSHOT AND RÉSUMÉ

Actors' headshots and résumés are the tools that make or break an agent's submission. To be successful, a headshot (1) must look like the performer walking through the door, and (2) must look professional. A "homemade" headshot cannot compete with the multitude of professional photos received by agents and casting directors. It will not be the one selected for an interview from the stacks of envelopes in an agent's office, or, for that matter, from the piles of photos ending up on a casting director's desk. An actor can sometimes get lucky with a roll shot by a camera-savvy friend in a neighborhood park, especially given the current taste for "natural" and "informal," but that kind of luck is extremely rare.

An actor's looks and credits are significant in this business, and getting auditions depends on the information conveyed by headshots and résumés. A casting director may bring a particular actor in to a director or producer because of that actor's looks. In pushing an actor to a casting director, an agent might cite the most recent credit listed on the résumé. Therefore, it is in actors' best interests to keep their photos and résumés up to date. Actors who don't, lose out on opportunities, and can sometimes even annoy the casting directors who are their fans. A casting director casting a commercial for a shampoo will flip if you walk through the door with your newly permed blonde bob when he expected to see the familiar straight, brown, shoulder-length hair in your headshot.

Recently we submitted an actor whom we had just signed, for a role on an episodic television show. The casting director called in our client for a different role on the breakdown—a much younger role. She was responding to the photo we had submitted, which had been taken five years before. (New photos were on the way but not ready in time for the submission.) Not wanting to jeopardize this audition opportunity in any way, but certainly wanting to avoid an uncomfortable first meeting between the casting director and our client, we suggested to the casting director that she bring in this actor for a more age-appropriate role. Without an updated photo, she was hard to convince, but when she met the actor, she gave him the different sides on the spot.

An updated photo can sometimes be just what is needed to jump-start a career. For example, a new headshot that illustrates a new age range can open doors previously closed—it's almost like being reborn. Many actors making the transition from thirties to forties find that an updated headshot representing them accurately sets up auditions that turn more readily into bookings. Now they are being called in for the right roles. This goes for any kind of dramatic change in look. A significant weight change or change in hair color launches an actor into a different type. A client of mine went from being a leading man trapped in a character actor's body to a leading man in a leading man's body when he dropped seventy pounds. With his new headshot opening the appropriate doors in casting, he booked more successfully. But these good results won't come without the accurate headshot.

Agents like to have a choice of contrasting photos from their clients, to use for making submissions. The description of each character in a breakdown (the look, personality traits, and storyline) determines which clients an agent submits and which photos he uses. The photo and résumé must prove—visually and experientially—the validity of the submission. The sexy, hot photo sent in for a contract role on *Guiding Light* won't be so convincing in a submission for Tom Joad in a stage production of *The Grapes of Wrath*, although the same actor should definitely be considered for both roles. Obviously an actor can't supply his agent with a different shot for each submission. For men and women, the choice of a headshot or a body shot can sometimes provide all the necessary contrast an agent needs for marketing. A total of two or three shots should cover the range. After all, we ought to be able to safely leave something to the casting director's imagination.

It is the actor's responsibility to keep his agent well stocked with photos and résumés. Agents like to have an ample number of these on hand so they can submit their clients freely without worrying about running out. When an agent calls a casting director to push a particular actor, the casting director usually asks whether the actor was submitted, then says she will look over the photo and résumé and get back to the agent. If the agent has not included a photo and résumé of the actor in the submission, the casting director will have nothing to refer to and the actor will be out of luck. Agents would always like to give actors fair warning when the stock of their photos and résumés in the office is low, but usually we have no way of knowing how many submissions will be made at a given time. It's helpful when actors have on hand a supply of *attached* photos and résumés—that means stapled or glued together, or photos with résumés printed on the back. Then they can deliver them same day their agent calls or, at the very latest, next day.

Actors go to professional headshot photographers to get professional results. The know-how of a professional who can light properly, provide interesting but unobtrusive backgrounds, and position the subject to promote body ease and the most flattering angles will save the actor time and money. Recently a client asked a friend who was not a professional headshot photographer to shoot a roll of film. They chose a playground as the backdrop. My client's face looks fine, but the wire fence in the background makes him look like he's in jail. Not appropriate for a headshot! When clients go for new headshots, at the suggestion of their agents, the agents will take time to discuss what they think would be useful in terms of their submissions. This discussion includes wardrobe choice and the purpose of the shot—theatrical, musical comedy, film/TV, etc. For the fellows, we usually want two shots: one for theater and another, more edgy look for television. For the ladies, we suggest upscale glamour shots if the talent fits into that niche, three-quarter shots showing physique (especially for dancers), and a good, intriguing theater shot—maybe two, with one more suitable for comedy and the other more dramatic. Within these general guidelines, an actor can come up with useful shots taken in the studio, or in natural lighting. What's most important is that the end product is professional and looks like the actor, and is interesting and clear in terms of type and attitude.

Headshot sessions are traumatic. That's why it's so important to find the photographer who is right for you. This person must be able to put you at ease and guide you to reveal your most intimate self to the camera lens, while managing the intricate technical requirements of a high-quality shot.

Any device that helps an actor be less self-conscious and more communicative will reveal more of that actor and bring him into focus. Photographers who feed specific images to actors, or ask questions that require them to use their acting skills, are most successful in bringing out their personalities. Actors are put at ease when directed to have a specific focus and a personal reason for communicating.

Regarding whether an actor should have color headshots or black-and-white, I think it depends on the individual. Many actors opt for a combination of the two. Some agents like color, some prefer black-and-white. As this book is being written, color headshots are the norm in Los Angeles and are just beginning to break through in other areas, like New York. I think they are extremely valuable for redheads, whose coloring is totally indistinguishable in black-and-white. Recently a client went in to update her headshot. She's a beautiful redhead with a wonderful skin tone and big blue eyes. When she found out that the new digital technology enabled her to get color prints without ending up in the poorhouse, she decided to make the investment. I submit her with new-found relish because I just love that new color photo. It's a real eye-grabber; next to the old black-and-white there is no comparison.

A word or two about résumés: For agent submissions, clients' résumés must clearly and thoroughly present the information. That's especially helpful for agents when we need to refer to something specific in our conversation with a casting director. The résumé should include any information that an agent could ever possibly use as a selling point—known directors, actors, writers, producers, teachers, awards, etc. Put your best credits on top, in an interesting but readable typeface; and throughout, selectively use options like boldface, italics, upper- and lowercase letters or caps only, in a way that will help the reader sort out important details. As was mentioned in Chapter Two, be specific and up-to-date about your special skills. For example, list the dialects you can really do, and list the musical instruments you can play now or with only a few hours of practice. When an agent, responding to a breakdown calling for tenors who play the sax, sees on your résumé that you are a tenor and can play the sax, he will submit you and expect you to perform when called upon to do so at the audition, which may be the very next day.

Agents want to be included in their clients' process of getting headshots and putting together résumés. One of my clients once tried a new photographer and brought her new headshots to the office. I felt that the shot she had selected was not useful for our purposes and asked to see the contact sheets from the session. Luckily I discovered a few that were perfectly fine, so the session was not a loss. Another client asked a fellow actor for advice in pruning her résumé. When she showed us the revised version, I was appalled: all of her important information had been deleted. She had taken the advice of someone who was well established in the business and could afford to pare down credits. Our client, pretty much a newcomer to the industry, needed to list all of the information included in the "training," "special skills" and "work experience" sections so that casting directors could place her. In both situations, I admonished my clients and reminded them to allow their agent to work for her ten percent.

Agents and actors collaborate to establish a winning tool kit of head-shots and résumés for submissions. Agents make submissions diligently and in a number of ways. These submissions are the crux of our business: if we don't suggest our clients for roles, we won't get auditions for them, and without auditions, there is no opportunity to book work

★

There's a project you really want to be seen for. When you mention it to your agent, she tells you that you were submitted, and asks whether the casting director knows you. You say, "Unfortunately, no." Next day you are amazed when your agent calls you with an audition. How did she do it?

Chapter 6

HOW DO AGENTS "SELL" ACTORS?

"Can you get me in?" is the plea that agents hear daily from their clients who are looking for auditions. These calls can range from timid inquiry to desperate indignation, depending on a number of factors. You see, actors know that jobs don't just materialize out of thin air—not unless you're a celebrity, or an actor so well established in the business as to receive offers of work without auditioning. Most actors know that they must audition to get work. And they know that they depend on their agents to get them these valuable auditions. In this respect, an actor's job security depends on his agent's persistent and effective search for opportunity.

For their part, agents recognize that getting auditions is critical to their own livelihoods, as well as to their clients'. After all, our daily bread, so to speak, comes from the commissions earned on actor bookings, and those bookings are, for the most part, the direct result of the auditions we obtain for our clients. Did you ever wonder why an agent spends so much time making submissions? It's because the more submissions we make, the more auditions we can get for our clients. The more opportunities our clients have to book jobs, the more money everyone stands a chance to make.

What does an agent say to a client when he asks, even demands, to be seen for a project? How do we address these inquiries ranging from, "Can you get me in?" to, "Why aren't they seeing me?" The agent simply says, "Let me make a call and find out." That phone call to the casting director is the beginning of the process we call "selling," or "pushing"—whereby we try to work our submissions into auditions.

I'd like to offer a tip here, if I may, on *how* to ask your agent about submissions and auditions. Requesting a submission for a project is perfectly fine. Actors do it all the time, and we agents expect it—although we recommend that our clients fax or email us the lists of projects they want to be seen for, rather than phone us, so as not to interrupt the flow of our work day. It's even okay to gently nudge your agent to follow up on a submission. What's not acceptable, and probably won't work in your favor, is whining or demanding to be seen, while dumping on your good agent your frustration and disappointment at *not* being seen. Actors must realize that there many reasons why they may not get in for a project—however perfect they think they are (and indeed may be) for a role. These reasons make no sense in other professions, but have a unique logic in the world of show business. And these reasons, certainly, lie beyond an agent's control. For instance, the fact that an actress has already played a certain part in a play may be the very reason that a director chooses not to bring her in. There she is— the actress—agonizing over the fact that she's not being seen for the role that brought her such great notices in Atlanta. Even after her agent has phoned, faxed reviews—done everything possible short of offering his firstborn to the casting director—the actress still doesn't have that audition for the Broadway production of the play. What she doesn't know, her agent finally discovers, after numerous calls to the casting director: though the actress thought she'd be one step ahead of the competition because she'd already played the part, the director wants to work only with performers who come to the material totally fresh. This is a reality that neither actress nor agent can change; it must be accepted by both. At other times, an actress who has already played a role could be just what the director needs—for one-week stock, or as an immediate replacement during rehearsals, to name two examples. What's certain is that to maintain a healthy relationship with his agent, it is advisable for an actor to realize that casting criteria are not the fault of his agent. In the end, it's always better to believe that your agent will try his best to get you in. After all—again— it is in everyone's best interest to do so.

SUBMISSION TO AUDITION

Let's take a closer look at how the "submission to audition" process occurs, to see just how an agent cultivates activity on the submissions he makes. Usually I make a submission with the hopeful expectation that the casting director will call me with audition appointments. When I'm selecting from among my clients for the characters listed on the breakdown, I'm casting the play, TV show, or movie, in my mind. I suggest actors whom I feel can legitimately be cast in the role and perform it brilliantly. I select the clients whose talent, training, and experience will justify the casting director's calling them in. I try my best to keep up with my clients' schedules in order to submit talent that is truly available for the project. Some clients need to stay in New York and can't work out of town. Some are on vacation during the shooting dates for the current episode of a television show. These are just a few of the factors that influence whom I select to submit for particular projects.

Many actors wonder what happens after they mention to their agent a project that they would like to be submitted for. Will the agent make the submission? Should the actor wait to hear from the agent regarding an audition? How does he follow up on his request? Assuming that the agent has agreed to make the submission, she will have sent it to the casting director by mail, fax, over the Internet, or by messenger. As for what happens next, many agents keep copies of their submissions in folders that are within easy reach for quick reference, when a casting director calls with audition appointments. When that call comes, the agent takes down the information regarding the audition, paying close attention to which actors are being called in, while checking that list against her list of submitted clients. Not wanting to seem ungrateful for the decisions already made, but desiring to make the most of this opportune conversation, the agent goes into high selling gear, trying to get more auditions, especially for those actors whom she feels are sure bets and have been overlooked by the casting director.

Most of the time, I send submissions to casting directors who are familiar with the agency and the actors we represent. These are CDs with whom I've developed relationships over the years. They know what to expect from my submissions, and I can usually forecast which clients they will audition. This is not uncommon; most agents have developed close relationships with certain CDs over time. Because of a connection with an agent and a fondness and appreciation for a particular actor, a casting director will sometimes go out of his way to help this actor obtain continuous work. I have overheard conversations between agents and CDs in which an entire season of work is planned out for a certain actor. Of course, the actor has to audition well enough to book the jobs, but the casting director is the one who provides the auditions— and the agent is the matchmaker who introduced them.

Sometimes actors mistakenly assume that an agent's solid relationship with a casting director is all that's needed to get them an audition for a project. A client of mine once asked me about a high-profile production in New York. This was the kind of job that only celebrities and very successful actors could afford to take: the pay was terrible, but the exposure at one of the top Off-Broadway houses was great. My client, a fine actor with solid training and good regional theater credits, asked me whether he had been submitted. I said he had been, but warned him that the producers would probably seek name talent. He then asked me if I had a good relationship with the casting director. I said I did, but reiterated that I might not be able to talk the actor into an audition for this one. The actor incorrectly assumed that my good relationship with the casting director would trump the producer's request for box-office talent. During the course of this uncomfortable conversation, I could see that my client was stubbornly refusing to accept the reality of the situation, and I could tell that it wouldn't be long before he would blame me for not being able to get him in.

When sending a submission to a casting director, I have great confidence in my clients' castability, which I feel is reflected in their headshots and résumés. I submit with the belief that should the CD open my submission and find that the look, credits, and training of my clients meet the casting requirements, he will definitely call some of them in for auditions. What I tend to forget, however, is that I, as do most agents, work in a vacuum. We may have total belief in our clients and their "rightness" for the roles being cast. What we *don't* know is the type of competition that our clients face in the submissions of other agents. I'm always slightly deflated when, after I've spent a good amount of time preparing a submission (carefully culling the appropriate clients, assembling their photos and résumés, and writing a persuasive letter—all so efficiently that the package reaches the casting director in time for him to look through it and make his selections), I get maybe one or two auditions out of the twelve suggestions I made. What I forget, at this moment, is that many other agents have done just as I did. I also sometimes find out, after making the submission, that the theater is obliged to cast some of the roles locally, which takes away opportunities for my clients to be seen. Of course, once I have secured these auditions for my clients, it's up to them to prove the validity of my suggestions by doing well at the auditions, and hopefully getting callbacks and job offers.

TIMING IS EVERYTHING

If I were to wait endlessly for a casting director to respond to a submission I'd made, I might lose out on opportunities to make business. Instead, like most agents, I routinely thumb through those folders where I keep the copies of my submissions. Checking up on submissions and audition activity is like watering plants: if it isn't done regularly, business will die. I gauge the amount of time I wait for a casting director to respond. This is determined by the type of project being cast and the audition date, which is usually stated on the breakdown notice. For example, it is common knowledge that episodic television shows are cast quickly, so I need to deal with them the day after I make the submission. Plays, on the other hand, usually take a week—sometimes longer. If I make a submission on a Monday for a play that is holding auditions the following Monday and I haven't heard from the casting director by Thursday, I know I should make a follow-up call immediately.

When I don't hear from a casting director in response to a submission, I quickly get over my amazement and make a follow-up phone call to try to get auditions for my clients. Sometimes the only way I know that I'm missing out on auditions for a project is when I get a phone call from a client who has heard through actor friends that auditions for that project are being scheduled now. This timely newsflash spurs me to make a follow-up call to the casting director. I usually begin my conversation with the simple question, "Did you receive my submission?" In this way, I can touch base with the casting director and innocently corroborate my client's tip that audition appointments are being set up. Depending on the CD's answer and how agreeable he seems to be to continuing the conversation, I might suggest that I re-fax the submission list (if he says he hasn't received it yet), hoping that some of the actors' names will ring a bell; or pinpoint a few of my top choices (if he says he has), so he can look more closely at those particular photos and résumés.

It's important that agents make these follow-up phone calls, because many times what they find out will determine their next step. Perhaps the casting director reveals that the project has been postponed, or will be cast in Los Angeles only, or that a particular role was cut from the script. Although the news may be disappointing at first, the agent is grateful that questions have been answered in a way that allows her to put the matter at rest and move on to follow-up on the next submission. On other occasions, the agent may discover just how overwhelming the numbers are. For instance, the casting director will explain that she has only four hours to cast a six-character play, and most of the audition slots are going to performers requested by the director. If an agent's client isn't one of those requested, the best that can be hoped for, according to the CD, is that an actor who is scheduled cancels, at which time she will try her hardest to replace him with the agent's client. This is important news that the agent would never have received without the follow-up call.

A casting director might not respond to an agent's submission for many reasons. It is the agent's job to investigate and discover what these reasons are, and then push like crazy to prove them wrong in order to get audition appointments. This is where an agent's selling skills—to charm, persuade, and assert—come into play. Pushing is selling, is talking up, is bending an ear, is going to bat for—is literally creating an opening where there was none to be had.

OBSTACLES TO THE SUCCESSFUL PUSH

Frequently, an agent must jump over many hurdles to make a successful push. One of the first, and perhaps the greatest, is actually getting through to speak directly to the casting director. You see, CDs are no dummies. They realize that an agent's job is to phone them and push to get auditions for their clients. In fact one casting director, who shall remain nameless, once stated (somewhat facetiously) that an agent's job is to push, while a CD's job is to say "no." This is a fairly accurate take on this aspect of the agent-casting director relationship. Casting directors expect an agent to try to get as many clients as possible into a casting session. It sometimes seems to agents that casting directors create a shield of assistants, interns, and voicemail in order to avoid taking agents' calls. That's why the first and most important directive an intern or assistant receives when starting work in an agent's office is to hold onto any incoming telephone calls from CDs. She is admonished to keep the casting director on the line at all costs, while vigorously tracking down an agent to take the call. Getting through to a casting director is usually so difficult that when a casting director actually does call an office, it is something like a miracle; therefore, an agent must seize this opportunity to sell. From a casting director's point of view, avoiding communication with agents makes sense. First of all, there simply isn't enough time in a day to take every agent or manager's push. If they did, they wouldn't have time to set up their casting sessions. Second, there aren't enough slots in a casting session to set up every agent or manager's choices. Clearly, a casting director must devise ways and means of protecting herself from the onslaught of hungry talent reps.

How do agents surmount this challenge of getting through to the casting director? By chipping away at her fortress. We re-fax submission lists as gentle reminders, in case our original submissions got buried under the piles of envelopes she receives. We leave messages with assistants or on voicemail, asking that she return our call. Sometimes we speak with an assistant or intern who knows to ask us for our pushes. This usually occurs at the networks during pilot season, when the process of submitting and pushing happens at breakneck speed in a frenetic feeding frenzy of agents, managers, and casting directors. Agents rattle off the names of the actors we want seen for a project, which the casting director's assistant or intern writes down, making sure to get the correct spelling. The assistant or intern then assures us she will pull the pictures of these actors from our submission to show to the casting director. Ever hopeful for the positive result of an audition, the agents hang up the phone and wait for the return call from the CD. When it doesn't come, we follow up the next day to do it all over again. Agents are driven people, and they believe that perseverance will win the day. For myself, I figure that at least my name, the agency's name, and most importantly, the client's name, are getting lots of exposure from all these phone calls, and that perhaps sheer familiarity will lead towards getting auditions.

In any sales business, it is the relationships between the players that determine activity, and developing these relationships pays off in many ways. In show business, for example, casting directors who usually handle theater projects occasionally are hired to cast a film. When this happens, the theater agent who has developed a relationship with this CD over the years has a chance to get those envied film auditions for his clients who mainly work in the theater.

One agent I know spends a lot of his time on the phone talking to casting assistants and interns. He goes out of his way to treat them with respect and develop friendly relationships with them. He knows they are the gatekeepers to a casting director's attentions and can therefore be potential allies. He is also planting seeds: many of these folks will grow within the industry. Yesterday's assistant or intern is tomorrow's independent casting director, and if an agent sticks around long enough, he will harvest the fruits of his labor. People are much more helpful when they are treated with respect and courtesy, and they remember who treated them well when they were just starting out.

When I do get a casting director on the phone, she will usually ask me for my top two choices. Here's where my selling expertise comes in handy. I quickly zero in on the best choices from my already selective list. For example, let's say a breakdown calls for a petite blonde with lots of personality. I have submitted my petite blondes (all with lots of personality), but if it's Shakespeare they want, I'll push Susie, who trained extensively at London's Royal Academy of Dramatic Art and is just back from working at the Utah Shakespearean Festival. If it's musical, I'll suggest Annie, a triple threat who recently became unemployed when her Broadway show closed unexpectedly. Let's face it: some actors do Shakespeare, and some sing and dance. And, yes, many do it all. Generally, as noted earlier, I submit broadly, giving the casting director freedom to choose from a wide range of possibilities. I follow up on these by pushing selectively and smartly when given the chance.

SOFT SELL, HARD SELL

Selling is one of my favorite aspects of agenting. It's very easy to speak enthusiastically about something you like. I can talk for days about the talent of my clients. Since I hold their talent in the highest regard and believe in the legitimacy of my casting suggestions, it is not difficult for me to speak enthusiastically and persuasively to casting directors on my clients' behalf. My pushes are not filled with empty rhetoric or hyperbole. They are justified. As for proving a point or backing up my rhapsodies, I cite recent credits, significant callbacks, screen tests, feedback from other casting directors, training—anything that I believe will sell my casting suggestion. For example, I know that many casting directors like to "discover" a talent. If an actor they give a break to becomes a big success, they can claim part of the credit. Sometimes I appeal to a casting director's ego by tempting him to "make a discovery today." This gives me an entrée to discuss an "unknown" actress, one who perhaps recently relocated to New York City or graduated from conservatory. If I play it right I will arouse the casting director's curiosity to the point that he will call the actress in to satisfy his own ego. In the end, I really don't care who takes credit for the suggestion that turned out to be a big success. I'm satisfied that my client got the audition.

Many agents fear that the current movement to conduct business electronically, over the Internet, will hamper our ability to sell talent. So much of our promotion is done over the phone. Personal contact is the modus operandi for many of us. While we realize and appreciate that the Internet and email save time, we truly hope that show business won't devolve into list makers huddled over computers, trading emails.

Some casting directors seem to like to be difficult and to challenge agents. I know one in particular who reacts negatively to *any* suggestion offered by an agent. Perhaps it's his way of testing the agent's belief in her pushes. Perhaps he enjoys his authority to say "no." Whatever the reason for this behavior, the agent must steel her resolve, stand firm in her push, get the audition, and hope her client will rise to the occasion and do well. Agents by and large push for auditions because they believe that any opportunity an actor has is better than none (even if he's still a bit jet lagged or sounds slightly nasal from the last remnants of a head cold). It's helpful when actors acknowledge that these auditions sometimes come from hard-fought battles, and that an agent's reputation rests on the talent and professionalism her clients bring to them. Any audition, especially when it results from an agent's push, is not to be taken for granted and deserves the actor's utmost preparation. Even agents with clout, those fairy godmothers to the common actor, work their magic sparingly. They might be able to get an actor into an audition on the heels of a celebrity client, but after that it's up to the actor to make the most of this opportunity and prove himself worthy of that audition and more. Clearly, a great deal rests on these audition opportunities for both actor and agent.

Sometimes an agent makes a push for an audition in order to introduce an actor and his work to a CD and director. The audition experience may be more valuable than the job itself. Here's a story about two graduating students from one of the top acting conservatories in the United States: Our agency signed them right after conservatory. They spent their first year out of school auditioning and getting callbacks, but neither actually booked a job. This is more common than not with student performers transitioning from acting school to professional life. Usually during the first year out of school, many actors not only face the challenges of living life (surviving on their own in a new city, etc.), but find themselves adjusting to how the industry casts them—which is different from casting in school. Big girls aren't necessarily cast as mothers, for example, and short fellows won't necessarily play children. We submitted our two recent graduates to many casting directors over the course of the year. We happily embraced the news of their callbacks because we knew that these would eventually lead to bookings—as they did. A director remembered the young actress from her audition for his production of *Picnic*, and cast her a year later as a lead in his production of a Molière play. The actor was too young for the role he went up for, but the director of that production remembered him from his audition and offered him a lead (without auditioning) in a Shakespeare play the following season. I recall the specific feedback we received from both of these auditions: "Major talent, well trained, not right for the role." One year later both actors had jobs in fine theaters, through the connections with casting directors that had been established by their agent. The CDs became fans of these two actors for life! The agents continue to build these clients' fan bases to include new contacts.

It's fun when a buzz starts among casting directors about a client. I once opened up an envelope that came to the office where I was working as an assistant agent, to find a very intriguing headshot of a young actress who had just landed in New York City from East Texas. She had had some training and a little experience, so on a hunch the office decided to meet her. It was pilot season and we started submitting her for projects. We pushed her for auditions and she auditioned very well. It wasn't long before casting directors at the different networks were talking to one another about her. The day after she auditioned for an ABC pilot, CBS staffers called, demanding to see this great actress that they had heard about from ABC. And so it went—a chain reaction of positive response, a bonfire of activity—sparked by the interest of a single agent. For the record, the actress booked a pilot that year and went on to become a major television personality.

The decision to push a client for a project will sometimes be based on the client's importance to the agency. If the client is a major earner for the agency, the agent will go at it full force. Every agent has a personal style of pushing clients. Some agents are very theatrical and like to dramatize their position. This approach is most successful when done with humor. One agent I know creates a verbal drama for her push, which is meant to entertain and soften the casting director at the same time. Another agent, an older gal, did most of her agenting in the days before casting directors even existed, when directors and producers called agents directly, requesting suggestions of actors for their productions. Eventually this procedure fostered the kind of agent who coyly offers solutions to a casting director's problems by way of suggesting clients. The older gal told the story of how a well-known director one time called her in distress. He couldn't find his young male lead for an odd new script by a young playwright from Harvard. After the agent heard the character description, she remembered a young actor she had recently met and said she thought he could do the role. When Jerome Robbins met Austin Pendleton, he cast him immediately in *Oh Dad, Poor Dad...*, and that's how that career got started.

Most agents are very straightforward in their pushes. They name the actors that they "feel strongly" about and cite the reasons why. Whatever powers of persuasion an agent has, this is his time to use them. I know an agent who manages to stretch every conversation she has with a casting director into a chance to sell talent. Since most CDs don't want to give agents a chance to go into overdrive to push clients, they do their business quickly; before saying good-bye, they allow agents only enough time to rattle off a name or two with some quick descriptive words. This particular agent, in her efforts to continue the conversation, refuses to adopt the pace of the casting director, and starts to ask probing questions about what he is looking for, or whether he is having any particular casting problems, forcing the casting director to engage in a conversation that usually leads to his giving this agent more auditions.

Casting directors are buyers. Agents are sellers. Actors are the product. And, of course, the number one rule in selling is that the customer is always right. The agent's challenge is to hear every "no" uttered by a casting director as a "yes"—regardless of how strongly the "no" is expressed. Even when that "no" is final, we must treat it like a "yes," or at least a "maybe." If our client is not right for this role, perhaps the casting director will remember her (because she is fresh in his mind) for the next role. We cannot allow ourselves to feel defeated, much less show our disappointment to the casting director. We must stay focused, stay positive, stay objective, and stay personable, ready to return shortly for the next round.

In the end, there is just so much an agent can do. No amount of charm, persuasion, or excellent reasoning will turn around a casting director who has decided to pass on an actor. It is very difficult for an actor to accept the words, "The casting director looked at your photo and résumé, and passed." It is equally difficult for the agent to hear these words from the casting director and then have to relay them to the actor. I knew I had become a full-fledged agent the day I countered the rejection of my push of one client by suggesting another client. *It became obvious to me in that moment that an agent's priority is to get auditions, not to push a particular actor.* In a New York minute, a pass on one client became an opportunity for another.

It is difficult enough for an actor to learn that his face and credits have not passed the submission test. Worse yet is that he never knows for sure what factored into that decision. When no amount of diligent and assertive pushing by an agent can uncover those reasons or reverse the decision, it is best for both agent and actor to accept the reality and move on.

Some submissions don't need to be pushed to bring many auditions. Others require constant cultivation to gain merely one or two appointments. In either scenario, clearly an agent works hard to get action for clients. Is our ten percent becoming any more justified in your mind yet?

★

You haven't heard from your agent in three weeks. Now, all of the sudden, you have three auditions scheduled on the same day. Luckily your agent seems very organized and thorough in preparing you for the hellish, but wonderful, day that tomorrow is about to be.

Chapter 7:

HOW DO AGENTS PREPARE ACTORS FOR AUDITIONS?

Calling an actor with an audition is one of an agent's most favorite activities. It rates right up there with giving the news of an offer or inviting an actor to sign with the agency. No one can doubt that getting auditions for clients is a top priority on the list of agent responsibilities. Until someone comes up with a different way for actors to get jobs, auditioning is it. Therefore, the manner in which the entire audition experience is handled from start to finish is absolutely critical to an actor's artistic and financial well-being.

An agent will do everything in her power to help a client prepare for an audition—everything from giving the actor exact coordinates of an audition site, plus suggestions of material if required, wardrobe choice, interview demeanor. Many times the audition comes to the actor through the agent's persistent pushing. She as well as the actor has a great deal at stake, and much to gain from the audition experience. Not only possible employment with salary and commission, but reputations and opportunities for future business are on the line. An actor who does well at the audition may be called back and, indeed, go on to book the job. The finances and the careers of all parties concerned will prosper from the credit. The job has a monetary value and it raises the actor to another level within the industry. Once a client books a day on *ER*, for instance, his agent can use that credit to get him into auditions for other television shows, or for more challenging roles on the same show. This holds true in the other areas of the business—stage, film, commercials, etc. The more work an actor amasses in a certain area, the higher his value becomes in that area. Higher value commands better jobs with commensurate salaries. By doing well at the audition his agent pushed to get him, the actor confirms his agent's taste in talent, thereby establishing her with the casting director as a provider of winning talent.

What should an actor expect from his agent in terms of audition preparation? What does an agent expect from his client? How much information does a casting director give to an agent about an audition, and how far in advance of the actual audition does the agent usually receive that information? In what different ways do agents prepare their clients for theater, television, and film auditions? In the handling of audition material, how might communication between agents and actors be improved to give actors every possible advantage for a well-prepared audition? These important questions will guide our discussion in this chapter on audition preparation. Let's begin by seeing how the system works.

CALLING OUT THE AUDITION

Agents and managers each submit to casting directors X number of clients for X number of roles in a project. The casting director confers with the writer, director, and producer of the project to come up with a list of the candidates they want to audition, then calls the agents and managers to give them audition appointments for their clients. These appointment calls include all of the pertinent information, like the date, time, and place of the audition, and the type of material required for preparation. The agents and managers call their clients with this information, many times leaving it on voicemail and instructing the clients to call back to confirm and corroborate the details. If this sounds like a game of "Telephone," ripe for all sorts of miscommunications and slipups, you're right. "Two-fifteen" can sound like "2:50," "Monday" like "Sunday"; there may be as many as five phone calls going back and forth between the parties before an audition is confirmed. Let's say a casting director calls an actor's manager with an audition appointment. The manager calls both his client and his client's agent to tell them about the audition. The client calls his manager back to discuss the audition and perhaps request a time change. The manager then calls the agent to ask her to call the casting director to get the time change. Is your head spinning yet? Honestly, the last thing an agent wants to do is make so many phone calls for one audition for one client. Agents want the process of putting out audition appointments to go as smoothly and efficiently as possible. This frees them up to get more appointments for other actors.

Let's look at the picture from the casting director's point of view: Say a casting director receives a double submission of an actor from that actor's agent and manager. How would the CD determine whom to call with the audition appointment? Agent or manager? Either way, someone is bound to be offended. To avoid this type of confusion and potential discomfort, casting directors ask agents and managers *not* to double-submit their clients.

For that matter, casting directors also ask agents to be sure to get clearance from their freelance clients when submitting them for projects. Let me review: A "freelancer" is an actor who works with an agent without signing an exclusive management contract. Freelancing allows the actor to work with several agents from different agencies at the same time. An agent secures ("clears") a freelance client every time he submits him for a project, to prevent double submissions to casting directors. The last thing a casting director wants to do is get caught between two rabid agents fighting over an audition appointment.

Most agents still use the telephone to call out their audition appointments. Since voicemail systems usually pick up their calls, many agents choose to leave only skeletal details in their message, like the project name, and the date and time of the audition, asking the actor to call back for more information. Bitter experience has taught agents to do this: they have taken too many phone calls from actors asking them to repeat all the details of an audition appointment, because the message was "accidentally" deleted.

When agents phone and reach a client directly, they tell the actor as many details about the audition and the project as are available to the agent. Along with the essential information—title of the project; date, time, and place of the audition; and description of the audition material and ways to obtain it—agents may choose to cite the medium (theater, TV, or film) and the name of the casting director, director, producer, or network; or to offer inclusive dates and location of the project. A Steven Bochco series is different from an Aaron Spelling series, and Shakespeare at New York City's Delacorte is different from an Anne Bogart piece at Actors' Theatre of Louisville. Agents believe that having this information helps actors properly focus their audition preparation. Sometimes in response to an agent's persistent probing, a casting director will reveal details about a project that prove significantly helpful to an actor in preparing his read. One time a casting director from a New York nighttime drama called the agency asking for suggestions of actors to potentially play a few judges. She specifically said that she was looking for a very natural, non-dramatic delivery. We knew not to suggest our wonderful Shakespearean actors, who are most comfortable playing in large amphitheaters, and we made sure to give the actors we did send in the specific adjustment the casting director had described to us in her initial phone call.

When agents call out the audition appointment, we do our best to give detailed information. After that, most agents feel the responsibility for preparation shifts to the person actually taking the audition—namely, the actor. They believe that it is the actor's job to get the sides, locate and read the script, learn the songs, and figure out where the audition is to take place.

An agent I know remembers when he was starting out as an assistant at one of the larger agencies in town. A senior agent told him that on no condition was he to spend time getting actors their audition material: it was their responsibility. While this sets the standard to live by, it doesn't always prove logical. If a client has no way of getting his audition material without the agent's help, the agent must step in—if she wants her client to get the job. An older client of mine doesn't have a fax machine and doesn't do email. Since we live within ten blocks of each other, whenever he has an audition I offer to print out the material and leave it with my doorman for the actor to pick up the next day.

That's what agents do to make the audition work. Here's what actors can do: They can try not to burden their agents with tasks that they can easily take care of themselves. Be aware of the many things you can do to make the collaborative process go smoothly and efficiently. After all, wouldn't you want your agent to spend more time getting you more appointments than taking care of the extraneous details that you can handle for the ones you already have?

One agent I know insists that his clients have one telephone number, and only one, that he is to call. He asserts that he just doesn't have time to call the service, cell, and home phone number for every audition he gets. It is important for actors to realize that agents represent more than one performer, and can sometimes get fifteen auditions at a time to call out. An actor can help out his agent enormously by taking down all the information concerning an audition appointment the first time it's given, and not asking the agent to repeat it. I would also suggest that an actor listen to the entire message left on his voicemail before calling his agent for audition details. Any action that requires an agent to repeat business needlessly is a terrible time waster. It does not foster an agreeable relationship with the agent, and ultimately hurts fellow actors, who don't get auditions because their agent is essentially making two calls on one client's audition instead of using his time to get other auditions. Being a self-sufficient actor wins points with your agent, and getting into his good graces couldn't be anything but good for your career! Having the reputation of being a low-maintenance client also helps at those times when your computer just crashed and you can't get your sides off the Internet. Believe me, I am much more willing to go out of my way to get a script for a client who is usually self-sufficient than for an actor who has problems with every audition and expects me to take care of every step of his preparation. See what you can do to ease the workload of your agent; it will pay off in the long run.

Before cell phones and answering machines, agents called an actor's twenty-four-hour "answering service" to notify him of auditions. Live people at a switchboard or a telephone wrote down the messages as they came in. These would be brief, like, "Message for Susie Q. Call her agent." An actor routinely phoned his service several times a day to "check in." When he picked up a message that his agent had called, the actor immediately phoned the agent to find out why, hoping the reason was an audition. If it was, the actor got details at that time. When a performer picked up his message after business hours, he had to wait until the next morning to call his agent for the information. Sometimes the loss of these hours reduced the actor's time to prepare for the audition.

With the advent of home answering machines, agents were able to make one call per audition per actor, leaving all of the information in one message at his home. These privately owned machines enabled actors to retrieve the information at any time, from virtually any place. At the same time personal answering machines came into the picture, voicemail services that functioned like an electronic switchboard, eliminating the need for a middleman, emerged. No longer were agents and actors at the mercy of slow-moving switchboard operators, or roommates and houseguests from out of town who accidentally erased phone messages. These technological advances gave actors and agents more freedom. Actors could retrieve messages and prepare auditions according to their own time schedules. Now that they were making fewer phone calls per audition appointment, agents could devote more time to other activities—like making submissions, negotiating deals, and giving advice and counsel.

Now actors have cell phones, and I suppose some agents even use email to put out audition appointments. Both technologies provide extremely mobile communication that increases personal freedom and saves time. Now an agent can reach a client on the other side of the world at 3:00 a.m. if need be, via cell phone and/or email. This instantaneous communication does not come, however, without its own set of problems: like "breaking up" reception, erratic volume levels, and delayed response time. Although agents prefer landline communication any day, they realize that the cell phone is not only here to stay, but is moving to take over. We just hope that advanced technology will eliminate these glitches, making communication a more pleasant and consistently reliable experience.

THE CASTING SESSION

In this chapter we have seen how agents have incorporated technological advances into their daily routine of putting out audition appointments. Let me now suggest a few things that actors can do to help the process run smoothly, thereby enabling more auditions to come their way and allowing them to better prepare for the auditions they do get.

Important enough to reiterate is that actors should try very hard not to accidentally delete voicemail messages from their agents. They should make their best efforts to get all the information the first time it's given, and to call to confirm an audition as quickly as possible. This is crucial for casting directors, who are paid to secure talent for casting sessions. They need to know before the casting session they've set up starts, whether they can expect the requested actors to show up at their appointed times. Casting directors appreciate a quick confirmation from agents so they can determine how many audition slots, if any, still need to be filled. It looks very bad for a casting director if there are holes in the session. There they sit with the director and producers in an empty rented studio while time ticks away. Somebody had to pay for that audition space, and unfilled time is wasted money. The people who hired the casting directors will blame them for any slots not filled by auditioning actors. Thinking the casting directors are inefficient, producers will question whether to hire them again. Because agents want to preserve their relationships with casting directors and get more auditions in the future, they urge their clients to respond quickly with confirmations, and admonish them for canceling auditions on the same day. We can hardly condone any reason for canceling the same day, other than family or personal emergency, or sickness. We know how very difficult it will be to get that actor into that casting director again.

I would also suggest that, as a general rule, actors try to accommodate their schedules to fit the time of an audition appointment *before* asking their agents to change it. I understand that people have complicated schedules. Many actors have day or night jobs with minimum flexibility. There are bound to be schedule conflicts, and one of an agent's jobs is, indeed, to manage schedules. However, what drives an agent crazy is when each appointment given to an actor becomes a Sisyphean task of making innumerable calls back and forth about time changes. Once again, the more time we spend accommodating schedule conflicts, the less time we have for getting more auditions.

Preparing the Audition

Let's move on to audition material: As an actor progresses from auditioning for non-union to union jobs, he discovers that the call for monologues lessens, and "sides"—which are excerpts of material taken directly from the play, TV show, or movie being cast—are used instead. (There are exceptions: Shakespearean festivals still ask for two contrasting classical monologues, one of them preferably in Shakespearean verse. New theater companies, when auditioning for members, generally require two contrasting monologues, usually one contemporary and the other classical. Legit agents auditioning new actors in their offices often want to see monologues.)

Most professional auditions require an actor to prepare a page or more from the project's script—the sides—which he obtains beforehand. How and when he gets this material depends on the casting director and the agent. Theater auditions are usually called in to an agent, and in turn to an actor, with a week's time to prepare. I know one casting director, however, who purposely waits until the day before the casting session to call out the auditions, in an effort to avoid last-minute cancellations. Sometimes the reason an audition comes in with a very quick turnaround time is project oriented. For instance, I frequently get *Law & Order* appointments on the same day. This happens because scripts are revised overnight and a new role appears on a casting director's desk in the morning, which must be cast by the end of the day. The casting director will call that morning, with apologies, asking if so-an-so would be available to come in at 5:00 that afternoon for an emergency casting session to meet the director and producer. At other times, these auditions come in at the last minute because an actor cancelled on the same day of the audition, causing the casting director to respond to an agent's push. If you are the lucky client being pushed, spare your agent your complaints about the lack of preparation time. Instead, respond with excitement and readiness. Drop everything and focus what little time you do have on getting the sides and preparing your audition. In these situations, an agent will answer any complaints with the quip, "Do you want to be an actor or a waiter?" because that's how an agent sees it. Sadly, some actors discover too late that such opportunities come too infrequently not to be seized upon immediately. Don't be one of those actors.

To truly appreciate the time-saving advances of the Internet in coordinating audition material, it's useful to take an historical tour of the process: In the past an actor had to travel by subway, bus, or taxi, or on foot, to the casting director's office during regular business hours, to pick up copies of the sides for an audition and/or to read the script. With the invention of the facsimile machine, casting directors began to fax sides to agents who, in turn, faxed them to clients. Agents were not happy—suddenly an entirely new time-consuming task was added to our busy workload. An agent I know who sometimes gets twenty auditions per project began to lose the will to live. Previously, he had prided himself on the number of auditions he got per project. Now he cursed his success because it meant spending much of his day at the fax machine, to the neglect of the breakdowns and other business, which piled up, undone, on his desk. I know what you're thinking: faxing sides is for interns or assistants. True, but not every office is equipped with these happy helpers. Clearly, what made the day easier for casting directors (who no longer had to provide sides for actors to pick up) and for actors (who could now receive sides on their home faxes, or at the nearby copy shop) played havoc with the agent's daily routine.

Today, we live in the age of computers and electronic information. When a casting director calls me with an audition appointment, he will say that the sides are posted on Sides Express, a website for agents and managers that is included in our subscription to Breakdown Services. Most sides on Sides Express are also posted on Showfax, the companion site for actors. To subscribe to Showfax, actors pay a nominal yearly fee, which is less than the cost of a single reorder of 100 headshots. Since this is, of course, a tax-deductible business expense, agents strongly advise their clients to include it in their yearly budgets. With websites like Sides Express and Showfax, agents, managers, and actors have access to audition material twenty-four hours a day, 365 days of the year, from literally anyplace in the world where they can find a computer and the Internet.

Without doubt a computer with Internet access is necessary for a performer these days. It empowers an actor to take charge of preparing his audition from the moment he receives his agent's call. Computers and Internet access have made the process of getting audition material easier, less time-consuming, and cheaper. Agents hope that all these "economy" advances will promote better audition preparation and lead to more callbacks and jobs.

Some actors like to audition cold. They don't want to receive the material beforehand because they think it will take away from a "spontaneous read." Others need to spend as much time as possible with the material. Whichever the actor's preference, it is based on his knowledge of his own needs and methods of preparation. As I mentioned above, the type of project—whether theater, TV, or film—will affect when an agent gets the information about an audition; that, in turn, will affect how an actor prepares.

COMMERCIAL AUDITIONS

Earlier in this book, in Chapter 2 specifically, I discussed how actors get commercial representation—mailings, interviews, follow-up, that sort of thing. In this section, I'd like to focus on how an agent typically prepares her client for a commercial audition and what the actor can expect to happen there. Commercial auditions are usually called out the day before, and the information given to the agent is scanty at best. Time, place, product name, dress, and role type are the details given to agents to pass on to their clients. "Upscale casual," "jeans," "straight hair," "ethnic [meaning big] hair," "doctor," "lawyer," "mom," "John Goodman type," are examples of the incoming clues with which an actor can fashion his role for tomorrow's audition for the Wendy's spot. When the actor arrives at the audition, he will most likely be handed a page of sides that he usually has about ten minutes to work on before he's called into the studio. Then it's through the door, find your "spot" to stand on in front of the camera, slate your name, read the copy or do the improv, say "thank you" and "goodbye." (In commercials, an actor "slates" his name by looking directly into the camera and saying his name out loud. This enables the casting director, advertising company, and clients to identify each performer—to essentially put a name to each face—when they review the audition tapes.) Commercial auditions don't require a great deal of preparation; in fact, they are over before you know it.

THEATER AUDITIONS

What information does an agent give a client to help her prepare for a theater audition? It usually consists of the character description, and of how to access the audition sides and read the entire script. Even for a classic like *A Doll's House*, I read to my client the character description as it appears on the breakdown, so she knows what direction this particular production plans to take. This is essential for the "high concept" productions that often are given to classical material. For instance, any type of gender bending can certainly affect an actor's audition preparations as he interprets the sides material and anticipates the audition experience itself. If the play is published, actors can read it at the library, or at Barnes & Noble, or can buy their own copies. If it is new and not yet published, they may read or obtain a copy at the casting director's office. Companies like New York's Lincoln Center Theater often make one copy of the script available to an agency for their clients. The agency either sends a messenger or one of the auditioning actors to pick it up and bring it to the agency's office. The incentive of borrowing the script overnight before bringing it to the office usually sets an actor off and running. During the next few days the agency becomes a reading room, with clients sharing the script among themselves, or taking it to the nearest copy shop to make their personal copies. The greater the number of clients needing to read the script, the more time an agent spends scheduling its availability. More and more frequently, casting directors are choosing to email full scripts to agents that we can, in turn, forward directly to our clients. This is another time-saving advance, courtesy of the Internet, that agents appreciate greatly. It cuts down on office traffic and the time-consuming task of scheduling reading time for clients, and it offers actors greater flexibility in receiving and reading entire scripts—many times in the comfort of their homes.

MUSICAL AUDITIONS

An audition for a musical project usually calls for an up-tempo song and a ballad, both in the style of the show. Sometimes actors are asked to prepare selections from the show itself. If the material is complex, preparation might require the services of a coach, and an agent can only hope that the client gets the material in time to prepare it thoroughly. Unfortunately, this is not always the case. One of my clients was called in to audition for a lead in a new musical at a very prestigious Off-Broadway theater. I was thrilled. However, with the casting director's apologies, the audition came in with only one day to prepare. This was not enough time for my client to learn the complex material well enough to perform it with confidence—however intensely he prepared. The audition was very important for him; it would have been his first time in front of a Tony Award-winning director. No amount of pleading on my part could persuade the casting director to postpone, and I'm sure she didn't call the audition out so late on purpose. Probably an actor had dropped out of the project, or perhaps negotiations for the actor who had been offered the role fell through at the last minute, forcing the casting directors into an emergency casting session. Ultimately, the circumstances behind the late call made little difference: at my client's request, I had to cancel the audition, and watch another actor in the role when the production went up. Looking back one always wonders whether correct decisions were made. An agent knows she can't *force* a client to audition if he feels uncomfortable about issues like the lack of time to prepare or even the material itself. At times, when we feel it is appropriate, we can reason with the client to "give it your best shot," but ultimately it is the client's decision. I've also found through experience that these late calls of auditions, even though they come with the casting director's apologies, don't usually favor the actor auditioning. He is rarely applauded for his courage in trying. He is expected to jump through hoops and give a great audition—the "emergency" of the situation is conveniently forgotten when the casting directors are looking for a quick fix to their problems.

TELEVISION AND FILM AUDITIONS

Audition material for daytime dramas, films, and television shows is usually sides from the script that are posted online or are sometimes faxed to the agent on the same day the audition is called in (not enough time to post them online). Material posted for a contract role on a soap includes a detailed biography of the character. Character descriptions for roles on primetime TV dramas are cryptic, to say the least. Many times when I'm giving a client an audition for one of these shows, I re-read the character description as it appears on the breakdown and struggle to make sense of the storyline so that I can give my client a sense of context for his role. Too often when my client reports back to me about his very quick two-minute audition, we agree that *context* had very little to do with the audition.

For episodic television show auditions, an actor usually reads first for the casting director. This "pre-screen"—a live audition that is sometimes videotaped—offers casting directors the chance to meet actors whom they do not know. If the person has been taped, the casting director shows the tape to the director and producer, who decide whom to call back. If it has not been not taped, the casting director decides whom to bring back to the director and producer, either later that day or on the following day. If called back, the actor reads "live" for the director and producer. Sometimes the auditions occur in one building. Other times the pre-screen takes place in the casting director's office and the callback occurs at the production studio. Pre-screens are given to actors who are not known by the casting directors. Actors whom the casting director knows go directly to the director and producer for their first auditions.

For film auditions, casting directors usually videotape actors reading sides from the script, which have been made available to them online beforehand. The casting directors show the tapes to the director, who chooses which actors he wants to meet. In these cases it is up to the individual actor to decide how much time he needs with the sides and whether he requires a coaching session. Unlike in theater auditions where actors can carry and refer to the material in their hands, on tape it is wise to nearly have the sides memorized, so you can look into the camera or interact directly with the reader, who is usually standing beside the camera lens. The people watching the tape want to see your eyes, not your forehead. Sometimes complete memorization is called for. A client who had a general audition for one of the networks was instructed beforehand to be completely off book. Complete memorization is always required for the screen test, which is usually the final callback. Since this is the last audition before the actor either gets the offer or doesn't, it is a replica of life on the set. In a screen test he'll be directed by the director, and in some situations—for instance, when vying for a contract role on a soap—will screen test with a cast member of the show.

Sometimes a casting director calls an agent, requesting an actor's demo reel or DVD. If the director responds positively to this sample of work, the actor will be called in for an audition and/or meeting. This casting procedure is used more often in Los Angeles, where most activity is film based. However, I seem to be getting more calls from independent films casting here in New York City, in which the first step of casting involves sending a demo reel or DVD of the client. Even Breakdown Services now offers options for actors and agents to include video slates (demos) on, respectively, Actors Access and Breakdown Express. The slates can then be electronically submitted to casting directors all over the world.

Some movie directors and even some theater directors—especially the Brits—like to meet and interview actors before "reading" them. It's a very civil way to approach the inhumane process of auditioning, and actors seem to appreciate it greatly. Actors who have reached a certain level of success and notoriety in their careers rarely "read" at auditions; they "take meetings" instead. However, a "meeting" can lead to an informal reading of the material if the director works his charms on the noteworthy player.

GOING FROM ON STAGE TO ON CAMERA

It is highly advisable for actors not to go to their first audition for projects in unfamiliar mediums. Many of my clients who are known primarily as musical theater performers go regularly from musicals to straight plays. They are gifted singers (and sometimes excellent dancers) who happen to be fine actors as well—they are well trained and have lots of experience in both kinds of stage performance. They also want to work in the mediums of television and film. They would be the first to say that on-camera acting is very different from stage acting, and takes some getting used to. Auditioning for a role on a primetime crime drama isn't like singing for Stephen Sondheim. Spending a day on the set of a soap opera is very different from performing at night on Broadway. No actor likes to feel at a technical disadvantage when auditioning; the experience is nerve-wracking enough when you're on top of it. Before auditioning for projects in a new medium, help yourself out: build some self-confidence by booking a coaching session, taking some classes, and getting some experience. I urge those actors who are given the opportunity to audition for their favorite television shows or film directors to take the time to *thoroughly* prepare their auditions, so they can show themselves at their best. Get into the best performance shape you can, because the possibility of future auditions could depend on this first impression. Many stage actors have done commercials. To build up their confidence when auditioning for television and film projects, they draw on the audition and work experiences they have had in the commercial realm. If applicable, make this your approach, too.

What does an agent expect from these first-time, breakthrough auditions? Agents don't necessarily expect the client to book the job first time out. They are happy for an actor to make an impression, and perhaps get a callback that can lead to more auditions in the future. The first time one of our clients auditioned for a role on *Law & Order: Criminal Intent*, the casting director refused to cast her in so small a role. The CD told us that she would keep our client in mind for a larger one.

What should an actor expect at these breakthrough occasions? Sometimes a casting director will spend some time "getting to know you." She is looking for you to be "natural" in order to evaluate whether you can play the level of everyday reality in a crime or medical drama; and she is trying to get a hook as to your personality, so she can figure out what future roles to call you in for. If you are meeting the head of casting at Warner Brothers, where looks and personality (and youth) play a big part in casting, don't play a game of twenty-one questions waiting for her to do the asking. Come ready to reveal your full personality. You can be sure she's taking notes. If you're a musical performer whom your agent has convinced the casting director of *The Sopranos* to meet, make sure to come up with the goods— you'll need to dispel the prejudice against musical comedy performers' working in nighttime television dramas.

PROBLEMATICAL AUDITION CIRCUMSTANCES

Should actors fly in for auditions? Should they take an audition if they're not feeling well? These are tough questions that really must be answered on a case-by-case basis. Many of our clients out on national tours don't fare well when they catch a red-eye for the last day of auditions for, say, the new Flaherty-Ahrens show coming to Broadway. One client working out of town had an audition for a good role in a new musical at New York's Lincoln Center. It was wintertime and his connecting flight was cancelled. Luckily he was able to book another flight and make the audition (after many phone calls between his agent and the casting director, arranging to hold the auditioners in the studio past the session time). But the stress of travel affected his performance and he didn't get a call back. Another client spent a small fortune flying from San Diego, where she was performing, to Los Angeles for an important one-time-only audition. The casting needs of the producers shifted at the last minute and she was never even seen. The trip was a complete waste of time and money. As for auditioning when you don't feel well: Singing through a cold for an important casting director or well-known composer doesn't earn brownie points. It just leaves a bad impression. In those cases, heartbreaking though it is, it's best to cancel (with as much advance notice as possible). At least you'll have kept open your options for another chance.

I've just cited two horror stories. Here's one with a happy ending: A client flew into New York City from Ohio, where she was performing in a Molière play, to audition for the replacement of a contract role on a soap opera. She was called back to audition for the executive director the next morning, before returning to theater for her Tuesday-evening performance. The day after the play closed and she returned home to New York, she screen tested for the role and booked it. She had never done daytime before. Her look, talent, and professionalism—and the fact that employment is always a confidence builder—all converged to yield this happy result. Auditioning when you're working usually brings good results, because your self-esteem is high and you're in the "acting" groove.

Sometimes a client working out of town can save money by putting himself on tape for the first audition for projects, and then flying in for the callback. This is true mostly for non-musical theater auditions, contract roles on soaps, and first auditions for film roles when the casting director is compiling a tape of actor auditions for the director to view. Admittedly, this option of putting yourself on tape has a moderate success rate, since tapes are very often poor substitutes for live auditions and actors don't always know technically how to make the best tapes. Also, there's no substitute for physically being there, meeting the casting director face to face, and participating in the mix of the actual audition rather than appearing as a virtual reality who's out of town. Certainly, for our client who got the soap, flying in for the live audition was an investment that paid off. One wonders whether sending in an audition tape would have lead to the same result.

Clearly, many factors influence the process of audition preparation. Agents want to do their utmost to help their clients prepare the best auditions possible. Sometimes, however, the situation is out of our control: we are at the mercy of the casting directors who are at the mercy of writers, directors, and producers. We can't get the material to actors if it is not yet written. We can't prevent the director of a show from being called for jury duty and moving up his casting session by a week. For these reasons and many more, actors would do well to develop auditioning skills that enable them to prepare their auditions thoroughly and economically, regardless of the situation. Face it: the requirements and goals of any audition are unrealistic. How can anyone expect an actor to produce a fully realized performance without the benefit of rehearsal? When the audition comes in at the last minute, the demands are even more unrealistic. It's important to remember during the stressful times of auditioning that agents are on your side, and that casting directors expect and hope that the actors they bring in will do well—because that makes the casting directors look very good to the people paying their salaries. Also, the enlightened directors, producers, and writers—should you be so lucky as to meet them—will evaluate an actor's skill level and professionalism in these auditions and see the possibilities that his creativity and rehearsal will bring to the role in performance. They will test their hypotheses at the callback, and getting that callback should be the actor's aim in the first audition.

It's the responsibility of casting directors and agents to provide an actor with the most helpful information possible, on a timely basis, so he can audition with confidence. It's the responsibility of the actor to use this information to prepare the best audition he possibly can. I advise actors to listen carefully to the instructions provided by their agents, and to prepare their auditions accordingly. A young actor once assumed that being given two specific pieces to prepare for an audition meant he had a choice. He prepared only one, and realized his mistake when the casting director asked to see both. This mistake cost him the opportunity to play a lead. He was cast in small roles in the production and asked to understudy the part that could have been his had he prepared his audition thoroughly.

Regardless of circumstances, it is the actor's challenge to come up with the goods. Be prepared, be professional, and don't apologize. Excuses are time wasters and can throw an unwarranted negative light on an audition. If agents, casting directors, and actors all do their parts diligently and thoroughly with an understanding and respect for each other's place in the process, we can all look forward to more casting sessions, with more callbacks, and more job offers!

★

Weeks after your audition, the happy call comes in. They want you for an immediate replacement on the national tour of *The Producers*. What the producers don't know is that you travel with your pet parakeet and plan to get married in three months. They'll find out soon enough when they speak with your agent, who's also going to do her best not to settle for minimum!

Chapter 8

HOW DO AGENTS TAKE OFFERS
AND NEGOTIATE CONTRACTS?

I t's a happy day when an agent receives a job offer for a client. Casting directors usually deliver these glad tidings, and depending on the type of project—theater, TV, or film—an agent will negotiate the deal either with the casting director, the theater's general manager, the film's producer, or the network's business affairs lawyer.

Let's look in greater detail at the process of getting an offer and negotiating a deal. Generally, first a casting director calls an agent to tell him that an offer is coming in. The casting director may, at this time, give the agent a few specifics about the potential offer, such as the name of the role the client is to play and the dates of the project. Next the casting director calls with the actual offer. Many actors don't know that frequently at this point the casting director has been authorized to negotiate the terms of the offer with the agent; the producers have entrusted him to deal with the agent on their behalf. This is true especially for jobs on episodic television shows and daytime dramas. For example, let's say a client books two days on an episode of *Law & Order: SVU*. This is usually the culmination of a process that began with the client's auditioning first for the casting director and then for the producer and director. When the director and producer got closer to choosing that particular actor for the role, the casting director called the agent to tell him of their interest. At that time, the casting director asked the agent to verify whether the client was available for work during the dates of the shoot. The agent then called his client with the news, checked out any potential conflicts, and got back to the casting director to confirm that his client was available and willing to do the job. Then the agent and client waited.

When he calls the agent with the actual offer, the casting director names the role and *approximate* dates of work because he usually doesn't have the "board" (shooting schedule) and can't be more specific. For roles on daytime dramas, business is done somewhat differently, because shooting schedules are put in place a week or two in advance. When a CD sets up an actress for an audition for an under-five or day-player part on a soap opera (read on for definitions), the casting director will give the agent the specific work date. When the agent calls his client with the audition, he makes sure that the actress is available to do the job if cast. A casting director would be very upset if he found out that an actress had auditioned for a job that she knew beforehand she could not do. Casting directors consider this a major time-waster, and they don't take kindly to it.

If an offer comes in as a scale job—scale being a minimum salary regulated by the relevant actors' union—the casting director generally offers to pay the commission over and above (on top of) that salary. That is called a "plus ten," as in plus ten percent. Sometimes, when the casting director doesn't offer the "plus ten," or an agent finds he cannot better a scale salary through negotiation, he will ask the casting director for it. This enables the agent to collect a commission, i.e., money for the use of his client's services, without sacrificing his client's salary—because the payment does not come directly out of his client's wages. "Plus tens" can be negotiated in SAG, AFTRA, and even Equity contracts.

Salaries for extra, under-five, and day-player work on daytime dramas are union regulated, according to the number of words spoken by the character. Extras have no words; under-five players have five lines or fewer; day players have more than five lines. The actor is paid according to the union minimum allotted to each category. Agents are usually guaranteed a plus ten percent on the minimum scale payment for under-five bookings, and negotiate over-scale payments for day-player roles. Salaries for series regulars on television shows and for contract roles on daytime dramas are usually negotiated by the network business affairs lawyers and agents before talent is screen tested.

For an over-scale job, when the discussion turns to naming salary, the casting director will first ask the agent for the client's "quote." A quote generally refers to the salary that the client made the most recent time he worked on the show. The quote serves as a jumping-off place for negotiating salary. In their negotiations with casting directors, agents generally try to better the quote each time the client works. They always go for a raise in pay and would certainly never accept less— never, that is, without a very good reason for doing so. Alluring offers would include a project that gave the client the opportunity to work with a well-known director, or a workshop of a piece that was coming to Broadway. A low-budget independent film may often offer great artistic fulfillment at the expense of financial satisfaction.

When a television casting director requests a client's quote, and the client has never worked on the show in question, her agent then looks through the booking records to find what the client earned most recently for a comparable job. For example, if Susie has never worked on *Law and Order: Criminal Intent*, but worked a day on *Third Watch* the previous year, the agent would refer to that salary as the established quote. When there is no evidence of a previous comparable booking, we refer to salaries from other types of jobs that could be relevant. For instance, say a client has never worked in episodic television, but has done a few different day-player roles in daytime drama. The agent might refer to what the actor made there when giving the casting director the quote. Or we may suggest a number based on the client's other credits and overall standing in the business. What an agent *can't* do is lie about the quote. Money amounts are traceable, especially with respect to shows on the same network, most especially when they're running under the same banner (e.g., the *Law & Order* franchise). It does no good to be caught in a lie. Even exaggerations are to be avoided.

I know an agent who held out once for a very large salary without having any evidence of a current quote. She made her stand based on her client's past credentials, which were significant, and refused to back down. (Typically, a negotiating agent asks for a significantly higher amount of money than she really wants. She does this expecting the casting director to counter with a modest improvement in the amount of money he originally offered. The CD's second figure generally will be close to what the agent really is after.) This agent was delighted when the casting director agreed to pay her client the full sum she had proposed. That win resulted from big thinking on the agent's part, solid persuasion, and definite moxie. Clearly, agents do have their purpose!

TROUBLESOME NEGOTIATIONS WITH CDs

Doing business with casting directors doesn't always run so smoothly. An agent can sometimes find herself in the awkward position of having to do battle with her friend and ally—her clients' champion— whom she relies on daily for those crucial audition appointments. When an agent heads into a complex negotiation with a casting director, she may wonder if this will in any way jeopardize their ongoing relationship. Whether asking for more money, better billing, or a special perk for her client, there's always a moment of fear: the agent worries that the casting director may punish her for all the "trouble" she's caused, by denying auditions to her clients in the future. An agent who did very well in negotiating a better salary for one of her clients tried to do the same for another with the same casting director on the same television show. Despite many phone calls back and forth in which the agent tried to justify her position, the casting director refused to budge, declaring, "Take it or leave it." At her client's request, the agent accepted the offer. When she didn't get any auditions for the following two episodes of the show, however, she couldn't help but wonder whether that had anything to do with the troublesome negotiation.

Agents also wonder what will happen to their relationship with a casting director if they pull their client from a job because the client received another better offer. Casting directors tend to be very territorial and to have tunnel vision about their projects. They tend to see theirs as the only projects of value. Agents submit their clients for many projects simultaneously, hoping that one of these submissions will turn into a job. Agents have no control, however, over *when* offers come in from the various casting directors. Certainly, before accepting an offer, agents research the status of other possible jobs, and most of the time we accept an offer for a client fully intending that he will do the job. However, if a Broadway offer comes in before our client signs the contract for a regional theater job that has been accepted, there is little doubt that the client must choose the Broadway show. Similarly, television and film opportunities trump theater. Decisions are usually based on money, although the length of a job can sometimes be important. An agent will advise an actor not to sacrifice a year's work in a national tour, for example, for the opportunity to work for a week on a film at scale. The agent will probably try to negotiate for the possibility of the actor's doing both jobs.

Here's an interesting situation: I have a client who has been offered a role in a play at one of those high-prestige, low-paying theaters in New York. The same casting director who booked him in this is also casting a major Broadway revival. I wonder how the casting director will react when he sees my client's name on our submission list for the revival. What seems obvious to me—that my client should do Broadway over the other job—probably isn't so obvious to the casting director. After all, he doesn't have to pay his rent on my client's salary and he also probably doesn't want to take time to re-cast the role he locked my client into originally. Casting directors can afford to do what's best for themselves. Actors want to do what's best for *themselves*, but not at the expense of their relationships with casting directors. Agents are caught in the middle, trying to appease both sides. Sometimes conflicts are unavoidable and there's nothing to do but get past the fallout from an angered casting director. Eventually he will call again to request a client represented by the agency. Then an agent knows the relationship is back on track.

Before each confrontation with a casting director, an agent wonders what's more important: this client's particular deal or the agent's ongoing relationship with the CD who so strongly influences the lives of *many* actors. We ask whether the two must be mutually exclusive. The answer can only be reached on a case-by-case basis, according to the particular deal and the available options.

NEGOTIATIONS

Let's go further into the area of negotiation in our industry. Negotiations occur primarily between two people who represent the interests of two parties. An agent speaks for the actor, his client; and the casting director, general manager, or other representative speaks for the producer of a project. During the course of a negotiation, agents may wear many hats, functioning as diplomat, protector, and advocate. When negotiating, agents use many different approaches to establish their positions and to make requests (sometimes even argue for demands) that are based on those positions. At one moment in the conversation, an apologetically coercive tack may be more productive than a smoothly seductive one; at the next, a stridently defensive response may prove effective.

I have a client of some prestige who commands top dollar when she works. Her value is based on a career that she has built over many years, consisting of impressive work in important projects with people of note, in all media. She is well respected by her peers, and her association with projects lends them value and weight. Recently she was asked to play a role in an independent film that interested her very much. The writer-director had corresponded with my client and me over the course of several years while developing the project and seeking financing. When she (the writer-director) had finally secured the money and was ready to start shooting, she called to tell me her good news and pleaded with me to secure my client's services for the film. Noting that my client was the only actress she had ever "seen" in the role, she said she would be greatly honored if my client agreed to play it. Tucked away in all of this "salesmanship" was the phrase, "Of course, you realize that we don't have a lot of money to offer... " The moment I heard it, I knew our love fest was heading into bumpy territory. The director's good words were very flattering and nice to hear, but in a business sense did not make up for the fact that this film was shooting under a SAG Limited Exhibition Agreement. This contract, similar to the Equity Showcase Code agreement in theater, enables filmmakers to employ union actors at a rate far below minimum. I knew from experience that my client had established a policy whereby she never worked for scale. She would never even entertain the idea of working for scale unless it were for one of her friends like John Sayles. I had to figure out how to bridge the gap between what the film director was offering and what my client was accustomed to being paid. First off, I agreed with the director about my client's value — not only artistically, but in terms of the benefits that the recognition of her name could bring to the project. I did this to reiterate my client's position as one of the top actresses in her category in the industry. From this position of power, I segued into asking how much money the production company had to offer my client. The director cited a pitifully low number: the mere minimum under the Limited Exhibition Agreement — not even one cent above minimum to at least show appreciation, preference, and respect for my client's reputation. My counter proposal gave a number that was closer to my client's quote. The director gulped and said she didn't know if she could match this request, but that she would talk to her producers to "see what they could do." Agents frequently hear that phrase in response to their demands, and sometimes even use it to initiate action.

For example, if a casting director or general manager refuses to budge on the money terms of a deal, an agent might say, "Well, Bob, see what you can do." Many times our negotiations will hang on a, "Look around and see where you might be able to find some more money." We usually do this knowing that the members of the creative team really want the client in the project, and presuming that they will urge the producers to come through with some concessions. How hard and fast an agent holds to a number during negotiations is the client's call. If the client says, "Get the best deal you can... but don't lose the job," an agent knows to drive forward with caution. Specific salary amounts are very clear instructions for an agent. Deal-breakers — requests that actors make which, if not met, keep them from accepting the offer — range from days off for important events like weddings, to housing that accommodates pets. These deal-breakers are always the actor's call; agents are merely the mouthpieces for their expression. In the case of my client and the independent film, the director went to her producers and came back with a plan to offer a deferred payment as part of a "back-end deal" that matched the sum I had mentioned in my counter-proposal. Back-end deals signify monies that come to actors after the film is sold to a distributor and the expenses and investors are paid off. Agents negotiate back-end deals with "points" — percentages of the profits of a film — and deferred salary payments, as a way to better the terms originally offered in these low-budget film deals.

A negotiation is essentially a coming to terms with terms. The person making the offer brings to the table a set of terms. For theater projects these generally include the role or roles offered to the actor, dates of the production — more specifically the date of the first rehearsal, first preview, and when the show opens and closes, including any potential extension. Also included at this time may be the type of housing offered, salary terms, and billing. If the offer is for an episode of a television show or film, shoot dates are given with an on-or-around start date and end date. Salaries, billing, and travel arrangements are also discussed now. These issues, and others, are like pieces of a puzzle that are shifted and adjusted during a negotiation, to create a design that satisfies both parties. The agent receiving the offer discusses its terms with his client, then responds back to the producer's representative in agreement or disagreement, and with suggested revisions. This back-and-forth movement of suggestion and response makes up a negotiation. How willingly the two parties work together to fashion a mutually satisfactory deal is key. Each stands to gain from working out the deal. A lot, of course, depends on the actor's position in the industry and his importance to the project.

One of the values of having an agent negotiate your deal is that he brings an objective overview of the terms being offered. He interprets these terms simultaneously, from a dual perspective: (1) he determines whether they are fair according to the actor's place within the industry —

years of experience, track record, and most recent credits; and (2) he reviews the terms in comparison with what is being offered to the other actors in the company, film, or television show. This goes for all terms and conditions. The agent's function is to investigate and protect. It's all very well to evaluate a salary, for example, out of context, but it's equally important to examine it in relation to the total picture, which includes the other players. Evaluating the correctness of a salary out of context is easy, because an agent is always well informed about his client's worth and standing in the industry. The second perspective, however, requires research and investigation in order to ascertain how the client's terms compare to those offered to others in the company.

Agents are investigators. They are fact finders. Where an actor might fear asking too many questions, lest he become a nuisance and perhaps lose the offer, the agent forges ahead with total confidence to perform this relatively routine part of his job. In order to position his client correctly in terms of salary and other conditions, the agent must first explore the playing field. We do this in a non-confrontational manner, for the most part trying to discover how much money is available, what the client is making in comparison with other actors, and what, if any, plan exists for a future life for the project. All of these factors influence the strategy and nuances of a negotiation.

Sometimes, an agent will ask the general manager point-blank where his client's salary comes in, in regard to the other actors'. In big musicals, for instance, or in other large-cast shows, union contracts establish tiers that denote salary range for the stars, leads, supporting leads, and chorus/ensemble members. An agent must determine whether his client is placed in the appropriate tier according to the size and importance of his role, and whether his salary is commensurate with that placement. Having this information is the agent's key to successfully explaining the deal to his client: it frames the picture clearly and correctly.

Agents generally negotiate for parity within a tier. This is especially important with certain musicals, when the policy of theater management refuses to allow agents to negotiate salaries above scale. In those instances, the best an agent can do is to make sure that no actor within the tier is getting a higher salary, although that won't stop him from trying to negotiate a perk for his client. If an agent doesn't do as well, if not better, than the other actors' agents in negotiating for his client, he might be out of a job. I remember a time when I almost accepted a deal prematurely. Having fashioned the deal to my client's liking, I was ready to accept it, when I was warned to make sure that the money offered was comparable to that offered the other actors in his tier. Though hesitant to re-open negotiations, I knew that this was the right thing to do for my client (and would protect me from the possibility of losing him). It's important to nail down the details of a deal very specifically and clearly *before* the contract is signed; an agent can't be too thorough. Otherwise, he might find himself the victim of dressing-room chatter and come face-to-face with a very unhappy client who could use any mistake or oversight on the agent's part as reason to seek other representation. In this instance, because I asked my questions tactfully, I was able to pull the necessary information regarding money from the general manager. This information led to making a few crucial clarifications and adjustments having to do with salary bumps and out clauses (permission to leave the contract for other work) in the final deal, which my client signed soon after and never had cause to dispute.

How much movement an agent can make within a negotiation is a clue to her client's importance and value to the project. When an agent discovers that her requests are being considered seriously, she can take this as a good sign. It either means the offer came in low and there is definitely room for improvement, or the producer strongly desires to have the actor on board and is willing to make concessions. Sometimes the actor is indispensable, sometimes not. When he is, the negotiation is enjoyable; when he is not, it is frustrating toil. Whichever the case may be, it always stands to reason that the actor benefits from having a neutral party speak for him — either venturing forth boldly after higher money and better terms, or casting a cautious glance over all terms, in search of absolute parity. The objective person — the agent — can explain the reality of the situation to the emotional person — the actor. In the end, it's always the actor's choice to say "yes" or "no" — i.e., to accept the job or turn it down. How an agent advises the client in making this decision is another story: the subject of Chapter 6.

TIMING AND THE FAVORED NATIONS CLAUSE

Timing is an important element of negotiating. This is true especially in deals offering terms that come in on a Favored Nations basis. "Favored Nations" simply refers to a leveling, or equalizing, of terms. It was originally created as a tool that an actor could use to ensure that no one of similar stature or playing an equally large role in a production was getting a better deal. It also became a way for actors who commanded large salaries to work at not-for-profit theaters for minimum without affecting their "quote." They could attribute the discrepant salary to the Favored Nations clause included in their contract. Unfortunately, while this might have done much to preserve the integrity of an established actor's quote, it did little for his self-esteem when he found himself being paid the same amount as newbies in the business.

Generally speaking, a Favored Nations clause stands for a negotiated agreement between a producer and an actor ("Actor A"), which specifies that if other actors in the production receive better terms than Actor A, Actor A will be entitled to those same terms. Terms covered in a Favored Nations rider include such items as salary, expense money, transportation, housing, dressing-room space, or even the care of one's pet. Sometimes the clause covers all terms and conditions; sometimes a single term, like salary. When negotiating a deal that comes with a

Favored Nations clause, an agent may benefit from the work of other agents, as each tries to raise the stakes and benefit from the successes of his predecessor. I know some agents who, when negotiating a contract that has a Favored Nations rider, specifically choose not to take the lead in asking for better terms, allowing the other agents to initiate the fight, and thereby piggybacking on their efforts. Here's how it works: I once received an offer for a client which, according to my evaluation, came in low on every term. The salary was low, the housing the bare minimum required by the union, to name just two items. The saving graces were the actual material — a Pulitzer Prize-winning play — and the production venues, which were good theaters in major cities. After asking for improvements on several terms and being rebuffed by the general manager at every request, I decided to let things be for a few days. When I returned to the negotiating table, the view had magically brightened. Apparently some of the other agents had responded to the offer with similar reservations and had pressured management for concessions. Thanks to the Favored Nations clause, these concessions applied to everyone: my client, along with the other actors in the company, benefited from the work of all these agents.

TIMING AND DAYTIME DRAMA

Did you know that the contracts for contract roles in daytime drama are negotiated before a client actually screen tests for the role? The deal is negotiated and put in place on the possibility, not the actuality, of a client booking a job. This is done so that an actor can start work immediately if chosen from the screen test. Salaries, guarantees, terms, any types of outs (leaves to do theater, film, or other television projects while under contract to the soap) — all of these are agreed upon in writing before the client actually performs the screen test. It seems like a lot of work for a far-from-definite outcome. These deals are tricky to negotiate because the agent doesn't have the benefit of knowing that his client is crucial to the project. He doesn't even know if his client will be offered the job. All he knows is that his client is one of a few actors who are screen testing for the same assignment — so he must base his negotiation totally on his client's current standing in the business. Experience, past credits, awards, or noteworthy recognition — Miss America title, Olympic athlete, for example—are just a few of the bargaining chips available to an agent in this case.

THE RULES OF THE GAME

Here are a few general assumptions and rules that an agent has to work with when negotiating a deal:

> Offers generally come in low, and if an agent doesn't ask for more money, she'll never know whether she can get it. Conversely, the person making the offer, whether he be a casting

director, a general manager, or a producer, expects an agent to ask for more money. He knows that she wouldn't be an agent if she didn't. It's all part of the buying-selling game.

No actor is indispensable. There's always a second choice. If you've ever produced a show or worked as a casting director, you know how important it is to get a backup choice for every role. Of course, there's always a *first* choice, too—but having a backup is crucial to protect the integrity of the project in case first-choice actors are not available, leave, are fired, or are let go. Sometimes casting directors select two backups, but when there's only one, and he seems about to be lost, many CDs will pressure the agent representing the first choice to accept the deal, to avoid having to go back to the drawing board. Casting directors work very hard to fulfill the demands of the producer, assembling the desired cast of characters while at the same time protecting the product by shoring up alternatives.

Deals shift and change. Before accepting an offer, agents confer with their clients to make sure that no outstanding issues need to be resolved, such as getting excused to attend the nephew's bar mitzvah in June, or finding housing that accepts a pair of pet canaries. Agents make sure to get everything agreed upon *in writing*. Even in a letter of intent, the terms must be in writing in case any wrongdoing calls for future redress or recourse.

It's important for agents to take very good notes during negotiations, to avoid costly oversights and misunderstandings. Once I received a draft of a contract and while looking it over discovered that the roles listed were incorrect; they weren't what we had agreed upon at all. Luckily, I had carefully itemized the various steps of the negotiation on the booking slip (the form on which we record the details of a deal), so a quick check confirmed my suspicions. When I pointed this out to the general manager, he was extremely chagrinned, apologized, and adjusted the contract accordingly. Mistakes *do* happen, as in this case. One can't be too careful when it comes to protecting a client; otherwise, there's always the possibility of losing him. An agent earns her ten percent by being careful and thorough in all aspects of negotiating.

My most favorite negotiations occur when I work very closely with the client to construct the deal. I've had clients who, having worked in the business a long time, are extremely knowledgeable about how it works and about what will personally satisfy them in a deal. They usually have a clear and accurate sense of the big picture, which enables them to make realistic demands. For instance, a client was offered a small but important supporting role in a new Broadway musical. This was a fellow who had worked for thirty years as an actor. He usually played leads in national tours and regional theater, and stood by for celebrities on Broadway. A character actor with singing ability, this client was excited to finally have the opportunity to be an original cast member of a new Broadway musical. The offer included a substantial amount of "covering," which means understudying. If memory serves, there were two understudy assignments along with his primary role. When giving me the terms of the deal, the general manager also mentioned the phrase "as cast." This gives management the option of expanding the number of assignments for a particular actor as the piece develops throughout the rehearsal process. It's up to the agent to put a cap on just how many roles this can include; management sometimes loses track. In this particular case, my client wanted very much to concentrate his energies on his primary role. No stranger to the stress and strain of understudying, he felt he could really only prepare and have ready at a given moment one additional understudy assignment. He wanted also to be listed as the first cover for that role. He decided this after I obtained a copy of the full script, at his shrewd request, which he needed to read in order to determine the different roles in relationship to each other according to size, challenge, and importance. I remember that in the course of my conversations with the general manager (which were not unpleasant), the GM defended the use of non-enumerated covers. "Non-enumeration" simply enables management to assign more than one actor to cover a role without specifying which actor is the preferred choice (i.e., which actor would be the first to go on). This is very troubling to actors. Understudying is difficult enough with its built-in anxiety; sharing an assignment with one, maybe two, other actors adds to the fear factor. It's a little like Russian roulette. No actor wants to deal with the additional stress of never knowing which cover will go on at any given moment. Non-enumeration also undermines performers' self-esteem: when preferences are not clearly indicated, it's hard to know where one stands in the estimation of management. Actors very much like enumeration. Management very much does not. It wants the freedom to make decisions spontaneously and would rather not lock an actor into a specific assignment if that's unnecessary. Management wants to be able to keep its options open until the final moment when it *has* to make a choice. In these instances, an actor struggles not to get paranoid.

Let's return to my client with understudy assignment woes: In our negotiations, the general manager tried to play down the likelihood of my client's being called upon to fulfill his understudy duties. Since my client was one of several actors covering each of the roles, said the general manager, the likelihood of his going on in either was slight. Because the other actors might be asked to go on in these assignments before him, my client needn't worry so much about preparing the roles. The general manager's laissez-faire attitude reflected a flippant, irresponsible, and illogical argument. It was as if he were saying, in so many words, "Okay, here's money to go on if there's an Act of God— but never mind about going on, because there won't be an Act of God." Of course, my client and I knew that an actor must always be ready to fulfill his contractual obligations; he should never give management grounds for letting him go. Being unable to perform an understudy assignment when called upon to do it would be grounds.

The general manager wanted us to "agree to agree" that the first role listed as an understudy assignment would be regarded as my client's primary understudy. I discussed this with my client—because that's what agents do: discuss with their clients feedback, clarifications, and alterations of a negotiation—and we decided to stand by our condition that he be assigned the first cover of one and only one role. Much to our surprise, we got our demand. Not only was that woeful "as cast" clause eliminated, but the other understudy assignments were struck. The icing on the cake was when management agreed to enumerate my client as the first cover for his one and only understudy assignment. Evidently, management had found ways to cover its bases by using other actors in the company.

Seeking to protect his clients, a good agent is always alert to a laissez-faire attitude's popping up in general managers and people in hiring positions. Sometimes an actor is hired to do a film or television show. Then before the contract is signed, he is asked to participate in an "informal" (i.e., volunteer, for no pay) read-through of the script. The producers, if unhappy with his performance, could recast his role, leaving this actor unemployed and uncompensated. Agents warn their clients against participating in these readings.

I once did a deal for a client that included a nudity clause in the rider. In extremely vague and general language, the paragraph gave the theater permission to take photos at any time. I was uncomfortable with the terms and asked that any photography or videotaping be used for archival purposes only. The general manager reacted as many do when faced with a watchdog agent making requests: he cited me as being the *only* agent who had found the language in the paragraph objectionable. This was supposed to shame me into backing down. I stuck to my guns and was very pleased when the contracts I received included amended language.

NEGOTIATING STYLES AND STRATEGIES
Because agents have different personalities, they have different styles of negotiating. I've known some agents who protect their clients' interests like lionesses protect their cubs. They suspect every detail of an offer and think their job is to smell a rat before they even see it. Other agents are gifted persuaders who find ways to lead a rigid producer to a sympathetic understanding of what must be changed. Still other agents

take a very straightforward path to justify requests logically, making negotiations look easy by doing them in a one-two-three manner.

Individual projects and clients also require different negotiating tactics and strategies. Doing a deal for a young actor's first Equity job in a regional theater is different from doing a TV deal for an actress who has been in the business for fifty years. These clients receive equal attention from the agent; they just get it in different ways. Many times an agent might cajole an offer from a casting director by promising a quick acceptance from a young client, knowing how important it is for this actor to get the experience of working. In this situation, the agent might devote his energies to shepherding his young client through the signing of the contract and running interference for any problems that might arise during the actual job. When negotiating a TV deal for an older client, however, an agent will devote most of her energy to fine-tuning the details of the contract, which could be complex and time-consuming.

Clearly, it is useful for actors to have offers of employment negotiated by agents. No matter how savvy an actor is about business, negotiating for himself can be problematic. Asking for more money, for an extra round-trip airplane ticket for your girlfriend, or for housing for your pet can be scary when each time you ask for something, you're afraid (either consciously or subconsciously) that the job offer will be pulled because you're being "difficult."

I know for a fact that no matter how much sleuthing an actor does to unearth details regarding his offer, the objectivity and experience of an agent can uncover more key points and provide more valuable ammunition at the negotiation table. Agents, because of their overall knowledge of and experience in the business, know what to look for and how to cover the territory thoroughly, whether negotiating for TV outs, special billing, or signing bonuses. Having a knowledgeable agent do business for you frees you up to be the creative artist you were meant to be. It's also good to have a person to whom you can report any negligence or wrongdoing during the term of employment—such as salary payment, honey wagon, or injury issues.

★

Well, now the offers are pouring in and your agent is negotiating three deals at the same time. You'll have to decide which one to take. Luckily, your agent is there to advise you.

Chapter 9

HOW DO AGENTS
ADVISE ACTORS?

There you are with three job offers on your plate: which do you choose and how do you make that decision? Two hundred different thumbnail-size photos of your face stare up at you from your desk: How do you decide which one to use as your headshot? That Off-Off-Broadway showcase you did in the fall is moving to Broadway: how do you know what to ask for when negotiating with the producers? Every actor, at various times in his career, needs advice from a professional. The student turning professional, the regional actor breaking into the New York scene, the New York actor taking a stab at pilot season in Los Angeles—these are but a few situations that call for the expertise and experience of an agent. This chapter explores several instances in which an agent plays a major role in advancing an actor's career.

When advising their clients on important career decisions, agents use their unique vantage point to objectively clarify and examine the variables of each choice. The purpose of all of this examination is to position the client appropriately according to his training and experience, and to determine whether the choice will move a career forward. Many different aspects factor into these decisions; good agents take seriously their responsibility for their clients' careers, studying each choice thoroughly. I think it would be helpful to see how agents evaluate the variables, working with their clients to choose the best line of action from the many factors at play.

Building careers is an agent's job, and positioning talent requires good judgment—judgment that comes from knowledge and experience. No matter how bright and energetic your agent may be, if he isn't knowledgeable about how this business works, his counsel and advice are of questionable value. Most agencies have several agents who represent the clients, each possessing special gifts. One agent may be an excellent negotiator, while another is a terrific seller. Each brings a singular perspective to the weekly staff meeting, or to the impromptu chat at the water cooler; this team know-how benefits the client who needs advice on an important career decision.

DECISIONS FOR YOUNG ACTORS

At the beginning of an actor's professional career, there are few job offers to be selective about. Actors starting out need to get experience and build their résumés, and agents work very hard to get auditions for their young clients so that they can get work. Young actors living in New York City, or in any other top industry center, struggle to beat out the tough competition to book jobs. Many young actors, having completed training at one of the acting conservatories, or in an undergraduate or graduate university theater program, rush to New York to perform in their industry showcase (a program of scenes, songs, and monologues performed for agents, managers, and casting directors), sign with an agent and slog through what turns out to be a desultory year of figuring out how to audition well enough to get callbacks—much less book a job—and how to survive in the Big Apple. When they first arrive, they enjoy a smattering of auditions that their agent has procured for them; and depending on their performance at these first calls, the auditions will either continue to come in or will dwindle to a few here and there. Of course, a lot also depends on the casting needs of the season. For example, the year after *Dancing at Lughnasa* played on Broadway, many regional theaters included this play in their seasons, offering an unusually large number of opportunities to young actresses. The same was true for young men when *Love! Valour! Compassion!* started popping up in regional theater seasons.

Some young actors have "model" looks that they are able to combine with the talent and skills needed to land a contract role on a soap opera. Others are able to sing and dance their way into the ensemble of a Broadway musical or a national tour. The vast majority of young actors, however, should be willing to audition for anything and take whatever job is offered, so long as it meets with the approval of their agents. Most of the jobs that young professionals tend to book are regional theater jobs or national and European tours of musicals. Summer stock, TheatreWorks/USA or other children's-theater tours, and cruise ships are also viable jumping-off points for the young actor just starting out.

Some actors take alternate routes in building their careers. We represent one such actress. After graduating from Boston University with a BA in theater arts, she came to New York, saw the competition she was up against for booking jobs, and quickly decided that she'd rather be working than waiting. She moved to Seattle and for the next ten years worked successively in theaters up and down the West Coast, where she played the great roles and developed into the leading lady she was destined to be. An agent from the office saw her work in one of these shows and urged her to come to New York. Interestingly enough, he had met with her after her college industry showcase ten years earlier, hoping to represent her then, and was pleased to see that his hunch at that time wasn't wrong. Her talent had blossomed because of all these work experiences, and her résumé, now with abundant and impressive theater credits, enhanced her saleability. He would have no trouble promoting his "discovery" because he had so many legitimate reasons to justify his pushes to casting directors. Only two weeks after she arrived in New York, she booked a job at one of the top Shakespearean theaters on the East Coast. This just reinforced what the agent had believed all along: "Talent is good, but experience makes an actor great." Clearly, for this actress, re-entering the New York market at this stage of her career proved to be an entirely different story than her first go-around ten years before.

Working is *so* crucial for a young actor—not only in terms of acquiring credits, but for making contacts towards future work, getting his sea legs, and keeping up his self-esteem. It's hard to call yourself an actor when you're not working. It's a vicious cycle: The longer an actor doesn't work, the less he feels like an actor. The less he feels like an actor, the harder it is for him to find the self-confidence to audition well. If he doesn't audition well…well. I met a young actor once whose New York agent had advised him two years earlier to leave his job playing a supporting role in a national tour, so that he could be in New York, where his agent could submit him for pilot season. When I met this actor, he was agentless and still trying to recover from the fact that he had left a good job, which he enjoyed doing, and hadn't worked since.

There is no doubt that acquiring credits on the résumé enhances an actor's value in the marketplace, both artistically and professionally. Agents like that. Many agents agree that an actor should go where the work is and make himself available for auditions when they come up. Remember the story in Chapter 7, about the actress who was performing in a Molière play in Ohio when she got an audition for a replacement of a contract role in a soap opera? She was willing to follow her agents' advice and fly to New York for the audition, which, happily, led to her booking the role.

As mentioned earlier, many times when an actor is working out of town and an audition comes through, his agent will ask the casting director if the actor may put himself on tape. It is presumed by all that the actor will make the trip in for a callback. Videotaping auditions out of town is not always easy. Locating a facility and a good videographer, and scheduling a session in order to get the tape to the casting director on time are some of the factors to contend with. However, when compared to making a plane trip that could cost a thousand dollars, handling the first audition in this way saves time and money.

Some people object to videotaped auditions, believing them to be no substitute for an actor's auditioning in the flesh. Others, however, think that an actor suffering from jet lag won't give a good audition anyway, so he might as well send in a videotaped audition that allows him the choice of a "best take." A client was working out of town on a three-month tour when an audition came through for the lead in a Shakespearean play that was to be produced at a 1,500-seat outdoor amphitheater. I knew it would be difficult for my client to fly in for the audition due to his time-consuming rehearsal schedule, so I asked the casting director if he would accept a taped audition. The casting director said yes, so my client videotaped his audition and sent him the tape. When I asked the casting director for feedback on this audition, he criticized elements such as vocal performance that I felt could not be assessed accurately from a taped performance. I have a feeling that my client chose to adjust his audition performance for the camera rather than provide a full-out theatrical display. What was lacking in vocal and language skills probably came through in emotional and internal dimensions that the camera picks up so easily. However, that's not what the casting director saw. In a case like this, if the CD had any influence over the director, there would most likely be no subsequent callback audition for my client.

Whatever you think about live versus taped auditions, it's important to note that some regional theaters actually build monies into the actors' salaries to pay for roundtrip transportation to and from New York or other home bases, during the run of the show (presumably on days off). Management expects actors and agents to schedule these auditions on the days off rather than disturb rehearsals or performances. Other theaters make available equipment to actors with which they can videotape their auditions. These theaters hope thereby to minimize disruptions caused by actors asking to be released to audition for their next jobs.

Many times the choices actors face have to do with working out of town as opposed to staying in New York City or L.A. Agents address this question according to an actor's training, experience, and life circumstances. As I mentioned earlier, when agents advise their clients, especially when choosing between multiple job offers, they must examine and interpret each case individually. A young actress just out of school, who recently had signed with our agency, received offers for two jobs at the same time. One was a paying engagement out of town and the other was a showcase of a new work in town. In discussing the choice with her, we first asked whether she had a preference. She said she didn't; both sounded great. We then examined more closely what exactly she would be doing in each job. The show out of town was a musical revue that was basically a string of songs from a particular time period, loosely woven together with a thin plotline. The new piece in town was a book musical with a story and specific characters. The production in New York seemed to offer more creative satisfaction, while the job out of town offered more money. We also took into account that this actress had recently participated in several workshops of new works in which she had performed in the ensemble. We determined that if she were to work for "free" again in New York, she would have to play a role. Positioning her in this way was necessary to move her career forward. Everyone concluded that this was just what the musical in town offered. The opportunity to create a role in a new piece that could possibly develop into an Off-Broadway show gave this actress a real chance for career advancement. We recommended that she take the non-paying job over the paying one, because we viewed the freebie as a career investment that could pay everyone big dividends in the future. Nor could we help but appreciate having a client with these happy choices of multiple job offers, because it meant that she was marketable and auditioned well.

CHOICES

As an actor's career progresses more choices come into play, and choosing correctly makes a bigger difference. Regarding the question of staying in New York City versus working out of town, for example, an agent may advise an actor to stay in the ensemble of a Broadway show because while in town he can access New York's opportunities for booking film and television work or for participating in workshops of new shows. All of these opportunities expand the horizons for work in other arenas, and that work can move an actor up the career ladder. Let's say a client is "hot" because of recent exposure from appearing in a theater piece in town. The agent will advise him to stay in New York to capitalize on any career activity that this exposure might stimulate.

It's ironic, however, that the very thing an actor aspires to—a great part in a great show in New York—is the very thing that can sometimes prevent him from capitalizing on all the exposure that comes from this job. For instance, many episodic television shows will not work around a performer's play schedule. Complex shows like *Law & Order*, which have many scenes, need to stick tightly to a schedule due to tech, location setup, etc. The producers are unable to adjust their shooting schedule to guarantee that an actor will make his half-hour call at the theater. Still, most actors on Broadway and in long-running Off-Broadway shows have understudies who are more than willing to fill in for a few performances.

Also, agents can address just this type of situation by negotiating with theater producers short-term outs for television and film work. Frustrating situations do occur, however. A client was performing in a show Off-Broadway that became the sleeper hit of the season. The production created an enormous sensation; its run was extended and the media blitz was on. Our client was getting a great deal of notice from the exposure. Unfortunately, we had to turn down an offer for a plum role on an episode of a television show because his understudy was not ready to go on. Being a team player and respecting the integrity of the production, our client refused to put the producers and cast in a precarious position: he declined the TV offer.

An actor runs into fewer problems with Equity staged readings or workshops of new theater pieces, where management generally makes best efforts to work around a performer's Broadway schedule. Being flexible enables management to use top talent to develop a piece in rehearsals and market it to possible producers in presentations. I have gone to scores of these workshops and have been constantly amazed at the level of talent assembled. An agent knows that these workshops are valuable in exposing actors to members of the industry and putting them in shows that might actually have commercial legs.

An agent will always try to keep every opportunity of work alive, sometimes brokering both theater and television jobs at the same time. For example: A client contracted a regional theater job, then during the few weeks before the first rehearsal went up for a featured role on a television show. She booked it but couldn't imagine doing it because she was supposed to be out of town, rehearsing at the theater. Wanting to make both possibilities happen, her agent called the theater to ask permission for the actress to arrive a day late for rehearsal.

Staying in New York is usually the right choice for actors whose careers have reached a certain level. They usually have résumés with extensive credits on national tours or in regional theaters, or have worked as company members at the country's top repertory theaters or Shakespearean festivals. To move their career upward to the next level, they will have to either move to New York or commit to staying there for some time in order to explore work opportunities. Building contacts by doing workshops and readings of new works requires a significant commitment of time. An actor must accept the fact that although a steady paycheck might not be coming in for a while, the investment will pay off in the long run. A reasonable agent will support this choice, recognizing that patience is required as long-term plans near fruition.

As agents, we try very hard to advise our clients to make correct choices, but show business is full of gambles. Not every decision turns out to be right, and hindsight, in many cases, is definitely twenty-twenty. One time a client turned down an offer to play the lead in a musical at a top regional theater with one of his favorite directors. He chose, instead, to continue performing in the ensemble of a Broadway show so that the producers might consider him when they began to look for the first replacement of the male lead, which he was understudying. He hoped that management would also consider him for that role in the national tour, if and when the show had one. His agents supported him in this gamble. Unfortunately, the show closed before a replacement was cast, and there was no national tour.

Here are some useful facts to know about working in New York: A Broadway Production Contract pays more than a regional theater job, while most salaries offered by the top Off-Broadway contracts barely pay for daycare. The money earned from working one day in a principal role on a television show, including residual payments (which are usually the same as the original payment for each of two or three re-runs), is more than a week's minimum salary on Broadway. Just one little factor in all of this cannot be ignored: the competition for any of these jobs is so stiff that steady employment in these areas is very unlikely.

Fulfilling Contractual Obligations

Whether a client is working in New York City or out of town, an agent will usually advise him to fulfill his contractual commitment. Choosing to stay on tour, for instance, shows the producers that the actor appreciates the job, honors his commitments, and is a team player. It may also score points for possible promotion to larger roles in the same show, or perhaps in the Broadway version to come. One never knows when a good relationship with the project's general managers, creative team, and casting director will pay off.

A client had been playing a supporting lead in the national tour of a very successful Broadway musical for a year and a half. His contract had been renegotiated once during that time. An offer came in for him to play a part in a major feature film helmed by an Oscar-winning director. Fortunately this actor had established good relationships with the tour's management and creative team. The timing for all of this couldn't have been better, because he had just received a very positive yearly performance evaluation. Because of his professionalism and his value to the company, this actor was able to obtain a leave of absence from the tour to do the movie. By the way, the film role came about from the connection he had made with the director on a TV series several years before. Can you see the connection here? *Work begets work because it creates a network of contacts.*

Recently a client called to say that he wanted to leave the national tour he had been on for six months. His assignment was physically rigorous and he missed being at home with his partner and creature comforts. We advised him to fulfill his contractual commitment of a year before seeking other employment. We did so in order to preserve our client's good standing with management, so that down the road it might consider him for a spot in the Broadway company. We also know that this industry has little regard for "quitters," and that no words from an agent can buy back good will after an actor has left his contract prematurely.

Sometimes an actor has to leave a company in order to force a promotion. An actress was the swing on the road for the national tour of a hit Broadway musical. She did this for six months, then renewed her contract for another six months. At the time of renewal her agents made it very clear to management that the actress wanted to move up to a performing spot in the ensemble. When it came time to renew the contract again, for another six months, we approached management with the ultimatum that they guarantee, in writing, that our client be offered the first ensemble spot that became available. When management gave us a verbal agreement that they refused to put in writing, we felt our client had no choice but to leave the tour. Not putting the term in writing gave us no possible recourse to hold them to it. She had played the good and happy camper long enough; it was important to take a stand and stick to it. Three weeks later an ensemble position in the Broadway company opened up, and management called us with the offer. Having taken a stand and because, of course, she was an excellent performer, our client benefited when something better came along.

Actors take jobs for reasons other than paying the rent. Paying off school loans and getting weeks for health coverage are just a couple more determining factors. A client of ours has worked mainly in the avant-garde theater. He's a marvelous actor—a true artist in every sense of the word—who never stops working, although the salary he pulls in isn't always a living wage. As agents, we vowed to get him a high-paying job, and we did. It was a small but important role in a big, flashy Broadway musical. Although creatively it couldn't compare with his usual fare, we were sure it contributed greatly to his daughter's college fund.

Sometimes choices are made by life circumstances. A client of ours is a wonderful actress, Juilliard trained and with experience. Recently she became a mother and chose to curtail her availability for jobs at regional theaters and for low-paying theater companies in New York. She couldn't go out of town and she couldn't work for next-to-nothing in town. The responsibilities of motherhood forced her agents to position her very specifically for the television and film market, which produced jobs that would satisfy her requirements. Sadly, because the competition is so fierce in this area, this actress doesn't work as much as she used to and runs the risk of losing the market familiarity she had established previously in the theater. We realize that although this is the reality of her actress life for now, and that jobs might be few and far between, things could shift quickly if and when she makes herself more available for a wider range of projects. Therefore, we are patient.

Agents are always looking for the choice that will further an actor's career. What makes the better choice could be a financial aspect or an artistic one. But sometimes the better choice isn't so clearly defined. I have a client who needs to be working all the time. Luckily for him, he's an excellent actor, truly gifted in many ways, and his periods of unemployment are few and far between. He spent years working outside of New York, building his résumé so that when he moved to New York he brought with him a background of training and experience. This actor is no stranger to the process of auditioning; he thrives on it. Every time he is momentarily unemployed, he auditions like a fiend until each day seems to bring in another job offer. When the dust clears, the actor and his agents discuss the various job offers to decide which one to take. The choices range from playing great roles in regional theaters to performing in ensemble positions in Broadway musicals with accompanying understudy assignments. Depending on a number of factors at a given time, any of these could be the best choice. For instance, once this actor was offered a job performing in the ensemble of a new Broadway musical while standing by for the celebrity playing the lead. This came at a time when he swore he would never take another ensemble job on Broadway again. He chose this ensemble position, however, over playing the lead in a play out of town, because we felt it to be the better career move; although it was an ensemble position, it gave him the chance to be in New York, performing in a new project with a well-respected creative team—folks he had never worked with before.

Sometimes money is a factor. The client might need to go with the job that pays better because he has heavy financial responsibilities. But it's not *always* the money. Actors choose jobs for artistic reasons, too— with the support of their agents, I might add. There are times when it's best to work at a regional theater in a dynamic role that offers the chance for creative renewal. I return to the client referred to in the previous paragraph: While he had the good fortune to perform the role he stood by for many times, he didn't have the opportunity to *create* the role. When the show closed he auditioned for many projects, and an offer came in for the lead in a challenging drama that was to be co-produced by two top regional theaters. (Coincidentally, many years before, this role had brought a Tony award to the celebrity our client had just stood by for.) Our client accepted the offer and embarked on what turned out to be a creatively rewarding experience. The impressive theater credit further solidified this musical performer's position as a dramatic actor, paying huge dividends by expanding his opportunities for jobs. I have watched this actor's work develop over time; it gets richer and better with each challenging theatrical experience.

OTHER KINDS OF ADVICE
Actors ask their agents for advice in a number of areas other than job opportunities. Take the headshot. We all know how crucial a good headshot is to opening doors. In fact, it's said in truth that the headshot and résumé are an actor's business card. Therefore, it makes total sense that an agent would want to advise a client on obtaining this valuable marketing tool. While agents don't necessarily wish to micromanage the entire process, we will, when asked, recommend specific photographers whose work we like, go over what kinds of shots we're looking for, and warn against certain pitfalls. For example, I know one agent who really dislikes those shots where the top of the head is cut

off. I know another who reacts very badly to busy backgrounds that distract from the subject of the headshot—i.e., from the actor. Agents generally advise their clients to meet with several photographers in order to see their books and determine who makes them feel most comfortable. After the photo session, when it's time to choose one or more pictures from the contact sheets to use as headshots, we generally ask our clients to spend some time with the contacts before coming to us. After they've asked their mother, father, sister, brother, best friend, lover, teacher…the world, for their responses, and have narrowed the choices down to a handful of favorites, we invite our clients to bring in the contact sheets for our response. We'd rather enter near the end of the selection process, when we feel that our opinion will be most effective. By then the actor has spent so much time poring over the contact sheets that every shot looks the same and he is at his wit's end, really needing help to make his choice.

Agents counsel actors in all areas—from headshots to taking auditions to choosing jobs. They offer advice based on their particular knowledge and experience. Just think about how invaluable your agent's suggestions could be for the preparation of your *Hamlet* audition if she happens to be a Shakespearean expert. Agents exist to answer questions, give support, and brainstorm on solutions to problems. A young actor came in to re-sign with the agency. During our meeting, it was agreed that the challenge was how to meet more casting directors. The agents encouraged him to find a good showcase in New York so he could invite industry people to see his work. He did just that. Becoming involved with a prominent theater company opened many doors and gave his agents something positive to refer to when talking this fellow up to casting directors.

Agents use their good judgment to position clients correctly in terms of employment and the auditions that can lead to employment. Regarding auditions, our "advisory" role becomes that of a screener. For instance, when a TV or film audition comes in for a client, we always ask the casting director if the actor will be reading or going on tape. This important information will influence the actor's audition preparation. When an audition comes in for an actor who is well established in the industry, an agent prudently asks the size of the role. The first person an actor will blame if he auditions for a role that he thinks is too small is his agent. Even though the casting directors have called him in for the part, he will assume that his agent submitted him for it—which many times is not the case at all. Most agents would never submit their clients for one-line roles on film, for instance. That's not where agents want to position their clients. While we're very happy to hear from the casting director, and certainly wouldn't want to offend her by turning down such an audition, we know how important it is to establish our client's position correctly. Instead of saying he doesn't do one-line roles, we refer to him as a fine actor who is available for supporting roles and leads. It's a subtle way to express this important distinction. If an agent doesn't make this clear, the casting director will continue to call the actor in for similar assignments. Although turning down auditions is difficult, in these cases it's absolutely necessary for an actor's business representative to protect him.

Agents protect their clients by differentiating between auditions that are pre-screens for casting directors, and auditions in which the client goes straight to the director. When a casting director calls in a client for a project headed by a director with whom the actor has worked many times before, the agent will suggest to the casting director that the client come in at callbacks, getting a pass on the initial audition entirely. Same is true for "pre-screens": An agent is thrilled when these opportunities occur for young clients who need to be seen by as many casting directors as possible to get work. However, more-seasoned clients are offended by the notion of having to pass judgment from a casting director in order to audition for the director. A seasoned actor feels that his résumé speaks for itself; if the casting director doesn't know who he is, the fault lies in her ignorance, not in the actor's record of training and experience. When dealing with auditions for seasoned clients, it's very important for the agent to find out whether the audition is a pre-screen; if so, the agent must convince the casting director to bring the client straight to the director. Agents need to act with sensitivity and perspicacity regarding how their clients see themselves in the business, and how the business sees them. We speak diplomatically to both sides, trying always to keep the audition alive.

There are times when an agent advises an actor to take an audition even when the actor doesn't want to. We know how valuable any opportunity is to be seen by a casting director. If there is a glimmer of a chance that the actor will do the job if booked, we encourage him to go in for the role. Here's a story illustrating that point: The writers of a very successful Broadway musical are friends of one of our clients. They are always encouraging her to audition for a particular leading role in this long-running show. Through the casting director, her agents keep a close watch for any possible openings for this part. (Our client had auditioned once for the role for the casting director, and that session had gone well.)When the role was opening up in the national tour, she was invited to audition for the entire creative team—clearly, a valuable opportunity. But before we could confirm this audition, we had to make sure that our client would really consider going out on tour. In talking with her, we discussed the many aspects: who would be at the audition, the fact that the part was not opening up on Broadway any time soon, how long the term of employment would be, and the ballpark salary. Although the actress has a house, a husband, a dog, and a successful commercial career, she was not dead set against going on tour. We encouraged her to audition. Then we confirmed the appointment with the casting director, explaining that while our client was definitely interested in the job, we could not guarantee at this time that she would do it, for the various reasons cited above. When the casting director said that he knew just how to position her for the creative team and producers, I understood him to mean that he would assure a second choice backup if our client were selected as the first choice but declined the offer.

Sometimes an agent works as an advisor in terms of audition technique, especially when clients seem to be having a problem with their auditions—e.g., they're not getting callbacks or the agent has received specific feedback from a casting director she trusts attesting to that fact. Based on my experience as a former actress and teacher, I usually advise clients to buy a copy of Michael Shurtleff's book, *Audition*. I'm one of those who considers it the bible on audition preparation. Written in the 1970s, it still holds true as a simple, logical, fool-proof system of twelve guideposts to follow in preparing auditions. May I tell you how Shurtleff came to devise this system? In the '70s, as a casting director for two very important New York City producers, he cast many Broadway plays and a number of feature films. Shurtleff loved actors and he made a point of seeing all the theater that was happening in the city, to scout out new talent. Over and over again he found himself discovering actors who were great in performance but failed miserably when he brought them in to audition for his producers and directors. Perplexed, he began to question his judgment of talent. Then he realized that there must be a difference between performing in a piece that the actor has rehearsed and doing an audition with minimal preparation time. After all, he knew that these weren't bad actors: he had seen them be great. It was then that he realized they simply had no idea how to use their talent to deliver good auditions. So he created his system of twelve "guideposts"—specific elements to focus on that give actors an organized method for using themselves quickly and efficiently in their audition preparation.

Along with suggesting the Shurtleff book, I might encourage actors who are struggling with their audition process, to work with an audition coach. This could be a teacher, a director, or even an actor who (1) works on general audition technique (breaking down a scene and making specific and strong choices, using yourself to connect to the material, entering and exiting a room, handling scripts in cold readings, working with less-than-friendly audition readers—things like that), and/or (2) guides the actor in the preparation of a specific audition. Some actors use different coaches for different mediums, e.g., an on-camera coach for on-camera auditions, a vocal coach for singing auditions. Sometimes coaching with a person before an audition gives an actor the opportunity to "try out" his ideas so he doesn't go into the audition completely unrehearsed. This builds confidence.

PERSONAL MANAGERS

Some readers may be wondering, "If an agent does all of that, then what does a personal manager do?" It's a good question and deserves some attention here. Crossover definitely exists in the job descriptions of agent and personal manager. I've been fortunate to work as an agent in two companies that foster close client contact. The first, in which I was an assistant and then a "baby" agent, serviced about twenty-five actors. In the business, this is referred to as a "boutique" agency. The agency where I currently work has approximately one hundred signed clients plus fifty or so freelance actors whom we submit mainly for musicals. This is a mid-size agency. In each of these firms, the agents function as agent-managers. They work closely with the clients and perform many of the duties that a manager would, such as offering advice on classes, headshots, wardrobe choices for auditions, etc. A wise person once said that an actor should only have a manager when he has something to manage. One wonders when that might be. Perhaps when an actor has a flourishing concert career, is also a regular on a television series, and does the occasional Broadway show or movie. At this point he probably needs a person to coordinate his schedule and organize his life. This person is called a personal manager. Of course, if an actor is young and brilliant, but inexperienced and without an agent, it might be productive for him to seek the services of a personal manager to help him choose classes, photos, wardrobe, etc. The manager would consider this actor to be an investment that will pay off when he matures. That explains why the term of a manager's contract with an actor usually starts at three years but can be as long as five years. That length of time might be needed for the "investment" to pay off. The manager also collects commission on all work booked during this time, whether he was directly responsible for the booking or not.

Many actors whose careers have progressed to a certain level but who want to get to that next level consider working with a manager as well as an agent. They feel that the additional attention devoted solely to the advancement of their careers will have beneficial results. These actors know that their agents are sometimes responsible to a hundred other actors. A manager has a much smaller client roster—usually ten to twenty-five actors—so he can give much more attention to the individual actor. This attention translates into arranging meetings with casting directors, producers, directors, writers—any kind of professional contact that could lead to career advancement. A manager can also be responsible for placing actors with agents and providing a wide range of career counseling that encompasses everything from wardrobe selection for the next audition to song selection for the spring concert tour. I knew an actor who had graduated from one of the top acting schools in the country. He proceeded to build a moderately successful career, but was forced to take a leave of absence from the business for family reasons. When he came back, some five years later, he hooked up with one of the most powerful (meaning having connections) managers in New York. It wasn't long before this actor was appearing in Broadway shows, guest spots on TV, and good supporting roles in feature films.

Agents have a love-hate relationship with managers. How the manager wishes to place her client in terms of agent representation will affect whether an agent chooses to work with that actor: Agents will not compete with other agents to *freelance* with an actor handled by a manager because a three-partner freelancing arrangement offers no protection for the agent's efforts; and the manager's active involvement renders the actor-agent relationship far too tenuous to lead to exclusivity. If, however, a manager introduces an actor to an agent with the purpose of seeking *exclusive* representation, the agent is more likely to take notice of the actor and consider representing him.

In Los Angeles, it seems necessary for talent to have an agent and a manager. Agents are extremely busy making submissions and doing deals for many actors in the very active film and TV market. Actors look to managers to consider the big picture while addressing the many little details needed to keep clients' careers on track and moving forward. I also think the opportunity for making larger salaries in the television and film market can support a commission of twenty-five percent (ten percent to the agent, fifteen percent to the manager).

I like to have personal contact with my clients. I feel that my knowledge and experience can be very helpful, and I enjoy advising my clients on every aspect of their careers. The managers with whom I have favorable working relationships respect my relationship with the client and promote a team structure. They are unobtrusively present. For example, they will call me to suggest a submission for the actor and help coordinate audition preparation, but they will not try to compete with me for the attention and approval of the actor. I have problems when a manager comes between me and my client and disrupts the connection I've established. A manager usually brings with him his own set of connections and industry players, which is what he offers the actor. If this network doesn't include the agent currently representing the actor, that agent could have a problem.

I am reminded of a young fellow with whom we started working shortly after he graduated from college. He was a unique talent, gifted in many areas, but not an obvious casting choice. As agents, we nurtured his career through a couple of rough early years, providing good advice and excellent support when needed. I remember one occasion specifically, when we spent a great deal of time on the phone convincing this young actor who was working out of town to come into New York to audition for a new Sondheim musical. He was very reluctant, being so involved with his current show and having limited funds for traveling to New York, but we convinced him. He was cast in the production. We were ecstatic and very much looked forward to building on this momentum. A manager saw him in the show and approached him, promising greener pastures that did not include us, his longtime, loyal agents. The young actor chose to leave the agency and go with the manager and his people, a move which to this day has done little to propel his career forward.

★

How great is it for an actor to have in his corner an agent who is very aware of and sensitive to his personal self-image and all the desires and needs that come with it. How wonderful to have an agent who uses her knowledge and experience to protect and promote the actor so he can accomplish his career goals. We have spent a great deal of time so far exploring how an agent does business, in order to shed light on the agent's value to the actor. Let's say an agent wants to work with you. And you choose her. The papers are signed. It's a done deal. Now it's time to talk.

Chapter 10

HOW DO ACTORS AND AGENTS COMMUNICATE?

Over the years I have been a panelist in many forums between agents and actors, in which agents talk about show business and answer actors' questions. In every panel I've ever participated in, agents uniformly agree that good communication between an actor and an agent is the most important ingredient in a healthy relationship. Its lack is the source of many misunderstandings, and pretty much of all the difficulties that arise between actors and their agents. Any research into a troubled relationship will usually point to some sort of problem in communication that has either evolved over time or erupted in a moment. Therefore, it's important to spend some time here discussing how to improve understanding and communication between actors and their agents.

The relationship between an agent and a signed actor is often compared to a marriage. It's generally agreed that the secret to a good marriage is respect: both partners need to respect each other as individuals in order to keep their relationship running smoothly. Any good marriage requires work. Relationships don't just magically happen: the most successful and long-lasting ones require constant care, adjustment, and give-and-take. In the actor-agent relationship, each person needs to value the other's existence and contributions to the partnership. The agent values an actor's talent, skill, and artistry. The actor values an agent's knowledge, experience, and business acumen. In an industry that is all about communication, clearly the various players rely on the art of communication to function successfully.

Of course, personalities and styles of communication differ, but everyone is aiming for the same overall objective: moving the actor's career forward. Some agents are very nurturing and relate to their clients like a sibling, or sometimes even a parent. Other agents are very businesslike, keeping a professional distance while getting the job done. They are equally effective. Actors come in many emotional shapes and sizes, too: Some can separate their art from the business with a relatively level-headed ease, while others struggle to protect fragile egos in the midst of commercial enterprise (read "are extremely needy"). Some are adults who behave like infants on and off the stage, while others seem extremely well balanced until an injustice is committed. Obviously, in order to successfully make business happen between people, an agent must be able to manage all types of personalities. Someone has to stay objective in order to think clearly in the best—and, more importantly—the worst of times. Agents are the rudders of a ship at sea, keeping the boat steady and on course in the heaviest storms. When your Broadway show closes unexpectedly, who's the first person you call? Your agent. When the director cuts your best lines from a scene during rehearsal, whom do you call? Your agent. Agents are in charge of crisis control in an actor's career. Daily. Whether it's capitalizing on something good or preventing something bad, agents try to remain calm and cool under pressure, making sure that whatever drama is to be remains *on* stage or screen. Actors need to know that their agent will be there solidly for them, no matter what. To use another boating metaphor: the stronger the anchor, the more rope is given an actor to go out and be creative.

An agent expects a client to be responsible—which is just another word for professional. What may seem obvious to most actors is evidently not so obvious to some, because certain misunderstandings between agents and actors keep recurring. For the benefit of future working relationships between actors and agents, let's spend some time here discussing several specific communication issues.

It seems to me that most of the problems in communication between agents and actors come from either ignorance or lack of consideration. Agents point to two things in particular that they feel would make business run much more smoothly day-to-day: First, they strongly advise actors to return calls from their agents promptly. Second, they advise actors to always tell their agents when they "book out" (plan to be out of town), whether on business or for personal reasons. Let me explain why both of these procedures are so important.

Recently I polled some agent friends and discovered that the telephone is still the preferred method of communicating with an actor. Personally, when I have an audition to call out I like to use an actor's service—preferably voicemail rather than a real person. The latter chews up so much more time, what with being put on hold constantly and having to repeat information endlessly. I leave a very thorough message with all pertinent details—which I expect to leave one time only. (Once again, actors: *please* try not to accidentally delete your agents' messages!) I ask the actor to call me back to confirm that he received my message, and to answer any questions that I might have asked. I expect him to do this on a timely basis, which usually means on the same day. I know this seems like a no-brainer, like something that an actor would unquestionably do, but you would be surprised at the number of actors who are delinquent in returning calls—from their agents, no less! This delinquency is curious, rather maddening, and, in many cases, can be downright dangerous for an actor, because casting directors will sometimes take away from actors audition appointments that are not confirmed the same day they are called out.

Offers of employment can be lost, too. The turnaround time for acceptance of most job offers is usually at least twenty-four hours. It's one of those unspoken-but-agreed-upon business practices. The casting director or general manager calls the agent with the offer for her client, allowing at least twenty-four hours before expecting to hear from the agent as to whether the client accepts, wants to negotiate, or declines the offer. At this point if he hasn't heard from the agent, the casting director will make a follow-up phone call, asking the agent for the client's response. Some organizations, however, unique unto themselves, operate with extremely quick turnarounds. I know an actor who lost a job on a cruise ship, for instance, because he didn't return his agent's phone call fast enough. Here's the story: The offer came in mid-morning. The agent, wanting to reach his client in a hurry, called his cell phone immediately. Unfortunately, he only got voicemail and did not speak directly to the client. The agent continued to call several times, leaving urgent messages at various other phone numbers, too, only to learn too late that his client had been working at a job that morning where he couldn't retrieve his phone messages. Agents are not in the habit of accepting or declining offers—or auditions, for that matter—for their clients without speaking to them first. Only if we have a special relationship with an actor that has developed over many years, do we have the authority to make these business decisions for him. Otherwise, we must speak directly to him before responding to casting directors, general managers, and industry players in general. In the absence of that "special relationship," agents protect themselves by continually keeping their clients in the loop, and not acting alone. The agent in the cruise-ship story was not in the position to accept the job offer without first speaking to his client. Unfortunately, by the time the agent's client returned his call, the producers had offered the job to a different actor, who had accepted it. While the agent felt this was a slightly abnormal and somewhat unethical business practice, it demonstrates to all actors the importance of returning agents' calls promptly.

CALLING TO CONFIRM

Certainly, agents can't fault actors who don't know agency protocol and procedures. Take this example, for instance: Let's say that for some reason (justifiable or not) an actor picks up a message from his agent late at night. The message gives the details of an audition scheduled for the following morning. But the actor neglects to call the agency overnight to confirm, because he doesn't know that the office has an answering machine that takes messages outside of business hours.

Next morning, the agent arrives at the office, already quite concerned that her client might not make this audition because she didn't hear from him the day before. She hopes to pick up his message on the answering machine confirming the audition—bad news: not a peep. The casting assistant at *Law & Order* calls a few minutes later to see if the actor is coming in. What's an agent to say? I suppose she could lie and say the actor will be there, hoping for the best. Or she could apologize for not having the answer and ask for a little more time so that she can call the client again. But what happens if she can't get the actor this morning either? Does she tell the casting director he won't be there? What if the actor calls the agent after she's turned down the audition? Does she tell him to go to the audition, then immediately call the casting director to tell him to expect the actor? What if the actor shows up at the audition after the agent turned it down? I can't tell you how inept an agent feels when she hasn't been able to reach her client in order to confirm these valuable auditions with the casting director, or when something else occurs that displays a lack of communication between actor and agent. Now, let's take this one step further: imagine the agent's distress when five of these situations are brewing all at once at the top of a morning, each urgently demanding attention. One can easily see how any confirmation left on the answering machine overnight would alleviate an agent's stress. Actors who can't plead ignorance to an agency's procedures, but know better, really should consider how they can help their agents be more effective, efficient, and less stressed. The actors will get better service.

BOOKING OUT

One of the most frustrating situations for an agent occurs when, having pushed a particular client to a casting director for a role, then having successfully obtained the audition, the agent discovers that the actor is out of town on a little vacation that he, oops, "forgot" to mention to the agency. I know, it's ridiculous: why would an actor call his service four times a day, or check his cell phone voicemail every three hours, but forget to tell his agency that he planned to take a long weekend in the Catskills from Thursday through Monday? Agents feel very foolish when the casting director finally gives us that audition appointment that we've begged, whined, practically prostrated ourselves for—and then we have to cancel it because our client is out of town. We are so embarrassed that we can hardly find it in ourselves to suggest another actor for the slot. After a mistake like this, the casting director may not entertain any pushes from the agent for a while. Due to one actor's negligence over one weekend, many actors stand to lose out for weeks. And this particular audition is a loss not only for the original actor who is unavailable to take it, but for the agent's other clients, because had she known that he was booked out, she would have pushed someone else from the start. If an actor is not available, the audition should go to another client. When trying to fill the slot, an agent will get annoyed if the client she pushes isn't around to fill it.

Some actors, when discovered to be out of town, excuse their negligence by implying that because they hadn't heard from their agents in a long time, they didn't think the agents cared about their whereabouts. Agents can read the oblique expression of resentment in this excuse. Unfortunately, it does nothing to address the fundamental problem of the moment, which is, the agent got the actor a great audition that the actor can't make. This business moves too quickly, when it moves, to allow for tactics of passive aggression. For the good of the relationship, actors should learn not to make assumptions about what their agents are doing for them. Actors really have no idea what actions are being taken to further their careers until they pin down their agents and ask. Although, admittedly, actors might not get the whole story even then—not every agent is forthcoming, all of the time. Still, it's very important for an actor not to assume that an agent's silence means any lack of interest or activity on his part. Sometimes getting just one audition requires sending out thirty headshots and résumés. And that could take six months. I'm not exaggerating; this has happened at our agency. I met a young actress whom I thought was very talented. She came out of one of the graduate acting programs, and the office didn't start working with her right away because we had made commitments to many other young actors. We felt we had to close the door in order to be fair to our new clients, and unfortunately she ended up outside the door. I asked her to keep in touch with me; she did, and a year later she requested another interview with the office. When I met with her again, I was very impressed by the amount of work she had obtained for herself without the help of an agent. This actress happens to be highly creative, very energetic, and likes to be active. This time the agency seemed to have a slight opening for her "type"—a young, quirky character actress—so we agreed to start submitting her for projects. Six months later, she received not one, but two calls from the agency, for two auditions on the same day, no less. You can imagine her surprise: She hadn't heard from us in months, and probably thought we had forgotten her. She had noticed that we hadn't even called to ask her for more photos and résumés. (Such calls are generally the sign actors use to reassure themselves that at least their agent is submitting them for projects.) We had been submitting her all along but it took six months for our submissions to pay off. Needless to say, the actress was ecstatic. She got callbacks on both auditions and it was only a matter of time until she booked a job.

To reiterate: always tell your agents when you plan to be out of town, even if it's only for a long weekend nearby, and make sure they know how to reach you. You never know when a call might come from Steven Spielberg—as one actually did for one of our clients, late one Friday afternoon. A casting director phoned our office requesting that our client put himself on tape with sides for a film that Steven Spielberg was producing. The tape had to reach Mr. Spielberg, who was staying in the Hamptons, on the next day. Luckily I knew how to quickly reach my client, who was traveling at the time; and being the resourceful actor that he is, he found a studio with a camera, received the sides by fax from me, made the tape, and sent it out without complication. All of this occurred without a hitch due to the excellent communication between actor and agent and the ingenuity and resourcefulness of this particular actor.

KEEPING IN TOUCH

Many times after signing agency papers, new clients ask how we would prefer that they keep in touch with the office. What method should they use to communicate with us, and how often? Once a week? Once a month? By phone, fax, post card, email? They want to know if it's okay to call us when they hear about a project they think they're right for. And may they call us for feedback on their auditions? Here's our response: By all means, if a client hears of a project that she thinks she's right for, she should call us to see whether it has appeared on the breakdown service yet, and whether she's been submitted. We would prefer that an actor call us with specific information about a project, like its title and perhaps the name of the casting director who is handling it. That makes our research much easier and faster. Vague rumors are extremely difficult to track down. Keep in mind, too, that many times an actor's information about a project is not as current as an agent's. Usually we really do have the inside scoop. Be prepared for the answer to your question to be either that the breakdown hasn't come out yet or the project is already cast, or the information given to the general public is inaccurate. An actress once called to ask about a new musical that she had read about in the trade papers. In answer to her questions about auditions and casting, the agent told her that it was not "new": it had been running for a year and was only looking for replacements in the ensemble—work that he knew she was not willing to leave town for. He had answers to her questions that not only gave her the right story but justified why she hadn't been submitted.

THE ACTOR NETWORK

Actors' Equity requires producers to hold open auditions for most shows under Equity contract, and actors can sometimes book jobs from these opportunities. For the most part, however, it is agent submissions that lead to the majority of actor bookings. Agents pay close attention when their clients call in to report that a casting director is putting out audition appointments. Their clients are getting this information from actors who are being called in. When an agent hears that auditions are going out on a project that the casting director hasn't called him for yet, he knows to phone that casting director to get some action.

The actor network can be a valuable and reliable source of late-breaking news; these situations are generally more productive than those exemplified in the preceding paragraph.

SEASONAL SUBMISSIONS

When clients phone to request multiple submissions ("I was looking at this year's list of LORT theater seasons and I saw some shows I'd like to be submitted for..."), I usually ask them to either fax or email the list to the office. This saves time and gives each agent in the office a clear and detailed list of the projects to research. Actors should know that agents don't usually make general submissions to theaters for entire seasons but tend, instead, to submit clients for specific projects as they come out on the breakdown service. Agents will make submissions to the casting directors who deal directly with the theaters. While we make every effort to remember the specific projects our clients want to be submitted for, we tell them honestly that we might need reminders at the time those projects are actually being cast. We may agree to keep an eye out for these projects when they appear on the breakdown service, but we also suggest that the actor contact the theater and casting director personally by mail to inform them of his interest in a particular project and to find out when the theater plans to hold its casting sessions. It is a good idea to list your agent and his contact information in your letter to the casting director and theater. In the end, an agent will consider any reasonable request made by an actor in a non-demanding way. Illogical requests, however—for instance, by the relatively unknown actress with modest credits who expects to be submitted for a Broadway show because she is "so right" for a role that she has always dreamed of playing—won't get the same attention. Why? Because such a request shows bad business sense, and the agent would feel foolish even suggesting it to the casting director.

FAXES AND EMAILS

One final note in this area of communicating with your agency office: When actors decide to fax or email a document to an agent's office, they should phone first to notify someone that it is on the way. Without forewarning, faxes can get buried and go unnoticed for days. I also like to know when a client plans to email information to me. I don't open unsolicited emails: it's my protection against viruses. And I refuse to be a slave to email because it takes away from the time I need to make submissions, put out audition appointments, negotiate offers, and return phone calls. One client, who is careful not to abuse email, communicates to the office through faxes. He is selective as to when and how often he does this, and is very thorough and articulate when he does. The fax may touch on a number of subjects, such as submission requests and negotiation points when we are doing a deal for him. After I have read over the fax and have separated the bits of "venting" from the issues that require an agent's action or response, I find myself appreciating this tool's effective economy of communication. A well-written email can also convey precisely this information; the advantage of a fax is its being hard copy—quick and easy to refer to and file.

Addressing Problems with Your Agent

Actors want to know how to keep in touch with their agents, especially if they've not been heard from in a while. If you haven't heard from your agent within a couple of weeks of signing, you might touch base by phone, mail, or email to verify whether this is, indeed, a slow time. In general, resist the vague "what's up?" calls. Try to find something specific to say, suggest, or impart. Even, "I haven't heard from you in a while; is it slow?" is better than, "What's up? Is anything happening?" Can you hear the difference in intent between these two expressions? One is fairly innocent. The other is obliquely accusatory. Any agent hearing the latter will suspect it prefaces a whining session that she would rather avoid. It's true, I've compared notes with other agents.

Try also to stay away from accusing, demanding, or suggesting (either directly or indirectly) any lack of diligence on the agent's part. Support your agent's efforts, ask specific questions, and always note what you yourself are doing to stir up activity—whether it be taking class, joining a theater group, or networking with directors and friends. As I've said before, agents respond better to pro-active team players! One agent I know specifically tells actors that it is their responsibility just as much as their agents' to find work and keep busy. If an actor finds himself between engagements and calls this agent to "check in," the agent wants to hear that the actor is taking class, doing a showcase, shooting a student film or is involved in a play-reading series with a new theater company—anything that implies the actor is taking action rather than sitting around waiting for his agent to wave a magic wand to make a career appear.

Actors never know if and when they should call their agents with a problem. One agent, asked when she preferred her clients to call her with a problem, answered facetiously, "Never." In truth, there are both good times and bad times to call your agent. The actors' problem is knowing which is which. Ask the agent. I always suggest that when a client calls in, he preface the conversation with, "Got a minute?" The agent will say either "yes" or "no." If he says "no," then ask when would be a better time to call. But most likely, unless he is involved in something that cannot be interrupted, he'll try to find out quickly what you need or why you're calling. When he does this, don't make it a mystery. If something's bugging you, say so—your agent wants to know. Please don't make us play a game of Twenty Questions. We don't have time for that. And please don't keep us in suspense by calling to ask us for a meeting and then not telling us what you want to talk about.

It's always best for actors to contact their agents at the onset of a problem rather than when it has reached full-blown crisis level. We are somewhat paranoid and know what "coming in to talk" usually means. Please understand that taking time out of our busy workday, which is devoted to getting auditions for you and all of our other clients, puts an enormous strain on the efficiency and productivity of the office. I know an agent who actually refuses to take meetings in the office with her clients. She claims that she just doesn't have the time in the day. She is, however, perfectly happy to discuss issues over the phone because, as she says, "That's what I do. It's my comfort zone." Spending time with a harried agent in the middle of an extremely hectic day is not going to do your case any good. Instead of being heard, you'll just be causing more problems, and you won't get thorough answers to your questions.

I urge actors to be aware of the workday flow and the sensitivity of the people actually doing the work. Agents are not insensitive to actors' needs and grievances, but we need to approach and deal with them at a time and in a way that's compatible with our daily workflow. Drop-ins really interrupt the workday flow and catch an agent unawares; this usually does not give you, the client, the best that agent has to offer. Also, it helps to pay attention to how your agent is receiving your call. When an actress once called one of our agents, she was totally oblivious to his lack of response to her questions. Even after she asked him "what was happening," and he truthfully told her he had just learned that a family member was very sick, she continued her self-motivated monologue. (And actors are supposed to be sensitive.)

Remember that each actor is one of many that an agent represents, and we try to give equal attention to all of our clients. If it's five o'clock in the afternoon and we've received audition appointments for a casting session for *Law & Order: SVU* the next morning, we must attend to that before we can discuss your "career." This does not mean we *won't* discuss your career. We should and we will. We just have to do so at another time. Try not to allow your temporary frustration and hurt feelings to fester and build into a resentment that isolates you from your agents. That won't do you or your agents any good. Problems should be addressed as they arise. They shouldn't be left to brew. The last thing an agent wants to hear on the answering machine first thing in the morning is a client's "goodbye" message—without having a clue as to where or when the problems started.

EMERGENCIES

When an actor gets lost trying to find an audition site, he should by all means call his agent to get the right address. Of course, emergencies require instant communication. But in the midst of a crisis, although this is difficult, the actor needs to separate expressing his anxieties from getting the solutions. Agents are understanding and experienced in handling egos in crisis. However, there is a limit to what we will tolerate. The better an actress manages her emotions, the better the service she will receive from her agent. Try to separate what went wrong from what might be salvaged, and treat your agent like the ally she undoubtedly is.

Relationship problems, submission requests, and evaluation and feedback issues can be complex and can be addressed by various means. One agent prefers to dialogue by email. Asked how often he checks his email, he replies, "Frequently." For him, it is an unobtrusive way to communicate. Another agent cautions *against* email—especially when the subject is a grievance. She urges actors to be careful with what they put in print, because it might come back to haunt them. As I suggested earlier in this chapter, it's wise always to notify your agent first before using email or fax to communicate. Emails are too easy for an agent to ignore and/or delete. Faxes can get buried. In either of these two instances, you will most likely be calling your agent first. Granted, these days you might just as easily get trapped in a labyrinthine voice-mail system—but as one agent puts it, "If your agent won't take your call, then find another agent."

PHONE MESSAGE ETIQUETTE

Here's something you might not even have thought about: phone message etiquette. Did you know that there's a constructive way to leave messages on the answering machine at your agent's office? First, think about the situation in which your agent is likely to receive your call. Let's say you've left a message late at night. Picture an agent opening up her office in the morning. No sooner has she stepped across the threshold but the phone starts ringing: Martha missed her connecting flight out of St. Louis, so she will be arriving in New York two hours later than expected. Should she still go to her audition? John never got the sides for this morning's *Rescue Me* audition. "Sorry, could you email them again?" Tom plans to drop in later to discuss his career. But he hangs up abruptly, leaving no indication as to when. And the day is off and running. All this occurs before the agent has even had the chance to check the overnight messages on the agency's answering machine. And she can see that the light is blinking—goodness, ten times! She starts to listen to the messages. Here's Ann with a voicemail message that goes on forever. It's a monologue describing the "kind of weird" audition she had yesterday. She rambles, with a sampling of vague complaints obliquely directed to the agency: something about having the wrong sides (the agent's fault), not being given the right address (the agent's fault), not being asked to sing both songs she prepared (the auditor's fault)...The agent, in crisis mode, is itching to get back to Martha's missed connection and John's missing sides. But she's listening patiently to what Ann wants the agency to do about her audition experience. Finally, Ann caps her message with something about her just wanting to let the agency know what was happening. The agent's reaction is, "Hunh?!" Ann didn't even ask for a follow-up!

Might I suggest leaving messages that have a more productive purpose? Even if you're calling in to complain or let off steam, try not to dump directly on the agents. Make the purpose of your phone call be solving problems rather than adding more guests to your pity party. And, by the way, those phone messages in which an actor is "just checking in," asking for a return call, probably won't get one. An agent has just so much time in a day for chasing the actors she needs for the concrete business at hand. When leaving phone messages on your agent's voicemail, remember to be professional and courteous. That means be specific, brief, and speak actions rather than complaints. This approach will get you the results you want. (Knowing what results you want will also help. Think like an actor: what is your objective in making this call?)

Doubtless certain actor-agent events and activities require a visit to the office. Signing employment contracts or agency papers, and showing new hairstyles or weight changes are some. Such visits are important and necessary, and should be scheduled at a time mutually convenient to client and agent.

REPORTING IN AFTER AUDITIONS

I love to hear from my clients after they've auditioned. I think actors like to "release" and let off steam following the intense process of auditioning, and I am glad to be that someone they call. Auditioning can be such a nerve-wracking experience. Even the best of the best crumble at the mere thought of it. I've seen seemingly shock-proof divas crack under the pressure of reading for a respected director. These calls also help me to do my job. They give me valuable information—who was in the room, what they asked the actor to do, how they reacted—which I can use later on if I speak with the casting director. It's important to know how the audition went from the actor's point of view.

CALLING FOR FEEDBACK

Wanting to know how they did in their auditions, actors are always asking their agents to get feedback from casting directors. One actor emailing my column in *Back Stage* asked whether it was customary for agents to seek feedback from casting directors. He mentioned in his email that he appreciated the number and variety of auditions his "new" agent was getting him. He also wrote that he was aware of his ratio of callbacks to auditions. He wanted to maximize the efforts of his thorough audition preparations—meaning he wanted to book jobs—and he felt that some feedback from casting directors would be useful to that purpose. At the same time, however, he did not want to seem ungrateful, needy, or in any way a "high maintenance" client. In answering his question, I attempted to lay out the entire issue of casting director feedback and how it affects the actor agent relationship. Let me share some of these thoughts with you here.

Until the powers that be come up with a different way to cast actors, auditions are it. I remember very well the experience of auditioning as an actress without an agent. You walk into a room, find a panel of nameless people, then shake each person's hand (if it's offered), while promptly forgetting his name. You perform your piece, then try to judge how well you did by the reactions from the faceless panel—they are a blur due to your nerves. Does a stony face mean you were awful? Do smiles and fawning compliments mean you've got the job? You leave the room with every shred of dignity you can muster, then call your service every fifteen minutes (these days, you'd probably check your cell phone) for a message indicating a callback. The day goes by, the week goes by— no word at all. Put a couple dozen of these experiences together over a few months and you're left with a big, fat question mark: no feedback and no way to evaluate how you're doing. It's like living in a vacuum. Unless you have developed relationships with casting directors and feel comfortable about calling them personally for feedback, the best thing to do is forget about the auditions as soon as you've done them. Otherwise you'll live forever in audition purgatory.

Having an agent alters the process somewhat. First of all, there's a person on your "team" who *can* make those uncomfortable phone calls requesting feedback. Actors need to realize that agents call casting directors for feedback only when a client isn't called back after an audition. Calling a casting director for feedback can be advantageous or detrimental, depending on several factors. I recently took a call from a client who was wondering "what was up" with a certain project. He had been led to believe by the director (who was also the casting director) that he was to receive a callback, but he was beginning to be concerned because apparently the appointment hadn't come in yet. He asked me to call to investigate this. I decided nothing ventured, nothing gained, so I might as well carry out his request. At that time, this actor was a new client of the agency, and this audition was for a long-term theater job with a nice salary—a job that I knew he was very right for and eager to do. I called the casting director and was shocked that he didn't even remember my client when I mentioned his name. I suffered my embarrassment quickly, offered to fax my client's photo and résumé, and did my super sales pitch. The next day the callback appointment came in. A frightening situation, to say the least. That callback might never have happened if I hadn't nudged the casting director, which might not have happened if my client hadn't nudged me.

There's a catch to calling casting directors for feedback, though. Let me explain: Agents don't necessarily assume that a client bombed at the audition if he does not get a callback. We know that so many factors affect final casting. Maybe the part is really pre-cast and they're just looking for backups; maybe the role gets cut from the script; maybe the breakdown went through a creative change, like the producers decided to go "ethnic" with a role. When agents call casting directors for feedback, we are introducing a negative perspective that may have no basis at all. By asking for feedback, we are reminding the casting director that the actor did not get a callback, and we are asking the casting director to find a reason to justify why this happened. She starts thinking that since the actor wasn't called back, he must have done something wrong. I can hear the wheels turning in the casting director's mind as she tries to come up with some kind of verbal appeasement. Usually the result is a pat phrase like, "They [the director, producers, writers] went a different way." Sometimes the casting director offers a subjective and vague comment like, "She just didn't do anything for me"—which, quite frankly, is not helpful. I wouldn't know how to interpret a statement like that, much less know how to pass it along to my client.

There is value in obtaining feedback from casting directors, especially in situations where it's necessary to evaluate a client's audition skills. I can certainly understand an actor's need to evaluate his own skills, especially if he's not getting callbacks. Calling for feedback is just one of the many things we do to keep an actor on track in his career climb. We all need evaluation to keep us on the path to success, and an agent can function as a lifeline in this respect.

FEEDBACK FOR AGENTS

Agents, as much as actors, want to learn any information that might help bring a client closer to booking work. I don't keep specific tallies of the ratio between each client's auditions and callbacks. What I do track are trends. If, after about ten auditions, I notice that a client hasn't received any callbacks, I decide to address the situation. I usually phone the casting directors who have been in on these ten auditions and whose judgment lines up with mine, and ask them for feedback. If they have the time they will refer to their notes, which are usually extremely specific and thorough. These notes provide valuable information and insights, which can prove crucial to the actor's success in booking jobs. At other times, when I am talking with a casting director about another subject, I might ask her for general feedback on a certain actor's auditions, when I know that she has recently seen him, and often. Usually the feedback is good, and there are no major problems—it's just a matter of time before the client starts booking.

If an actor *does* have an audition problem, such as a noticeable lack of preparation or readings that lack specific choices, most casting directors will volunteer that information without my even asking for it. For instance, a casting director who is a longtime friend of our office called to offer some feedback on one of the young conservatory grads that we had recently signed. She liked his work very much but thought he wasn't doing the best for himself at his auditions. She felt they lacked specificity and commitment. Her purpose in calling us with this information was to stop the trend—to get this actor onto the right track as soon as possible so he wouldn't waste a year auditioning badly. Another time, a casting director, after viewing an audition tape for a sitcom pilot, mentioned that she thought the actor needed to find a sense of humor and lighten up. He was too serious and she wondered if he had that quick take needed for situation comedy. This was useful information for the actor, who went on to take classes in improv and theater games.

Having said all this, I must add an important caveat: agents will not risk jeopardizing their relationships with casting directors by calling for feedback after every audition. We don't want to be pests. Plus, the more time an agent spends tracking feedback on auditions, the less time she has to secure other auditions.

The actor whose email launched this discussion on page 151 noted that he'd had one callback out of eight auditions. He wanted to know if he should call his new agent for feedback, and if so, how he should do it. I could appreciate his concern about how he was doing. After all, his new agent was getting him good auditions, and he wanted to start booking. I said, by all means, *yes*, he should speak to his agent. Then I gave him an appropriate way to do this without coming off as "high maintenance." I advised him first to be sure to thank his agent for the wealth and variety of the auditions she'd obtained for him. Then I suggested that he ask, very directly, how the agent thought he might be able to get more mileage out of these auditions, and that he state very clearly that he very much wanted to improve the ratio of callbacks to auditions and start booking jobs. At this point, it would make perfect sense for him to suggest getting helpful feedback from trustworthy casting directors. His agent would feel appreciated, I believe, and would want to take an action to help his client book jobs.

I have a client who has been auditioning for several months with no callbacks. I can tell it's beginning to bug him. He brings "guilt" gifts to the office and responds sheepishly to our calls giving him auditions. I asked several casting directors for feedback. Since they kept bringing him in for auditions even though he hadn't been getting callbacks or booking jobs, they could find no reason for this drought either. We suggested he take an audition class with a casting director; he did so and soon ended his drought. I guess this means there's always something to be learned.

Sometimes it's just best to forget about an audition and move on. How do I know when that's the case? It depends on the project, the client, and the casting director involved. In episodic TV, where casting goes so quickly, if my client has a pre-screen with the casting director at noon and isn't called back for the director/producer session later that day or the following morning, I can assume there's no further interest. I will be very cautious in determining when to touch base with the casting director and "casually" ask how so-and-so did. Perhaps I'll wait a few days before asking—when I know the episode's been cast and the next one hasn't started casting yet. To take another instance: if callbacks aren't coming in for a new client—say, one of the students recently signed out of the leagues—I will call into a casting director I trust. If any client has been called in for something unusual (for example, a client who mostly does straight dramas has auditioned for a musical), I might phone the casting director the next day just to inquire how the actor did. I would certainly feel no discomfort about asking for feedback in this particular instance, especially since the casting idea came from the CD in the first place.

Some casting directors see themselves as "directors" and "star-makers," relishing the position of importance they give themselves in developing a favorite actor's career. They see themselves as totally necessary to the actor's success. One casting director I know is a huge fan of a certain young actress; he brings her in for everything. At times he sounds like a personal manager mapping out her future. As agents for the actress, we don't mind this casting director's managerial spin...as long as he continues to call in our client for auditions. Usually, we advise our clients to try to incorporate whatever adjustments such casting directors offer during the pre-screen. Once an actor passes the evaluation of a casting director, he has acquired a powerful fan. Most CDs take diligent notes and can be very constructive. For example, when I asked a certain casting director for feedback after a client auditioned for a musical, he suggested that my client add Broadway standards to his repertoire of pop-rock winners. That was valuable and constructive information that I hope my client will act upon—especially before he auditions for that particular casting director again.

Of course, whatever feedback I do receive passes through my agent filter before going to the client. I don't see the good of sharing a casting director's feedback if it is vague or nasty. Given the subjectivity of this business, all comments must be taken with a grain of salt. "Not funny" gets translated by me into "polish up those comedy choices." "Stiff" becomes "over prepared," with the remedy being, "allow yourself to make riskier, more spontaneous choices." "Didn't do anything for me" becomes "raise the stakes," or "make stronger choices and don't be afraid to commit to them." Sometimes "add a sense of humor" becomes "turn on that sex appeal (which I know you have)"—which can loosen an actor just enough to get callbacks.

In short, an agent's asking for feedback is not as simple as it seems; it requires the deft hand of a researcher, analyst, and diplomat. Who said agents don't work for their ten percent?

✳

Speaking of ten percent, let's talk about money!

Chapter 11

MONEY MATTERS

This book is about agents and actors and how they work together to make business. Actors are artists, and agents are their business representatives. The playing field is show business and the goal is to make a living at all of this. Along the way, actors may strive to do great art, acquire health weeks for medical insurance, or shoot a student grad film to get some tape for a demo reel. What separates the amateur from the professional is that the former does this for sheer satisfaction, while the latter views acting as his job. Once an actor turns professional, he has chosen to perform for his livelihood. That's what it means to be a professional. Doubtless an actor can work within the industry without the help of an agent. But clearly any attempt to make a living consistently over time requires working on the level at which agents are the shepherds watching over an actor's career. These shepherds lead actors to career goals presented by casting directors and producers while protecting them from the obstacles that come up along the way. Certainly any movement up the ladder in New York or Los Angeles requires the aid of an agent.

ACTING FOR MONEY

So far in this book we've talked about actors and agents in terms of their working relationship. We've discussed their responsibilities to each other, and how they go about finding one another and booking employment together. Because this book focuses on acting in terms of show business, it is necessary to spend some time discussing how the players get paid. We have now come to that time. You've heard the expression, "There's no such thing as a free lunch." That becomes the motto of the actor who has crossed over to being a professional. Once he has become a professional—acting for money—he may become very stingy about donating his artistic services, because his acting now has monetary value. His agents are close by to negotiate the price of the goods and the terms of the transaction. Livelihoods are at stake here; therefore, issues about money do, indeed, matter—as the title of this chapter suggests. The subject of money brings up a variety of important issues that significantly influence the relationship between actors and agents. It's helpful when actors know the protocol for handling such business activities as agent commissions, "thank you's" and gifts, and invitations to shows and opening nights. "Getting it right"— following protocol—as one agent says, can make all the difference in an actor's career. This chapter means to clarify financial issues, answer questions actors may have, and justify the ways in which agents prefer these matters to be handled by actors. Let's start with the subject of agent commissions.

AGENT COMMISSIONS

People pay to see actors perform. Actors are paid to perform. Agents are paid when their clients perform and get paid. Depending on the structure of the agency, agents are paid in one of three ways: they receive either a weekly salary, a commission for the jobs they book, or sometimes a combination of the two. Since an agency makes money on a commission basis, it makes money only when its clients are working— and sometimes, depending on the salary amount, not even then. Many of our clients, for instance, do "freebies": non-paying workshops or showcases. They participate in these projects for various reasons: to perform in New York City where casting directors can see them, to get in a new project that might develop into a money-maker, to simply keep the creative juices flowing. Since agents can't make a commission on a salary of zero, these freebies are booked entirely for the development of an actor's career or artistic soul—and, on some rare occasions, both. The actor and agent alike hope that these projects will lead to a financial payoff down the road...and the agent hopes that when this happens she will still be representing the actor.

It is important for actors to understand that during the time agents are helping them secure employment by making submissions and phone calls, setting up auditions, and handling callbacks, they are virtually working for free, because they receive no payment for their services until their clients actually book jobs. Consequently, agents don't see paying commission to them as a matter of choice for an actor. These commissions are our livelihood, and the actors' performing unions back us up on this.

All three actors' unions are very clear on the subject of commissions. The AEA, SAG, and AFTRA Exclusive Agency Management Contracts, which both agent and actor sign in agreement, state that an actor agrees to pay to the agent commission on *all* monies received on jobs booked "directly" or "indirectly" during the term of the agency contract. This means that when an actor signs with an agency, he agrees to pay commission on work that the agency generates for him, as well as on work he books for himself. Many actors, when they sign with us, ask whether they are obligated to pay commission on jobs they've booked for themselves during the term of our contract. The answer, according to the management contract they sign, is "yes." When an actor is signed to an agency, he pays commission on all jobs booked during the term of the contract. The general rule is that salary is always commissionable, along with dubbing, fitting fees, holding fees, overtime, and travel time; while items such as per diem, living expenses, and meal, prop, and wardrobe allowances are not. For a more detailed listing of items that are commissionable versus non-commissionable, you may go to your unions. Note that commission is paid on the gross — the amount of money received before taxes are taken out.

THE PACKAGE INCLUDES THE PAST

An actor once wrote to my column with a particular commission question that I think is important to share at this time. After having worked in regional theater for many years, he moved to New York and signed with an agent. He wondered if he was expected to pay commission to the agent on any jobs that came in through the personal contacts he had established over the years. Many actors, like this one, view their professional lives as two separate entities: life *before* agent, and life *with* agent. They don't realize that what they bring to an agency at the time of signing is the sum total of all their experience up to that point, and that the journey onwards continues from there: the past influences the present and the present holds influence over the future. An actor offers his talent, experience, and contacts. These comprise the finely tuned "package" that attracted the agent's attention to begin with. In signing, the agent has committed herself to build on this foundation and enable the actor's rise to new heights. The two embark as equal partners on a business relationship that is mutually beneficial.

Here's a short story that addresses this particular issue: A colleague of mine and I traveled to Boston to see a client we had put in a show. While there we took in another show, at a neighboring theater. We had done business with this theater company over the years, booking our clients in its productions and representing many graduates of its training program, so we were curious to actually view some of the work. We saw a marvelous production of *The Cherry Orchard* with a particularly brilliant actor hitherto unknown to us. He had spent twenty years honing his craft in prominent regional theaters throughout the country. When we met him after the show, we convinced him that the time was right for him to move to New York City.

He signed with the agency and we embarked on a full assault of the New York casting community. We submitted him for every project for which he was remotely right. We were not wrong in our hunch. Each office we submitted him to responded favorably, first on the basis of his photo and impressive credits (and our sell), later on the word-of-mouth from casting directors dishing with each other. He spent three months in New York auditioning like crazy. Although he got lots of callbacks and great feedback from the casting directors (obvious from the continuous calls that came into our office asking to see him for projects), he didn't book a single job during that time. When he received a job offer from one of the many directors with whom he had worked over the years, he decided to take it. He pointed to family obligations and the need to make some money, plus his artistic need to act. After all, he had been performing steadily for many years, and a life of auditioning without booking or working was beginning to affect his confidence. He needed to do a play. The agency understood all of that; we were very sympathetic. There was no mention of any commission coming our way because his being signed to the agency *obligated* him to pay us commission, and we felt entirely entitled to it. This commission would be payment for the work we had already done and would continue to do while he was away working. We had just invested three months of our time introducing him to the New York market, and now he planned to go out of circulation for two months. It was appropriate that some money come into the office during the time he would be out of circulation as part of our client roster. When an agent makes a commitment to represent an actor and the actor goes out of circulation, the agent loses out on the opportunity to submit this actor and make money—unless, of course, being out of circulation results from booking a job that the agent receives commission on. The commission coming in serves as a retainer of sorts and goes towards keeping the agency in business—specifically, in business for the actor. Our job is to represent the client's interests on the current contract of employment that he is fulfilling, while also seeking opportunities of employment for when that job ends.

When an actor has had a long-standing relationship with a regional theater, it is sometimes possible for his new agent to ask for a "plus ten" on a job, especially if it's to return to play the company's Scrooge, as he's done for the last five *Christmas Carols*. In these instances, the producers are so appreciative of the actor's past service that they will generously pay the extra ten percent to support his career-building step of acquiring an agent. Keep in mind that it is always a good policy to mention such long-time relationships to your agent at the time of signing, so as to avoid any misunderstandings down the road. We had a client once who came to us after having spent a decade as a company member at one of the top regional theaters in the country. At the time of signing with the agency, at his request we agreed to accept a five percent (rather than ten percent) commission on any jobs he did at that theater during the term of our contract.

Decreasing Commissions

The Actors' Equity Exclusive Agency Management Contract provides a specific ceiling for salary that determines commissionable versus non-commissionable jobs. The contract states that when an actor's salary for a job falls below a certain number, the actor is excused from paying the agent the standard ten percent commission and is allowed instead to pay him a $100 fee. Every year many legit agents note with dismay that the ceiling amount determining commissionable jobs gets higher, while our commission rate remains the same ten percent. As salaries for commissionable jobs become higher, one might suppose that they would promise higher commission earnings for agents. But this supposition would forget the simple truth that higher salaries bring tougher competition and fewer chances of bookings. On the other hand, startup jobs that young talent need to book, to begin their journeys as professionals in the business, usually don't pay commissions— leaving the agent with no money for all her work. In the end, this harms actors, because more and more agents refuse to work on these projects. They simply can't afford to, and that leaves much of their client base jobless and frustrated.

As a side note, I might point to a trend in another part of the business, which affects employment and money-earning opportunities for actors and agents. As I write this, economic adjustments are being made in the daytime-drama sector that directly influence an actor's pay, and thereby an agent's commissions. One agent has noted sadly that the activity in this arena used to be enough to support an entire agent desk at an agency. Times have changed: These days new contract roles have dwindled to maybe two or three a year on each of the soaps, mostly in the eighteen- to twenty-five-year-old bracket. I recently met up with an agent who's been in the business a long time. He is a manager now, specializing in the youth market. When I asked him how he was doing, he said, "Great! I have a couple of kids on the soaps!" That's fine for him, but those of us who handle adult talent are finding more and more that the soaps write supporting players as under-fives rather than as day players, which, of course, impinges on wage and commission earnings for actors and agents. Quite frankly, for the agent, there is little financial gain in suggesting clients for jobs that don't pay a commission. Would you want to work for free? At least a salary with a plus ten would more be acceptable. A casting director from one of the soaps called me once looking to book a particular client of mine. This client happened to be unavailable for the day's work, so I suggested another actor whom the casting director did not know. I faxed the actor's photo and résumé over, did my sales pitch, and the casting director decided to set him up to audition the following day. The actor got the job and the offer came in at a time when AFTRA (the union with jurisdiction over the soaps) was adjusting its salary minimums. An actor who is paid scale under AFTRA is not obligated to pay agent commission, but I wasn't aware that the day-player salary offered for this job was the new minimum. I thought it represented scale plus ten. (See page 112 for a definition.) When it came time for the actor, who was a freelance client, to pay us commission on the job, he asked AFTRA what to do. It advised him not to pay anything, because his salary came in at minimum. This was upsetting to us. This actor booked this job as a direct result of our suggesting him to the casting director. I don't think our not asking for a plus ten (an innocent oversight on our part) was grounds enough for not paying us a commission. Had the actor seen it differently and paid us a commission willingly as acknowledgement and appreciation of our efforts on his behalf, he would still be a client of the office today… which he is not. An actor's approach to paying commissions—whether generous or stingy—affects the actor-agent relationship. When an agent senses that an actor is trying to avoid paying commissions, we take notice and are less willing to submit that actor for other jobs.

Returning to Actors' Equity's jurisdiction: another area in which its management contract differs from the other unions' involves commissions on Production Contract salaries. This contract—Equity's most lucrative—pertains solely to Broadway shows and national tours. Under a Production Contract actors are usually paid minimum salaries during the rehearsal period, so they are allowed to pay their agents five percent commission at that time. During performances, when the salary increases, the commission rate goes up to the standard ten percent. This makes total sense to an agent because minimum rehearsal pay is usually half of what minimum performance pay turns out to be. On the other hand, AEA's ruling that allows chorus members to stop paying agents commission after one year of performing in a show disturbs agents. Although this protects actors from lazy agents who put their clients in ensembles of shows and "forget" to service them while collecting commission, it ignores agents who continue to service their clients in these assignments and have come to rely on this commission to help cover salary, budget, or office overhead.

Our office booked an actor in the ensemble of a Broadway show where he remained for several years. Although we continued to service him with auditions for other shows and the occasional audition for a TV or film spot, as per Equity rules, he stopped paying us commission on the theater job at the end of his first year in the show. It didn't seem right to his agents that this actor was benefiting from the agency's resources without having any financial obligation for its solvency and continued existence.

Somewhere along the line agents got a bum rap. They were given the nickname of "ten-percenters," implying that they stop at nothing to get their ten percent, while providing very little service for it. A lifelong client of the agency tells the story of how he got his first agent when he moved to New York City thirty years ago. He was offered a job in a Broadway show through the recommendation of a friend. The same friend advised him to attract an agent by offering him the contract to negotiate. The actor found an agent who agreed to take him on as a client and negotiate the contract. What the actor later found out, however, was that the agent hadn't done any negotiating—in fact, he had settled for a salary that was much lower than the other cast members' and had proceeded to collect commission without offering much service during their time together. An actor would want to avoid working with that kind of an agent.

But agents can be taken for a ride, too, so most are very cautious about taking on an actor who holds out a contract needing negotiation as bait for representation. If we have no previous knowledge of the actor and his work, we will pass on the opportunity, unless the actor comes highly recommended by a significant source. If we have a prior relationship with the actor but know at the outset that the contract in question is virtually non-negotiable, we might agree to negotiate the deal for five percent (half of the standard ten percent commission), at the same time agreeing to represent the actor's interest on all business pertaining to this contract while also submitting him or her for future projects. A freelance client who had been working with the office for several months, enjoying many introductions to new casting directors through lots of auditions, was offered an ensemble position on the first sit-down company of a Broadway show in a major city. She booked this through a contact she had established before working with us, but as a matter of good will and insurance of our working relationship, agreed to pay the agency five percent commission. Since the deal came in at scale with no room for negotiation, we agreed to handle the negotiations at renewal time, when we felt we could better the terms, thereby earning a full commission. We also agreed to continue to submit her for principal roles in other shows.

Contracts for ensemble positions with Disney shows, popular Broadway productions, and cruise ships, among others, usually come in at union minimum or a salary with absolutely no negotiation. In these situations the best an agent can do is run interference on any problems that develop along the way regarding salary payment, part assignments, dealing with general managers and stage managers, etc., then go for better salary and terms at re-negotiation time. Sometimes, however, agents can break through. We had a client once who was offered a principal role in one of the "Special Production Contract" touring shows that enable producers to hire union members for significantly smaller amounts than the standard production contracts. The salary came in as very low, considering the importance of the role and the customary amount one would expect to be offered. Both the casting director and general manager stated that there was no negotiation, but the agent *was* able to negotiate a higher amount and several perks. At times like this, it's especially good to have an agent negotiating your contract.

Refuting the Stereotype

It's hard for agents to refute the persistent misconception that we are money-grubbers. Too often we hear stories like this one: An actor was performing in a national tour and his agent wanted to see him in the production. The actor asked management for a pair of comps for his agent, who was making a special trip to see the show. The general manager refused to provide comps, stating that the agent was gypping his client and could easily pay for the tickets; besides which all agents were just money-grubbing…(you fill in the expletives). The actor defended his agent, who also happened to be a personal friend. He described how the agent had devoted his entire career to working in the legit theater, and how anyone in the business should know that this hardly pays for luxury living. The general manager eventually relented, coughing up a couple of tickets. Most agents I know work extremely hard, because they have to. Our livelihoods depend on our success in seeking out auditions for actors, giving them plenty of opportunities to book jobs.

One agent expressed the feelings of many of us when he justified the payment of commission on all work gained during the term of an exclusive agreement. He stated that in doing so, an actor pays for all the efforts that the agent has made on his behalf that haven't resulted in commission-bearing employment. Unlike lawyers, for instance, agents don't charge by the hour for their services. The submissions, phone calls, faxes, and advice-giving aren't paid for until the client actually books a job. In essence, much of the time agents work for free; we are paid for our services only when our clients actually make money for their work. Understanding this concept is crucial to understanding the mind of an agent. Actors, while expecting their agents to get them many auditions on a daily basis, don't notice that it can sometimes take months before these auditions result in commission-bearing work. Clients often fail to realize that they have been receiving free service from their agents until the moment when the work is booked and the commission paid. That an actor would question paying commission on jobs when he finally does book them seems totally illogical to an agent. These commissions are the return on our investment in his career.

The agent-actor freelance relationship is murkier. When an actor free-lances with several different agents at the same time, he pays commission to the agent who books him on a particular job, usually signing a special management contract issued by the union to cover the business end of that job. Sometimes it is difficult to establish where and when and by whose efforts a connection leading to employment was first established. During the time they work with an actor, agents make many submissions and phone calls, and take other actions that push a client to casting directors. That's why agents prefer the protection of working with signed clients under a management contract that allows them to contractually collect commission on all work booked during the term of the contract. Say that a job is offered directly to a client—that is, the casting director or general manager phones the actor instead of the agent (trying to avoid a negotiation, perhaps?). Who's to say that job offer didn't start with a connection made by the agent months or even years earlier? If that client has been signed to the agency throughout those months or years, the commission goes to the agency. If he isn't signed, the job's genesis is hard to trace and remuneration depends on the actor's sense of loyalty.

As a freelancer, you may work with more than one agent. Although it's difficult to trace back connections, including an agent in the "business" surrounding a job offer supports and strengthens whatever relationship you have with that agent. Plus, the actor stands to gain much in the way of expert advice and career-enhancing action. Let me give two examples that illustrate this point: In the first, our agency booked a freelance client in a job at a theater in Maine. The actress loved working there—it was her home state and many family members resided there—and the producers enjoyed having her as part of the company. When that same theater decided to cast her in another play later that season, they called her directly with the offer instead of calling the agent who had booked and negotiated her previous job. Being an actress of integrity and wanting to solidify her relationship with the agency, she brought the contract to the office and offered to pay us commission on the job. She knew that it had resulted mainly from the business connection established previously by the agency. She felt the money was due the agency, and she was right.

Another freelance client handled a similar situation very differently. One spring I called this actress with an audition for a summer job. She informed me that she was unavailable because she was returning to do a job at the theater I had booked her in the previous summer. I was totally surprised to hear this because neither the theater, the casting director, nor my client had ever called me to discuss the offer. During our conversation, the actress made no mention of paying us commission. I felt cheated because I had been responsible for connecting her to that theater in the first place, and was entitled to collect commission on any monies emanating from that business relationship. My not wanting to see a future introduction end in the same way led to an estrangement, ending the relationship we had been building over several years.

Some actors feel strongly that they have a stake in the financial security of the agency that services them. They pay their commissions happily as a gesture of thanks, knowing that this money helps to keep the agency functioning. We represent an actress whose specialty is playing a particular role in a play that is done frequently throughout the States. She has worked with the agency for many years and is extremely thankful for our efforts on her behalf. Recently she booked a high-paying job through us, which she hopes to repeat for many years—

in a major holiday show in New York. Last summer this actress worked various jobs that came to her directly through her own connections. She offered to pay us commission on them as a way of thanking us for all the hard work we had done on her behalf and that she hoped we would continue to do. Agents appreciate such generosity, and their appreciation shows up in a renewed sense of purpose and dedication to promoting an actor's career.

I would caution actors against keeping employment secrets from their agents. True: many folks are strapped for money. Sometimes it's very hard to take that ten percent out of your paycheck each week and send it to your agent. But doing business on the side—participating in projects without your agent's knowledge or involvement—will backfire at some point, either financially or in terms of your working relationship with him. An actor I knew had so many connections from his days in the avant-garde theater that he was continually doing projects. Many times his agents had no idea what he was up to, even though they continued to submit him for and book him in productions. One of his "mystery" workshops went the distance and found itself having a series of presentations in New York under the auspices of an important Broadway producer. His agents found out about this workshop when they began to negotiate a job they had booked him that turned out to be a total conflict. Ultimately, it was the agents' involvement in scheduling and keeping a dialogue going between the producers of the two projects that enabled the actor to do both. More importantly, the agents made sure to negotiate a buy-out clause in the workshop contract. They knew that high-prestige workshops in New York offer actors the chance to develop material to the level that it can attract a celebrity's attention for future productions. A buy-out clause protects an actor's involvement in a workshop by stipulating that he gain financially from subsequent productions even if his part is recast with a different actor. It became very clear how fortunate it was for this actor that his agents had stepped in at the right time. When he saw a different celebrity in the audience at each performance, he began to realize that they were checking out his leading role for a future Broadway production in which they would potentially star. He was disappointed, of course, but relieved to have that buy-out clause. Whether or not he intended to avoid a financial responsibility to his agents on this project, it was clear that without his agents handling the business on it, he might very well have been left with nothing but a fine memory when all was said and done. When it comes to paying your agent commissions, being penny wise but pound foolish can look a lot like biting the hand that feeds you.

How Agents Get Paid

Let's turn now to a discussion of how agents get paid. A talent agency is a licensed employment agency that books actors in jobs and receives payment in the form of commissions on the salaries of those jobs. As noted earlier, agents are paid either a base salary (pooled from commissions), a commission, or a combination of the two. The money that comes to them as commission is usually part of a larger sum that has been split with the agency. Splits range from sixty-forty to thirty-seventy.

All three unions state that an actor should pay commissions to his agent when monies are received by the actor—which means *as soon as you get your paycheck!* At small- to medium-sized agencies, commissions sometimes pay for the company's overhead. I remember attending a meeting once in which lots of agents were discussing a variety of issues. When it came time to focus on collecting commissions on small theater contracts, an agent from one of the big agencies magnanimously spoke on behalf of the struggling actor, making a case to forego collecting commissions on these small salaries. An owner-agent from a mid-sized agency leapt to his feet to vociferously defend his need and right to collect these commissions. He said it was all very well for the big agency to waive these moneys it perceived to be mere drops in a bucket. He explained that for most agencies like his, these commissions were not only the result of hard labor, but many times kept the electricity turned on.

How actors are paid and how they pay their agents' commissions differ with the type of job. Most theaters pay the actor directly. Payroll departments of television and film projects usually send the actor's paycheck to the agency. It then gets sent to the client who will, upon receipt, send a commission check back to the office. Sometimes—and this is true for large commercial agencies with talent payment departments—the paycheck is put through the agency's account, and a check for monies minus the agency commission is sent to the actor. Many agencies do not have a business affairs or accounting department to take care of collecting commissions when they are due. Actors who are good business partners pay their agents on time without a reminder. Doing so is part of a solid actor-agent relationship.

Not paying commission and letting things slide will only lead to an erosion of your relationship with your agent. Your agent will resent having to chase down a commission that he's already earned; and the longer you resist paying it, the more you'll resent having to pay it. Don't let things get to that point. If you know you have a problem with money, try to get a handle on it. If things are unusually tight for you financially, call your agent to work out a payment plan. You'll find that if the situation is dealt with openly, as between partners, he is really very understanding about collecting commissions.

One client we work with knows he has a problem with money, so he asks us to make sure each theater that employs him includes an "agency clause" in the contract. This is a clause in the rider attached to the employment contract, which allows the theater to deduct the agency's commission from the actor's salary and send that commission directly to the agency. Many actors, like this client, request this clause because it relieves them of the responsibility of paying their agents directly.

Producers working under SAG and AFTRA contracts don't usually separate commissions from actors' paychecks. They will pay a "plus ten" (the commission on top of the actor's salary) on a scale job, for instance, but that money will usually be included in the paycheck sent to the actor. It's up to the actor to do the math (divide the gross salary by eleven) and send the commission check to the agent in the return mail. In some cases—especially on long-term film shoots that were booked at scale plus ten—the payroll departments of the production company will send a separate check to the agency for the entire commission. Sometimes an altogether separate entity—a talent payment service—will handle the payroll needs of a production.

A final thought on commissions. If you nickel-and-dime your agent, you will surely turn her into a "ten-percenter"—someone who works only for the money and not in the interests of building a career. If you begrudge your agent her due, you will force her to be a money-grubber. It's foolish for actors to weigh the number of bookings against auditions as a means of evaluating their agents' effectiveness in order to justify paying their commissions. An actor can never be fully "paid up." There will always be more auditions than bookings due to the competitive nature of the business. You can't blame your agent and a lack of auditions for your lack of bookings. If you don't think your agent is doing her job, or if you question the validity of having an agent at all, then it's time to reevaluate your relationship with her. Alternatively you can always experience an open call at Actors' Equity, where lining up outside in the cold beginning at seven a.m. won't necessarily guarantee you an audition.

Thank You's and Gifts

Several questions have come my way, through my column and from my clients, about the protocol of thanking agents and casting directors and giving presents. Actors want to know what is appropriate to give to an agent or casting director, and when such gifts are expected. They want to know what particular situations might call for a bouquet of flowers, for instance, above and beyond the customary verbal, "Thank you." They wonder whether the giving of a gift can ever be misinterpreted as a bribe for more activity. Since this chapter relates to "money matters," these questions find their place here.

First, let's look at the bigger picture: Show business is a business of relationships. The activity moves interdependently among the various players: actors, agents, casting directors, directors, writers, and producers. All work together to provide entertainment to the public. Nobody stands alone: Without writers, producers have no product and directors would have no job. Directors would also be jobless without actors—as would agents and casting directors. Conversely, actors need agents and casting directors to boost them up the ladder of success. You might have done the very first reading of a script two years ago in a famous playwright's living room, but when the play lands an Off-Broadway production and you want to audition for the part you read at the reading, you probably won't be able to reach the casting director without an agent—even though the playwright knows you and the director adores you. Your husband might be directing the world premiere of a new play at the Guthrie Theater, but you will probably need to get an appointment from the casting director to be seen for "your" role. There was a time when professional actors could gain access to important producers without help, but that era was on the way out fifty years ago.

Agents work hard to nurture and maintain their relationships with casting directors. The routine activities of submitting, phoning, and pushing build the relationship between salesman (agent) and buyer (casting director), and actors benefit when that interplay is effective. Routine advances in the careers of actors are generally acknowledged between agents and casting directors with verbal thanks and praise. When a casting director calls in a client whom I submitted for an audition, I thank him for the appointment—and try, at the same time, to get more auditions for other actors. When the casting director agrees to see a client I've pushed and the client gets a callback, the casting director might offer praise to which I respond with a polite, "Thank you"—resisting the temptation to gloat over the victorious result from my push. Agents encourage their actors to maintain relationships with casting directors by thanking them, usually through notes in the mail. Once in a while, a casting director goes beyond the call of duty to do something magical, like giving an actor a second chance after he bombed at the first audition. Or sometimes a real career breakthrough occurs, like a client booking her first TV pilot. In such cases, special acknowledgment, usually by the actor, is required to show appreciation and celebration.

I still believe that thank-you notes are the most appropriate way for actors to follow up on first interviews with agents and on meetings and/or auditions with casting directors. They show good manners and appreciation for the time given. I would suggest that actors try to avoid making them sound or look like corporate outpourings from a well-oiled marketing machine. That diminishes their individuality. Keep them brief, handwritten, and personalized. These thank-you notes work on many different levels. Such correspondence builds a bridge of communication in the time between meetings and auditions, thereby reinforcing the relationships that will sustain and, hopefully, move an actor's career forward. It builds on the first impression of your initial meeting, and welcomes the hoped for follow-up meeting, or even audition. Whether on photo postcards or attractive greeting cards with the actor's photo postcard enclosed, these notes enable an actor to express thanks for the meeting and/or audition, while getting his face and name noticed again without any demand for response—something both agents and casting directors greatly appreciate.

Giving presents is a trickier matter. Certainly, it is up to the giver to determine what, when, why, and to whom a gift is given. Let's be clear from the start: Agents *don't* expect clients to give them gifts for doing their normal day-to-day activities. A verbal "thank you" is just fine—plus paying your commissions on time, of course. Casting directors don't expect gifts, but aren't averse to receiving them. However, if a really big win occurs for which an agent feels somewhat responsible, some sort of acknowledgment in the form of a gift is appropriate. That gift should, of course, correspond to the nature of the win. Customary gifts are flowers or bottles of wine for the individual agents, or champagne for the entire office. Sometimes all it takes is recognition in the *Playbill*. (A mention at Tony or Oscar time is okay, too!) An actress booked a role in a reading of a musical that happened to be one of her agent's favorite musicals of all times. The agent's coaching had really helped her get that role. His being mentioned in the *Playbill* meant a great deal to him; it made up for the lack of commission on this prestigious but low-paying New York job.

Here are some examples of situations and the gifts offered as thanks: After struggling for many years in the business, a client booked a contract role on a daytime drama. The lush floral arrangement that was delivered to the office was a perfect expression of her gratitude for her double good fortune—the job itself and loyal agents who had stuck by her during the lean years. Another client, who booked a lead in a TV pilot, treated herself and her two agents to a wonderful lunch at a four-star restaurant. It was a grand celebration for all. Many clients bring treats from the nearby bakery to the office when they deliver headshots and résumés.

Can an actor ever go too far? Can generosity be misconstrued as obsequiousness? Let's just say it's important to keep a realistic perspective of how the business works in general. Part of an agent's job is to meet new actors. The same is true for casting directors. Anything beyond a verbal or written thank-you for a meeting and/or audition is questionable. Any gift, whether simple or extravagant, might put the agents and casting directors on the spot, embarrassing them rather than making them feel appreciated. Giving a gift in these circumstances could be interpreted as being more like "buying favor" than expressing thanks.

A word or two to those folks who drop off "care" packages filled with a hodgepodge of trinkets, candy, and thirty picture postcards of the actor seeking representation. While I haven't the heart not to accept the package brought to the office by an optimistic actor, I react very strongly against this form of solicitation. First of all, I'm a legit agent whose policy is to meet actors only after I've seen their work. A photo postcard—whether delivered personally or by mail—isn't going to make me change that policy. Second, I am highly selective about whom I choose to meet in the office, and the time spent in that meeting is real office time. It's time that I take away from doing business for my exclusive clients. It's time that can't be bought with an assortment of knick-knacks. This type of package might get more response from an agent like me if its purpose were to advertise a showcase in which the actor was appearing, giving me an opportunity to see his work.

Everybody likes to feel appreciated: whereas actors live for applause, agents flip to their client's program bio, hoping for a mention. It is good business for actors to make every effort to have these important players at their side at key events. They fit right alongside mother, father, wife, husband, or life partner. Agents want to be at opening nights—to celebrate the actor's good fortune and to protect their exclusive relationship from prowling competitors. When actors make sure to include their agents in such "hurrahs" (which management oftentimes neglects to do), they are spreading a great deal of good will that will benefit their own careers. I remember an incident from early in my agent life: I had just begun working at an agency and was meeting and establishing relationships with all of the clients. Suddenly I was called out of town to Florida on an emergency, to care for an ailing parent. The phone rang one morning, and when I picked up the receiver, the voice on the other end belonged to one of the agency's clients. He was calling to invite me to the opening night of the Broadway musical he was rehearsing. I can't tell you what an enormous impression was made on me by this phone call with its generous gift. The personal invitation and the fact that he had thought in advance to include me, a relative stranger, in this festive occasion (at great personal expense), established a bond that has influenced the excellent relationship we have had through the years—a relationship of mutual care, dedication, and respect. That the musical was written by my favorite composer was icing on the cake. It was a night to remember—my first Broadway opening and opening-night party at Sardi's.

Most times other than opening nights it's really the thought that counts, and a simple verbal or written expression of thanks is enough. If you do decide that giving a gift is more appropriate, remember that a smart gift doesn't have to be expensive. Be creative. The secret to effective gift giving is research. To discover what your agents would like, ask them discreetly, poke around for information from secretaries, listen to hints, and observe behaviors—then make choices according to your budget. Some presents that I have had the pleasure of receiving have included a gift certificate to a bookstore, a massage at a fancy salon, a plant (one holiday time a client gave each agent in the office a bonsai tree—very unusual), Grandma's home-baked chocolate-chip cookies, a yoga class, and movie tickets.

★

Whether you do so with words or a gift, remember that by thanking the folks who helped you get to where you are, you'll be renewing their attention so they can help you get to where you want to be. It's what you want to do to build a long-lasting relationship...for a long-lasting career!

Chapter 12

HELLO AND GOODBYE

For all of us the start of each experience, challenge, or moment offers the potential for something great to develop. Actors and agents are ever hopeful that each connection they make within the industry will lead to something good, that each "hello" will have a positive outcome. When actors and agents come together, actors are usually the more needy, but over time the partners develop a mutually beneficial relationship. Actors and their agents hope for long-term careers and long-term relationships or partnerships with each other. In some instances, the most productive relationship will be a long-lasting one between one actor and one agent or agency. In other cases, the partnership will healthily grow to a point, and then one or both participants will find that growth needs to continue in another direction, perhaps with another partner.

AN OVERVIEW

We've spent so much of this book detailing individual aspects of this important partnership. It's time now to put them all together and view the relationship in its evolution from first moments to transitioning times. The "hello's" and "good-bye's" of the actor-agent partnership, and what happens in between, are part of a greater universe. After all, "hello's" and "good-bye's" shape show business: each new production gives us a new family that, eventually, we leave behind. We all live in this reality.

No doubt about it: courtship is exciting. Actors who approach me for representation are for the most part polite, courteous, and respectful. Agents going after talent are attentive and complimentary, enthusiastic and full of purpose. Exclusivity, or "marriage," holds the expectation of great things and promises a long-lasting and deepening bond of purpose. The agent and actor click glasses of champagne at the time of signing and together they press on to realize a career's potential. The work has begun. What follows are the ups and downs of wins and losses brought about by the overall give-and-take of a personal and business partnership. Some partnerships last forever. I've known actors who have had one and only one agent their entire professional lives. Other associations have limited life spans. Familiarity can breed complacency and disinterest, and through the years keeping the romance alive gets harder and harder. Some alliances reach a certain point, then can't seem to break through to the next level. For example, we represented an actor for a good ten years, beginning at the time he graduated from acting school. When he decided to leave the agency, we felt that perhaps the timing was right for all of us. We realized that we had hit a ceiling of sorts in terms of submissions and bookings. He had been turning down whatever jobs had come his way, holding out for what he hoped would be better opportunities, and actually hadn't worked for a long time. We agreed to divorce.

Relationships go through hard times, and sometimes never recover from them. Situations develop that can sour an actor-agent relationship: myriad auditions that bring no job offers, a hard year financially, your entire network of friends moving forward in their careers while you remain in a holding pattern understudying celebrities—many circumstances can turn an actor from hopeful to despairing, and the first individual to feel the heat is the agent. The relationship between an actor and agent—this professional marriage—is easily influenced by the vicissitudes of the business. There is no way to forecast its duration or whether it will withstand the punches that show biz throws its way. At the beginning, all you can do is hope for the best.

AUSPICIOUS BEGINNINGS

I love beginnings. There's nothing like making a "discovery" and possessing the wherewithal to make something happen for an actor. I can see a show and witness a brilliant performance, then perhaps end up helping to create a career or propel a lagging one. How does the courtship actually begin? The day after the performance I call the membership department of one of the unions—usually Actors' Equity because it is the easiest to get through to—and ask for the actor's contact number. If I'm given a service or cell phone number I will call him. During the call I introduce myself, refer to the performance I just saw, and ask whether the actor has representation. If he doesn't, as I've expected because the union gave me no agency contact, I will invite the actor to the office for an interview to "explore" possibilities of working together. Most actors are very excited by this prospect.

If the union gives a legit agency as the contact number for an actor, I most likely won't make the call. I am not in the business of stealing other agents' clients. It's a karma thing: I don't want to do it because I don't want it done to me. That's pretty naïve because it happens anyway, but at least my conscience is clean. There are times, however— at opening-night parties, for instance—where I might find myself on the buffet line, standing next to an actor whom I think is extraordinary, and ask whether he has representation. When he tells me has an agent, I might venture to inquire whether he is happy with his representation. If he says he is, as most actors do (after all it's opening night, so everybody is happy until the party thins out too early—a sure sign that the reviews aren't good), I will tell him how much I enjoyed his work, give him my card just in case he might find himself looking someday, and move along the dessert line. It's called planting a seed, and it's really quite innocent. Every agent does it.

Agents can go to great lengths to track down talent they want to represent. One time I patiently kept in touch with a young singer over the course of two years, until she became free to work with me. I had first seen her in an audition evening at her acting school, and thought she was very talented, if perhaps a bit green. At this point my choice was one we agents often have to make: do we take on a young actor whom we feel is very talented but lacks professional experience, or do we wait until he's more seasoned before working with him? In the former scenario, we stand the chance of spending a year submitting, phoning, and doing all the prep work that launching a career requires, without earning a penny for our efforts. In the latter scenario, by the time the actor is ready to be launched, he might have already found an agent who dared to invest in his career, and we would have missed our chance. That is precisely what happened with this actress. After graduating from acting school, she booked a job on a cruise ship. When I called her six months later, on her return, I was dismayed to learn that she had signed with another agent. Some months after that, she called to tell me that she feared she had made a big mistake in signing with the other agent, and she asked if would I reconsider representing her. I invited her to sing for the other agents in the office, who responded favorably. After making sure she was legally free of her contract with the other agency, our office started representing her exclusively, planning to sign papers at her first booking.

Beginnings are leaps of faith. When an agent starts working with an actor, she has no real idea of what will happen. This business is such a gamble; it's as much hunch and luck as anything else, and although actors might wish it so, agents don't have crystal balls. Certainly, they can predict general patterns and scenarios of career development: Jobs in regional theater can lead to work in New York on and Off-Broadway. An appearance in a successful New York show can gain the notice of television and film casting directors, leading to work in those mediums and possibly a move to Los Angeles. However, many a career does not take a linear path to success, and beyond a general educated and hopeful guess defies an agent to anticipate its journey.

When an actor starts working with an agent, he, too, is making a leap of faith. He must trust his instincts for making the right choice, and believe that the agent will do her utmost to make things happen.

After all, isn't it in everybody's best interests for her to do so? Even in the slowest of times, an actor must believe that his agent is working to change the tide. He must realize that in this business, nothing stays the same. An actor's life can literally turn around overnight. One day you might be wondering how you'll pay the month's rent. The next day you book a position in the ensemble of a national tour and your challenge then is to find a subletter.

Audition Cycles

Many actors wonder what happens after they've signed with an agent. How long does it take before things start to cook? When should they begin to worry? What should they do if they don't hear from their agent for, say, three weeks?

A newly formed alliance with an agent takes a while to bear fruit. Variables include the time of year, where the actor is positioned within the industry, and just plain what projects are auditioning at the time of signing. In any case, actors should expect a startup lag of at least a couple of weeks before the headshots and résumés included in the agent's submissions yield auditions. Casting directors need a little time to notice that an actor has been added to an agent's client list. Of course, the agent will usually promote this addition by chatting up the actor to the casting director at the appropriate moment.

June and July are customarily slower months because the industry slows down for summer vacations. Broadway shows are up and running, capitalizing on whatever Tony Awards they've won from the big celebration at the beginning of June. Regional theater seasons running from September through May are supplanted by summer Shakespearean festivals and summer stock theaters that were cast in the spring. True, indie and feature films that are set in the summer take advantage of the appropriate weather; and in New York City, where television episodics used to go on summer hiatus, now many series shot for cable seem to pick up to shoot their full seasons during the summer months. (Los Angeles customarily devotes the summer to episodic television.) Overall, though, the industry is slow.

August and September heat up with the casting of fall and winter projects and the return of network TV's episodics after their summer hiatus. We had a newly signed client once who spent the summer after college driving a cab to build a nest egg. He moved to New York City in the early fall and dropped by the office one day shortly after his arrival to say, "hey." I picked up the phone and immediately got him two auditions. Ah, the power of an agent—or maybe I was just lucky that day. The real point here is that especially during the slow times actors should remember casting is cyclical. There are weeks when the breakdowns are heavily musical, and there is, indeed, a TV pilot season. Summer stock auditions come in a flurry, while regional theaters cast fall, winter, spring, and summer shows periodically throughout the year. A client can sometimes have three auditions in one week, followed by callbacks, then face three weeks of relative silence from the agency. Mostly this has nothing to do with the actor's talent, or how he did on past auditions. There just aren't any new ones. It's how the casting cycle works out.

AUDITION PROBLEMS

An area of concern for actors and agents alike are auditions—those pathways (or obstacles) to bookings. As I noted earlier, legit agents generally decide to represent an actor after seeing him in a show or showcase, or after viewing a demo reel of television and film clips. True, our office and others like ours set aside time for singing auditions specifically, because they are easy to organize and provide an economical way to judge talent. However, when it comes to straight acting, we would rather see an actor perform in a show with other actors than do a monologue in the office. We view the latter as an artificial and incomplete rendering of his work. The problem with finding talent in shows and showcases, however, is that although an agent might be captivated by the actor's work in performance, she has no idea how he auditions—and by this point in the book we all know how important that skill is in building an actor's career. The agent *assumes* that the actor must audition well—after all, he did book the show she just saw him be brilliant in, right? But this is not always the case. Sometimes actors get jobs through connections, without having to audition. A member of a resident theater company, for instance, is usually assigned his roles for the season by the artistic director. Many of the best regional theater actors coming out of the great repertory companies across the country have been acting for years without having to audition once. That's one reason that being a company member of a resident theater is so enticing. (Having a steady paycheck is another.) Agents who find great actors in performance take their chances regarding the actors' auditioning skills, so we monitor these when we start working together.

When an actor is in denial about his faulty audition technique, an agent has a very serious problem on her hands. After many auditions result in no callbacks and trustworthy casting directors report specific problems, an agent knows that attention must be paid. We once represented a lovely actress. I had seen her be wonderful a number of times in performance, but we had it on good authority that her audition skills needed tweaking. Refusing to admit having a problem, she left her agents at a loss as to what to suggest, and we could only watch the audition opportunities and job bookings dwindle. When a client resists facing facts—especially facts presented by people who are in a position to initiate job opportunities—it usually leads to a parting of the ways between actor and agent. A lack of bookings due to a lack of auditions frustrates an actor. Either he leaves the agency in search of different representation (which does not address the audition technique problems) or the agent decides not to re-sign him.

DROPPING CLIENTS

Sometimes agents "fire" clients. If an actor doesn't pull his weight financially, the agency can opt not to renew its exclusive management contract. One agent estimates that the agency where he works spends $1,000 a year to subsidize each client. This figure represents the cost of all the submissions, phone calls, other marketing expenses, and office overhead that comprise an agency's investment in an actor's career for one year. This agent strongly supports his agency's policy of dropping actors who, after a certain amount of time, haven't "earned" back that investment.

I know of an actor who was signed to an agency in Los Angeles and doing pretty well. Or so he thought. Until he discovered that his idea of doing well—working consistently in a few plays, doing supporting roles in films, making guest appearances on TV shows, and having a recurring role on a popular nighttime drama—wasn't good enough for the agency. Looking for talent that booked "higher" roles, it decided to let him go. Does this mean that no one is ever truly secure in his representation? Not necessarily. It just points to the fact that each side of the partnership is not immune to the other's evaluation. Each can take action to switch partners.

ASSESSING YOUR AGENT

When an actor doesn't hear from his agent in a few weeks, several questions run through his mind. Is she submitting him? If not, why not? If so, why aren't the casting directors biting? The actor might begin to question his agent's effectiveness. I would suggest that before you take action on a similar assessment, you do some investigating. Ask your friends in the business how they're doing. If, for instance, everybody is complaining about how slow things are, why should they be that much different for you? I remember one year when three Broadway shows closed within a week and an Off-Broadway show with great reviews announced its untimely closing. Such events have repercussions in the industry, affecting everybody's lives. Oftentimes actors, each so involved with his individual survival, don't see the big picture; therefore, they lack full understanding of the larger forces that might be affecting their personal struggles.

I think problems in the actor-agent partnership start when actors begin to blame the direction their careers are taking on their agents. True, an agent does bear responsibility for the development of a career—after all, we make the submissions, we get the auditions, we do the deals, we advise. However, an actor's talent and particular gifts are the stuff of which that career is made. Agents develop the structures; actors provide the materials. Together they build careers.

Actors leave agents for a number of reasons. They want more auditions, more TV and film work. They feel neglected by their agents. Sometimes significant others can cause a rift, sometimes a manager, sometimes other actors. No matter where the sense of dissatisfaction, frustration, or restlessness originates, the ramifications are unsettling.

A young client who came in to say goodbye went to great lengths to tell us what wonderful agents we had been. When we asked why he was leaving and what he thought his new agents would do differently for him, he replied that it was a matter of auditions. The new agents promised to "get him out more." We asked him where his new agents had seen his work to be able to know how to submit him and fulfill this promise. He said that all that they had seen was the monologue he did for them in their office. We thought this odd because we knew that the actor had worked consistently for seven years in jobs we had booked him in since he signed with the agency after graduating from conservatory. He had appeared in international and national tours, on Broadway and on some television programs, most recently participating in a number of high-profile New York workshops. There had been ample opportunity for prospecting agents to "sample the goods." This actor chose to sacrifice an agency that had invested time and energy in his career for seven years; we had introduced him to various casting directors and had made significant efforts to see his work in performance (sometimes traveling great distances to do so). Now agents who were virtual strangers to him would reap the benefit. Aside from the possible opportunities that this agency's L.A. office might offer, the move made no sense at all.

An agency that devotes a lot of its energy, resources, and time to developing talent faces situations like this again and again. We struggle for years to build the careers of actors who inch up the ladder of success by climbing the alphabet of LORT theaters from D to B+, or who rise from ensemble roles in national tours to featured roles in Broadway musicals. Then just when the client seems to be on the verge of a big career breakthrough, we learn that he is leaving our agency for one that has promised him more. As much as I love beginnings, I hate these endings. They make an agent question all the hard work she has done, or will continue to do—for other clients, because she feels robbed of enjoying the reward of the big career breakthrough. We wonder how seven years of hard work get traded in so quickly, and how we could ever have allowed ourselves to be in this position—with someone else reaping the financial rewards of the structure we had helped to build during the lean times. It's not just the money, though: it's the partnership—the marriage. We have a personal relationship with each client and, frankly, it hurts to be left for someone else. We still believe that we can do more for the client than the interloper (particularly one who hasn't bothered to see the client's work). We grieve over the loss of the past, but also over the loss of the future we imagined together.

It's only natural for an actor who's not working to develop a roving eye for agents. For that matter, few actors *with* jobs and agents are immune from flattery. It's human nature to be enticed by the attention of—or an offer from—a new-found suitor. But beware...

We had a client who was doing quite nicely, working steadily in good theaters and making a good living. Out of genuine interest and support, we traveled long distances to see some of that work. I remember one time when our trip to see him in *Long Day's Journey into Night* took longer than the play's performance. (And that was just one way.) One of the jobs we booked him in was at a theater in Florida where a celebrity was playing the lead. When the celebrity's agent came to see the show, he made a play for our client, who completely caved in to his attentions and promises. The actor left us for greener pastures and a couple of years later I bumped into him at a performance space in downtown New York, where he was directing a one-act. When I asked him what he had been up to, he mumbled very sheepishly that he hadn't acted in a while.

Actors, be cautious: There are agents who feed off the emotions of performers, wooing them with promises that can't be kept. Whether it's the thrill of the chase with its momentary high of capture, wishful thinking, or misguided helpfulness, these agents appeal to the insecurities of an actor who may or may not be feeling neglected by his current agent...but who certainly will be if the bug is put in his ear.

These agents prey on actors with the common desire to work more in television and film. Every New York actor demands his day on *Law & Order*, declaring that all of his friends are on the show—why isn't he? A responsible legit agent answers this demand in one of several ways, depending on the client's level of experience in the business. If the actor is a beginner, the agent will stress the importance of learning on-camera technique and acquiring some experience in front of the camera. She will explain how difficult it is to find work in this highly competitive arena. After all, how likely is it that an unknown would be cast as a series regular on a nighttime drama, when well-known TV and film celebrities are playing one-scene roles? Films are just as competitive. As I've noted earlier, film casting in New York City is actor specific (the casting directors come to New York to see specified actors at a producer, director, or writer's request). Even indie films—once the bastion of film-career breakthroughs—no longer offer opportunities for unknowns to break through; instead they cast actors whose names lever funding and publicity. In New York, if an actor has New York theatrical credits or strong regional theater credits, a crossover into TV and film might be possible through the submissions and pushes of a determined agent. The same holds true in cities like Chicago or Baltimore, where local casting directors pull from their pool of actors for projects shooting in the area. How successfully these casting doors can be opened has a lot to do with type and luck. Hundreds of pretty young women are competing for a handful of suitable roles on television, whereas blue-collar men in their 40s seem to have their pick of roles on each TV breakdown.

Legit agents commonly complain of those clients who leave them after years of successful career building, for an agency offering TV and film opportunities that never come through. The former agents continue to see their former clients in theatrical productions that they could have easily placed them in, and the years go by without evidence of that "promised" TV or film breakthrough. I advise all actors to be very careful and to always weigh the pros and cons of their choices thoroughly before making any big decisions. Bigger, more expensive, and flashier doesn't necessarily mean better. One client left her loyal agents of five years to sign up with a new agency that promised TV and film opportunities. After a year's investment with no return for their time and money, the agency dropped her.

DEALING WITH OBSTINATE CLIENTS

Part of an agent's job is to offer counsel to clients. For this we rely on our good judgment, derived from knowledge and experience. Particularly frustrating for an agent are those times when a client refuses to consider the opinions and justifications offered by the agent to resolve dilemmas or promote career advancement. When a client begins to question or doubt this advice, especially after hours of consultation, there is little an agent can do to prevent the inevitable. These "differences" of opinions usually lead to a dissolving of the partnership. Where does this doubt or questioning come from? Perhaps from a protective manager, a jealous spouse, or an uninformed parent. Whatever the doubt's source, generally in these situations both actor and agent suffer from the ending of their relationship.

I am reminded of a client whom I had to convince to perform in a two-character play. Her stage partner would be a brilliant actress who was one of the great acting teachers of all time. My client didn't want to work for free and this production was starting as a showcase. I pointed out that the job was invaluable because she'd learn so much from working closely with this legendary actress; she had to do it. Convinced, our client went into the showcase. Later, while the production was negotiating to move to an Off-Broadway house, she auditioned for a contract role on a soap opera. She made it all the way to screen test—which she refused, because she didn't want anything to interfere with the play! What a reversal—and this coming from an actress who always screamed poverty. Using every angle of logic we could lay out, we tried to persuade her to screen test. If she booked the soap opera role, she could do both—after all, didn't the actress she was performing opposite play a recurring role on a soap? Screen testing for the role didn't guarantee she would get it, but the test itself was another career boost. Nothing ventured, nothing gained, so she might as well give it a shot. We tried very hard to help her see the extraordinary good fortune of having the possibility of both jobs—a gift not to be ignored. Our client would not budge. It was such a shame, such an opportunity lost. A couple of years later, after this actress had garnered some positive industry recognition by doing the play, she left the agency. She complained that she didn't have enough film and television opportunities. We were too polite to remind her of the screen-test episode.

Switching Agents

Before trading in your current agent, make an effort to address problems. First of all, it's not so easy to get a new agent. You might think twice before leaving your current one, and try to resolve problems or explore ways to get more out of the relationship. This is a time to set up a meeting. Every actor wants more—more auditions, more jobs, more money; it's human nature. Agents know this. However, we don't like to be caught unawares. Remember the actor who left the agency to go to virtual strangers who had only seen his audition monologue? When he came in to say goodbye, we had no idea he had been unhappy or even wrestling with the decision to leave us. He had never said anything. His announcement came as a total surprise. That's scary. Had we been given the opportunity to discuss his "audition problem" with him, we might have been able to find a number of solutions. But he came to us with his mind made up, his decision to leave a *fait accompli*. Rather than brainstorming with the agents who knew him well, this actor chose to switch agents. Instead of working to heal his wound, he put a Band-Aid over it. His move, giving the illusion of career activity, would offer only temporary relief, not a lasting cure for his audition malaise. Ironically, our final piece of business with him was giving him the two auditions that had come in for him that morning.

In your "problem-solving" meetings with your agents, try not to be general or emotional. Be specific and use examples. Justify your position and clarify the issues you've come in to discuss. If you're not getting in for auditions, ask your agents why casting directors won't see you. Offer up a list of casting directors who don't know you but whom you would like to meet. Explore career-building tools, like new headshots or New York showcases that give CDs a chance to see your work. Invite a discussion of audition feedback. Use the meeting to strategize rather than complain. Have this meeting at least once before you make the decision to say, "Goodbye." Of course, if you are desperately unhappy in the relationship, or have cause to believe your agent is unethical and harmful, or have already had these meetings but to no avail, then, indeed, it might be time to move on.

Seeking New Representation

Every day at the agency I get a photo and résumé or a phone call from an actor who is dissatisfied with his current agent. "They're not getting me out enough," "I want to do more TV and film," and, "They never have time to talk to me," are but a few routine complaints. Every agent has heard these; although they may be true, using them in a meeting in which you are seeking new representation will only wave red flags. The prospective agent will wonder what's to stop you from saying the same thing about her to another agent in a year's time.

For this very reason, agents are cautious about taking on clients with "agent baggage." We're careful to find out what that baggage is. Here's an example: I invited an actor to the agency once for an interview after seeing him perform in a show in which a client of mine was playing a lead. When my client informed me that this actor was seeking new representation and asked if I'd like to meet him, I said, "Yes," because I thought he was very talented. We started the interview by my asking about the status of his current representation. He said he had been freelancing with an office for several years and throughout his career had never really had an "agent home." Steady work (often long assignments out of town) had precluded the need to sign with an agent. We dug deeper and I discovered a residue of hurt feelings: the various agents with whom he had established freelance relationships had never asked him to sign. A thorough discussion revealed this actor's desire to be exclusive with an agency that truly wanted to commit to him.

He went on to describe his plan for success, beginning with his assumption that getting a good role on a television show would lead to a starring role on Broadway. He had seen this phenomenon first-hand as a performer in Broadway shows that were vehicles for TV stars. The three of us in our meeting with him took turns explaining that because his credits were mostly theatrical, with a modest showing of TV and film work, his road to success would more than likely start with exposure in a high-profile role on or Off-Broadway, building on that toward appearances on television and in films. He listened carefully to what we had to say and was grateful that an agency had taken the time to explain how the business worked, specifically in regard to him and his career. We offered to work exclusively with this actor and asked him to approach our partnership totally fresh, with no past association to less-pleasant situations. He accepted our offer and shortly thereafter booked a lucrative long-term job.

Whatever circumstances lead you to seeking new representation, you can be sure that the prospective agent will canvas the entire territory of your past agent relationships before deciding to take you on as a client. Accept this as a sign of interest and be prepared. When an actor doesn't give a reason for seeking new representation in his cover letter, I address this issue at the top of our interview. Getting answers to this question will help me assess whether I'm the agent who can truly make the difference. When asked what the problem is with your current agency representation, try not to get personal. Be honest and specific about your grievances, but make every attempt to move quickly from your complaints about the past to your hopes for the new relationship. In other words, stay positive. For example, let's say an actor tells me he thinks he's not "getting out enough" (i.e., not getting enough auditions). I would want to be very careful before claiming that I could do better for this actor. However, when an actor with a résumé of solid credits relates horror stories about agent negligence in the form of lies, ignorance, apathy, or carelessness, I know this actor is an attractive candidate for representation. He is currently in a bad situation and I feel very secure in claiming that I can do better for him. An actor who came in to interview with us one time explained that casting directors were beginning to call him at home to give him his audition appointments because his agent was "forgetting" to do so. Shocked and appalled, we immediately offered to sign him. Because we knew that he was a good actor with an impressive résumé and obviously had fans in the casting community; our decision was not hard to make.

One final word of caution: do not take meetings with prospective agents unless you are truly shopping. Taking up an agent's time on a whim or a fact-finding mission will make enemies rather than friends of these important allies. Agents get very angry when they feel that their time has been wasted. In response to a single incident, they might choose to entirely forgo interviews for a while, thereby punishing the truly needy candidates. Recently a young woman came in to interview with the office. We had been interested in representing her right after she graduated from acting school, but she had decided to go with another agency. She was now looking for "new representation" and had sent us a letter requesting an interview. During the course of the interview we discovered that she had already decided to stay with her current agent. Her reason for taking the meeting with us was to tell us "in person" and at the same time pick our brains about representation in Los Angeles. Since neither of these had anything to do with business with our agency, we considered this interview a huge time waster. But it reminded us of how important it is for agents to find out before setting up an interview whether an actor truly is "seeking new representation."

THE BELIEF OF AN AGENT
Sometimes, no matter how talented we agents think an actor is, we can't seem to make anything happen; that's so perplexing for everyone. Other times, a conversation with an agent reassures an actor by the very fact that attention is being paid; this can save a relationship. Addressing problems, finding solutions, and settling on encouraging strategies can help an actor turn things around to break through to a booking. Here's a heartwarming story: A client's agency papers were up for renewal. He hadn't worked in many months. When he came into the office, he was obviously very despondent, at a crisis point, and did not know what he could do to stimulate action in his career.

We encouraged him to "act" in any way he could. We suggested that he audition for showcases, send out his photo to grad school film projects, take a class, join a new theater group, do play readings—anything to get involved. And we decided to re-sign him for one more year. We must have given him the pep talk he needed, as well as our vote of confidence by offering to re-sign him, because a couple months later he booked a leading role in a first-class production of a classic American play, in which he performed opposite a celebrity actress and received rave notices.

★

The cycle of beginnings and endings never really ends. There's a story apocryphal, perhaps—of a famous actress who left her first small agency when she grew to need a bigger one with stronger and wider-reaching connections. Years later, having developed the star power to attract offers and no longer needing the added clout of a bigger firm, she returned to her original agency. I'd like to believe that this story is true. It illustrates the combination of loyalty and career building evident in the best of actor-agent partnerships.

EPILOGUE:
ADVICE TO THE PLAYERS

This book is about actors and agents. It's about show business: how to get inside and how to work with the industry players once there. It's written by someone who spent time being frustrated on the out-side and wanted to "give back" once she got on the inside.

When an actor sits across the desk from me during an interview, to question me about the agency in terms of how we "see" him and what we intend to "do" for him, I sometimes can't help thinking, "You don't know how lucky you are." I know that thousands of actors stand in line for hours at an open call just to get an audition slot for a role that, if not already cast, probably soon will be cast from among the actors submitted by agents.

One day last fall our intern came into the office carrying so many bundles that I thought she had metamorphosed into an octopus. She had a knapsack, a handbag, a rollaway suitcase, and tucked under her arm a large object that looked like a yoga mat except for its pro-truding steel spikes. I thought it might be one of those modern archery bows that I had seen in the Summer Olympics, and asked if that were so. Very kindly ignoring my inane suggestion, she explained it was a folding stool that she carried with her to open calls so she could sit in-stead of stand in line. Out of curiosity I asked her what time she had gotten up that morning. She said she was in the line outside the Actors' Equity building by 7 a.m. She had signed up for a few calls and hoped to go back at lunchtime to audition.

In the office later that afternoon, one of the agents had a lengthy telephone conversation with a client, trying to convince her not to cancel an important audition. The actress wanted to beg off because she hadn't prepared the material thoroughly. The agent encouraged her to go, since canceling same day is bad behavior and could seriously undermine the agent and actress's relationship with the casting direc-tor—not to mention that this was an important audition not to be missed. Our intern listened in silent disbelief: Such an audition would be manna from heaven for her; how could anyone treat it so casually? Didn't our client know how hard it is for the rest of the acting population to *get* auditions?

Show business is tough, with or without an agent. It would be fine if we could all be the "artists" we studied to be. But we do this for a living, which is where the difficulty starts. Competing for jobs wreaks havoc on art. Clawing your way to the top—success?—takes determination, guts, and a willingness to endure humiliation on all levels. I'd like to share the four things I have learned in my actress-agent life that really make a difference in keeping a balance in this topsy-turvy business:

a positive attitude and sense of humor;

a willingness to seize the day;

the necessity of not taking rejection personally;

a true sense of self-confidence.

Exploring these will be the happy ending of this book.

Attitude is so important. Have you ever noticed that positive people are magnets to good fortune, whereas grumps are just so many sour apples? I don't advocate a Pollyanna attitude that ignores reality, but a sense of humor can ease your journey along the rocky road of show business. A person who can sense, or see, the humor in a situation is less likely to feel controlled by it or helpless before it. Humor comes in many forms, from the ironic shrug to the belly laugh. When things get too bad, or seem completely unfair—when there's little to laugh about—that's when a person needs a sense of humor most. Obstacles are such a problem: you seek to go above, under, or through them, yet the roadblocks seem insurmountable. A sense of humor, however, just might give a person enough perspective to step back and see a way around the obstacle, making it irrelevant. A sense of humor can sometimes minimize a disappointment, opening you to a new vision that guides you through your upset. It can also help put your disappointments behind you so you can move on. This business has no patience for resentments and grudges. It races ahead, leaving you behind licking your wounds. The normal reactions of anger, self-pity, and bitterness do not effect change. They are nonproductive and self damaging. Truthfully, you can't control a reality that has already happened. What you *can* control, though, is your reaction to it. When nothing else can be done to alter your circumstances, it's best to acknowledge and accept this fact, then move on. Actors are devastated when they don't get cast...especially after three callbacks. Agents feel the disappointment, too. You have to see the positive aspect of getting as far as you did, and believe that the connection made will pay off down the road.

Easier said than done, I know. And it doesn't help that the numbers are so unfair. A client of ours who was about to direct a show was working with a casting director who had assembled an assortment of excellent actors for him to see. Our client told us how devastating it was to realize how many wonderful performers are unemployed. This business is filled with them! In the end he chose actors with whom he had worked previously: familiarity was the deciding factor. (It often is.) That *we* knew this didn't help all of the actors who weren't cast in the production; they either assumed that they had done poorly or didn't know *what* to think. They still may be gnashing their teeth, torturing themselves trying to figure out what went wrong, when nothing really went wrong at all. Maybe some were spared this agony when their agents told them what they learned from the casting director—that the director had cast someone he had worked with before...or maybe they didn't agonize because they had a sense of humor and knew how to put their disappointment behind them.

Realizing how tough the competition is in this business puts you on notice to take seriously every opportunity that comes your way. When your agent calls with an audition for *Law & Order*, you must drop everything and make every effort to get there. These opportunities are precious. Actors are self-involved and not logical; it goes with the territory. Anyone who expects them to be different is in for a lot of disappointment. Getting to an audition is half the battle. Preparing thoroughly and doing your best at the audition is the rest. That's all that can be asked. (Though a little luck couldn't hurt, either.)

A wise actor I know attributes his longevity in the business to his decision not to take rejection personally. If he had, he says, he wouldn't have lasted as long as he has. Rejection is part of the business. Many actors audition for a role. Only one is cast. When working out this notion of not taking rejection personally, an actor must decide on his personal definition of success. After all, at the end of the day, you and only you are the one facing yourself in the mirror. Life and art require constant evaluation because they are constantly evolving. Nothing stays the same. The goals of yesterday can—indeed, may need to—change today to bring a better life tomorrow. The only real truth is the clock ticking on the wall and the dream that you conceived ten years ago, which inevitably alters with time.

It's your life. It's your career. You are the star of your movie. Actors need to nurture their self-confidence. Self-confidence comes from knowing what you are doing. Think of all the activities in your life that you do really well. You have confidence in your ability to do them, right? The word "confidence" is related to the verb "confide." When you confide in yourself you trust yourself to provide answers. That trust comes from knowledge and experience. Although actors are great at bluffing (after all, they're actors), a person can't fake real confidence. The secret to having confidence is knowing your stuff. Knowing your stuff comes from studying, learning, dissecting, and absorbing. A good reason to take classes. But becoming an expert by truly *owning* the knowledge you've obtained comes from experience. All the classes in the world can't add up to the experience of a season of one-week summer stock!

Becoming an agent was a natural outgrowth of what I did as an actress in business for herself. Instead of making submissions for myself, I do it now for hundreds of actors for a multitude of projects. I enjoy prepping actors for auditions, selecting headshots from contact sheets, going to shows and showcases to support my clients and case out new talent. I enjoy making things happen. Answering questions from actors in the "Ask an Agent" columns for *Back Stage* forced me to dissect and understand the mechanisms of show business. What I have distilled and attempted to put forth in this book is, I hope, helpful to anyone interested in working with an agent and having a career in show business. It's meant to be—and it comes with the most sincere wish of *"Good luck!"*

INDEX

Photo by Michelle Hannay.

A New Yorker born and bred, MARGARET EMORY has worked in entertainment management as a talent agent for the past fifteen years. She is currently at Dulcina Eisen Associates, in New York City. Margaret graduated with honors from Princeton University, where she was elected to Phi Beta Kappa, and subsequently from the Neighborhood Playhouse School of Theatre. Her New York acting studies also included work at the Stella Adler Studio. She has been a performer and director; headed The Shakespeare Workshop—a national Shakespearean company; served as an adjunct professor at Marymount Manhattan College; and is a member of New York Women in Film and Television. Her writing credits range from being a published song lyricist, to creating and running "Write On!" a series of writers' groups.

Margaret founded and continues to conduct the Emory Seminars— a program on the business of acting that she has taken to the North Carolina School of the Arts, the University of North Carolina (Chapel Hill), and the University of Michigan, among others. In New York, she currently teaches classes in soap opera acting and is a frequent guest at Actors Connection, TVI Actors Studio, One on One Seminars, and the Creative Acting Company. Margaret created and writes the popular "Ask an Agent" column for *Back Stage*, where she can be reached at Askanagent@yahoo.com. In her spare time, she is an avid early morning tennis player.